Masters of their Craft

Masters of their Craft

The Art, Architecture and Garden Design of the Nesfields

Shirley Rose Evans

The Lutterworth Press

This book is for Leslie and Robert

The Lutterworth Press
P.O. Box 60
Cambridge
CB1 2NT

www.lutterworth.com
publishing@lutterworth.com

ISBN: 978 0 7188 9323 1

British Library Cataloguing in Publication Data
A record is available from the British Library

First Published, 2014

Contents

List of Illustrations

Dates are given where known.

Nesfield Family Tree

Theophilus Nesfield (1664-1727)
of Staxton, nr. Scarborough, owned 700 acres at Willerby, Yorkshire
m.
Anne Woodall (daughter of John Woodall) of Scarborough

- Samuel (1694-1774) of Staxton, Willerby and Scarborough, farmer and landowner m. Anne Topkin of Scarborough
  - William (1731-1810) Vicar of Wickhambrook, Suffolk. Rector of Dalham, 2nd Wrangler Sydney College, Cambridge (1757) m. (1) Sarah Barniston (widow, d.1764) (2) Anne Martin (widow of Foxearth Essex, d.1805)
    - Twins, Leonard (d.1810) William (d. young)
    - William (1758-1828) Perpetual Curate of Chester-le-Street, Rector of Brancepeth, Co. Durham, 15th Wrangler Caius College, Cambridge (1781), Chaplain to King George III m. (1) Elizabeth Andrews (2) Marianne Mills
    - Charlton Gilbert (d. young)
    - Anne m. James Hustler of Sudbury, Suffolk (issue)
  - Theophilus (1735-1806) of Glaisdale, Scarborough, farmer at Harwood Dale (no issue)
  - John of Amborough House, Scarborough (1739-1866)
  - 2 daughters
- William of Staxton m. Anne Heggison of Scarborough
- John (Rector of Thormanby, Yorkshire) A.D. Sydney College, Cambridge (1729) m. Sarah (no issue)
- 5 daughters

William Andrews
(1793-1881)
m.
Emma Anne Mills
(1807-1874)
daughter of Henry
Foster Mills
(Chancellor of
York Minster) and
Alicia Henriette

John
(1796-1807)

Sarah
m.
Frederick Cookson
(Attorney, Leeds, later
took Holy Orders)

Frances

Charles (Jesus College,
1821, Rector of
Stratton and Headon
m.
Eleanor Collinson

Anne (d.1860)
m.
Anthony Salvin

Elizabeth (Bessie)
m.
Revd Charles Cookson

Robert William (d.1887)
m.
Lucy Underwood (daughter of
Captain Underwood, Estate
Agent to Duke of Rutland and
Master of High Peak Harriers

Henry William (b.1812)
died aged 11 of croup at his
school near Ripon, plaque in
Ripon Cathedral

Marianne
m.
Charles Albert Darley
of Albany Park,
Burtonfield, York

William Eden (1835-1888)
m.
Mary Anetta Blackwell
(no issue)

2 daughters
(d. young)

Arthur Marhkam (1841-1874)
m.
Fanny Catherine

Henry William
m.
Violet Hill (issue)

David William
m.
Katherine Mahoney (issue)

Markham Family Tree

William Markham (1719-1807)
Archbishop of York, Prebendary of Durham (1759), Chaplain to King George II (1756)
m.
Sarah Goddard (d.1759)

Alicia Henriette
m.
Revd Henry Foster Mills
(parents of Emma Mills, wife of William Andrews Nesfield)

Mills Family Tree

Henry Mills
m.
Elizabeth Fenwick (daughter of William Fenwick of Lymington, nr. Alnwick, Northumberland)

William (no issue)	Henry Foster Mills of Helm Park and Willington Hall, County Durham m. Alicia Henriette Markham (parents of Emma, wife of William Andrews Nesfield)	Marianne (2nd wife of Revd William Nesfield)	Jane m. Dr Britten (Headmaster of Durham School)	Eliza m. Captain Salvin (parents of Anthony Salvin)	6 more children

Emma Anne
m.
William Andrews Nesfield

Acknowledgements

My association with the Nesfield family has been a long and happy one and continues today. Firstly, therefore, I want to say how grateful I am to the Australian Nesfields, Robert, Sheila, Markham and Emma, for allowing me sole access to their Archives.

Also, I want to take this opportunity to thank the Kent and Hampshire members of the family for their help and encouragement over the years. My thanks go to the owners of the various estates, county record offices and university libraries who have allowed me access to their archives and to reproduce material held by them. A special thank you to Professors Michael Tooley and Timothy Mowl and to Jane Brown for their continuing support. My thanks to Adrian Brink at The Lutterworth Press for having the foresight to appreciate that the Nesfields were such an important part of the cultural scene in the mid-Victorian period. Also to my editors, Emily Reacher and Bethany Churchard, for their professionalism and patience, especially with my lack of computer skills.

My special thanks and love go to my own family, Stephen and Jean Evans, for their help, interest and forbearance over the years – with a particular thank you to my husband, Leslie.

Introduction

The Victorian age was a long one. It lasted from 1837, when Queen Victoria came to the throne, until 1901, the year of her death, and inevitably during that time there were many changes. The field of the arts was no exception. During the middle years of the Victorian era, the Nesfields (father and son) produced horticultural and architectural designs for some of the wealthiest and most influential landowners in the British Isles. Although they never formed a partnership, each pursuing his own career (Nesfield Snr as a landscape gardener and Eden Nesfield as an architect), the commissions that gave them the most pleasure were on estates where they were able to work alongside each other. In such cases, Nesfield Snr constructed the gardens, sometimes with the help of his second son Arthur Markham Nesfield (1841-1874), and turned the estate lands into what he considered perfect pictures. His first son, Eden Nesfield, delighted in designing intimate little buildings around the estates. He also restored and designed manor houses and renovated churches.

William Andrews Nesfield, pencil by James Duffield Harding, c. 1840.

William Nesfield Snr was born in 1794, and was a product of the Georgian age. Society at that time was arranged in a paternalistic, hierarchical manner, with a small landed elite at the top of the pyramid and the majority, consisting of the labouring poor, at the bottom. He was successively an army officer and a watercolour painter of rural, picturesque scenery before taking up landscape design. The skills he learned from these earlier professions were to stand him in good stead when he began to develop the landscapes of his wealthy clients. Eden Nesfield was born and died during Victoria's reign, but was a true Edwardian in his lifestyle and outlook, as were his friends and colleagues: bohemian and free-thinking, they forged their own ideas. Eden's social and professional circles included architects, craftsmen, painters, writers and poets, who formed the vanguard of the Aesthetic and Arts and Crafts Movements in London.

William Eden Nesfield, pencil by Jacques Emile Edouard Brandon in the style of Hans Holbein, 1858.

Eden was strongly influenced, however, by the art and design he had encountered in the family home, where his father designed strictly formal gardens that often included as a centrepiece a *parterre-de-broderie* (embroidered garden) reminiscent of those developed by André le Nôtre for the Sun King, Louis XIV, at Versailles. These influences helped fuel his desire to become an architect, and he was to remain enraptured by rich ornamentation of all styles, from the Gothic to the Japanese. It might appear that the philosophies of father and son were very different; William was concerned with overall effect, ensuring that the strictly artificial features in the environs of the house corresponded with its man-made architecture and led the eye towards the informal landscape beyond. Eden, on the other hand, was concerned with more minute detail. His affinity was with the early Arts and Crafts Movement. However, they are actually a good example of how two seemingly opposite ideologies can happily co-exist. In their case, their love of the picturesque scenery that could be found in the countryside of the British Isles, which they painted and sketched throughout their lives, brought them together. This interest, together with a shared romanticized view of the past, made their contribution to British landscape gardening and architecture unique.

1.

Early Days

To be born in the middle of winter, in the inhospitable, cold and windswept conditions associated with the northern counties of England, may not be considered the most auspicious start in life. Fortunately for William Andrews Nesfield, who came into the world on 19 February 1794, the poverty and hard conditions associated with the coal-mining areas of industrialized County Durham were not to be his lot, for his parents were not humble cottagers; on the contrary. William was the eldest, much-loved son of the Revd William Nesfield (1758-1828) and Elizabeth (née Andrews, 1770-1808). They lived at the time of his birth on the idyllic Lumley Park estate, which had been the original deer park belonging to the Earls of Scarborough, and, as the eldest, he held a special position within the family, 'with every fault leniently judged.'[1]

At the time of his birth his father was perpetual curate at the church of St Margaret and St Cuthbert in the ancient town of Chester-le-Street. The church was built in the eleventh century and contained fourteen effigies of members of the Lumley family, deposited there in 1594 by the family antiquarian John, Lord Lumley. Set on the River Wear, Chester-le-Street was once an important garrison town for the Roman legions, and it is where St Cuthbert is believed to have rested from 882 until 995 before being taken by the monks of Lindisfarne to Durham. The Revd Nesfield, after being educated at Caius College, Cambridge and ordained a priest in 1789, was also Rector of St Brandon's Church in Brancepeth and St Michael's, Witton Gilbert from 1800. He was one of the Prince Regent's chaplains, volunteer chaplain of the 68th Foot, and played a prominent role in local affairs as a trustee of a local charity and senior magistrate for the county.

Elizabeth Nesfield was the daughter of John and Elizabeth Andrews. Her father was a well-to-do landowner who owned Shotley Hall in Northumberland and a town house in Hallgarth Street, Durham. When her father died in 1792 he left Elizabeth, and each

1 Eliza Anne Salvin, *Reminiscences & Notes of By-Gone Years*, Directorate of Education Services, London Borough of Barnet Libraries Department, Manuscript Accession Number 6787/7/.

of her four sisters, £7,000; a considerable sum in those days.[1] In 1800 her inheritance enabled Elizabeth's sister Anne (1773-1841) to marry Charles Ingoldsby Paulet, 13th Marquess of Winchester (1764-1843), thus moving the Nesfield family into the strata of the aristocracy.[2] Tradition and lineage were important to the Nesfields, who could trace their ancestry back over 800 years to Dagobert II, a member of the Ariano-Celtic church and a prince in line to the Merovingian throne. Dagobert had married Imagne de Nessfeld, the daughter of a Saxon landowner, and from these illustrious beginnings the Nesfields descended. Over the following centuries they were listed as minor landowners who, by the seventeenth century, were living in Yorkshire. Theophilus Nesfield owned 700 acres of land at Willerby and Staxton, near Scarborough. His son Samuel (1694-1774) was William's great-grandfather, and his grandfather, another William, was vicar of Wickhambrook, and Rector of Dalham in Suffolk.[3]

The Revd William Nesfield, oil by Ramsey of Newcastle-on-Tyne, 1813.

In 1796 a second son, John, was born to the Nesfields, and in 1800 the Revd Nesfield moved the family to Durham. He had by that time been appointed as rector in the nearby village of Brancepeth, but as the rectory was not ready for them they moved into a house opposite Elizabeth's mother in Old Elvet, a prosperous area of Durham. The city, encircled on three sides by the River Wear, is set on a peninsula and dominated by its medieval cathedral and the castle, which was the residence of the Bishops of Durham. Both the cathedral and the castle are embraced by a single street, which is divided into the North and South Baileys. At No. 3 South Bailey, in one of the finest Georgian houses built in 1730, Sir John Eden lived. A friend of the Andrews family, he had been a witness to the signing of the Indenture drawn up at the time of the Revd Nesfield's marriage, and was ultimately to become godfather to William's eldest son.

1 Indenture drawn up 22.3.1793 at the time of the marriage of William and Elizabeth Nesfield, Durham University Library, Special Collections, SAL 66.

2 *Amport House: A Short History*, (Royal Air Force Chaplain's School, 1986) p. 12.

3 Information from the late Dr John Nesfield and Mr John Davis, both of whom were descended from William Nesfield's brother, Charles.

Framwellgate Bridge, Durham, watercolour by William Nesfield.

Once William had commenced his career in landscape gardening, he was to maintain that he had learnt more about trees during the visits he spent with his father on the Eden's country estate, Windlestone Hall, Rushyford, near Durham, than at any other time.[1]

During her short life, Elizabeth Nesfield gave birth to nine children, six of whom survived into adulthood: William, born in 1794; Sarah, in 1801; Frances, in 1802; Charles, in 1803; Anne, on 19 October 1805 and Elizabeth on 2 March 1808. Anne's birth was later recorded as being: 'in the old cathedral town of Durham . . . the baby just ushered into the world, when the autumn leaves were falling and every blast brought them rattling down from the trees, that lined the paths on the woody banks of the Wear.'[2] The birth of the final child, Elizabeth (Bessie) unfortunately resulted in the death of her mother on 2 March 1808, and she was buried in St Oswald's churchyard in Durham.[3] Her son John had already died in 1807, after catching a chill from bathing in cold water on a hot day.

On 17 June 1808 the Nesfields moved to the rectory in the unspoilt village of Brancepeth. It was situated a few miles from Durham, its cottages straddling the one main street that

1 This was the birthplace of the former Prime Minister Sir Anthony Eden.
2 Eliza Anne Salvin, *op.cit.*
3 Death Certificate of Elizabeth Nesfield, County Hall, Durham, EP/DuSO 157.

led not only to the rectory and church, but also to the imposing medieval castle, which had been the stronghold of the powerful Neville family. In 1809, the Revd Nesfield remarried. His new wife was Marianne Mills, daughter of Lt. Col. Mills, who lived at nearby Willington Hall. According to Anne Nesfield's daughter, one of Marianne's first acts after the marriage was to take Bessie from the cottage where she had been placed after her mother's death: 'as she could not bear to have the little motherless babe an exile from her home.'[1] Three more children were born of this union: Marianne, on 10 June 1810; Henry, on 30 June 1812; and Robert, on 8 August 1815. The children apparently led a happy, carefree life at the rectory. They were fond of running over the fields to Willington Hall, where they could play in the large garden, and where the housekeeper is reputed to have baked the best cakes the children ever tasted. Their maternal grandmother, the mother of the Revd Nesfield's first wife, was a most eccentric lady, who came visiting the rectory from Durham with her pockets filled with sweet-meats, which she invariably forgot to give to the children. It was said that their consternation was great when she started for home with this delicious treat still in her capacious pockets! Their summer holidays were spent at Seaton, a quiet seaside town on the east coast, the Revd Nesfield and Marianne going on first in a gig to secure lodgings and the children and Miss Caldecleugh, the girls' governess, arriving later in what was known as the 'Old Coach'. This coach was a battered affair that Marianne had acquired cheaply from a livery stable in Durham. It was said of Miss Caldecleugh that, 'though an excellent person and invaluable in the position she occupied, she was not accomplished, nor could she teach anything beyond the mere rudiments of common education.'[2] The Revd Nesfield, therefore, made arrangements with a French master from a school at Witton-le-Wear, a Monsieur Moens, to visit once a week.[3] He came to breakfast so that the rector could take the opportunity of speaking French with him. Miss Caldecleugh was, however, so well thought of by the family that when Anne Nesfield married and moved to London, the governess went with her as a companion, and was eventually left an annuity of £20 for life in the will of the Revd Nesfield.

As the children grew older they attended balls and concerts in Seaton where, whenever possible, they were joined by the Hustler brothers, the sons of the Revd Nesfield's sister, who lived in Bury St Edmunds in Suffolk, and who were being tutored by him before going to Cambridge University. Anthony Salvin (1799-1881), Marianne's nephew, was also a member of the party. Salvin ultimately became William's brother-in-law and without his friendship and support William would probably never have taken up landscape gardening. Life at Brancepeth was a happy one: Anne Nesfield's daughter wrote that her mother, after marrying Anthony Salvin in 1826 and moving to London, 'did not like her new way of life at first, clearly missing the busy country rectory full of family and friends.'[4]

1 Eliza Anne Salvin, *Ibid.*

2 *Ibid.*

3 Sarah, his eldest pupil, was nine years old when Monsieur Moens first came to give lessons to the Miss Nesfields at the Rectory. Eliza Anne Salvin, *Ibid.*

4 *Ibid.*

While the rest of the family grew up in Brancepeth, William was, at six years old, sent as a day boy to the grammar school (now the University Music School) on the Green opposite the cathedral in Durham. The headmaster at the time was the Revd Dr Brittan, the husband of Jane Mills, Marianne Nesfield's sister. In later life William was to recall that he had been 'a very surly old fellow and a desperate flogger.' His time at the grammar school proved to be short-lived, as it had always been assumed that he would follow in the footsteps of his father and paternal grandfather and enter the Church. In 1801 the Bishop of St David's, who was a Prebendary of Durham and a friend of his father's, suggested that he be placed at Winchester College as a scholarship boy. However, as a Latin examination was required to enter the main school, for which he was not prepared, he was sent instead to a preparatory school in Hyde Abbey, a suburb of Winchester, under the Revd Mr Richards. The journey from County Durham to Winchester was later described by him as follows:

> The journey to Winchester was in those days most dreary and fatiguing. First the journey to London from Durham in the 'Highflyer' stage coach occupied continuously 2 days and 1 night. On arrival in London my Father went to his old quarters 'Ibbotson's Hotel', Vere Street, now the district Post Office. He remained there a few days to show me London, tho not old enough to appreciate it. Our journey to Winchester 63 miles occupied 10 hours in a long coach. Like the modern buss, neither steam nor telegraph dreamt of in those days.

For a 7-year-old boy, plucked from a privileged position within a close and loving family, this was a traumatic experience, as he later confirmed: 'This parting with my dear good father was most painful and rendered me very sad for many days, which caused me to be quizzed by the other boys.' Indeed, so unhappy was he that he and another boy were persuaded by their room-mate to run away. They made for Andover, but, whilst taking refreshment at an inn, the Head Usher appeared and took them back to school. William sadly reported that: 'We were packed into a post chaise and delivered into Old Richards' relentless hands for a very severe flogging and confinement for several days indoors.' During the time he was at his preparatory school, which was nearly two years, he reflected that he was a stranger to his parents, the journey back to County Durham being too long and expensive to undertake. During the holidays he boarded with the Revd Chapman of Micheldever, near Winchester, and spent two vacations with his maternal aunt, Lady Winchester, at Amport House near Andover, which he enjoyed.

In 1803, after what he described as 'a sharp examination, particularly in Horace which I was best up to rather than Ovid or Virgil', he was admitted to Winchester College. However, after one year his father decided that there was little to be gained for his remaining so far from home and decided to remove him. He was far from sorry, having no regrets that he would no longer have to suffer 'the fagging, bullying, bad food on wooden trenchers (not plates) chapel twice every day and on Sundays 3 times, besides going to the Cathedral twice.'

His journey back to County Durham was not lacking in incident as the coach he was travelling in was upset near Leeds, in fog:

> . . . fortunately the coach was proceeding at a walking pace, the Coachman sang out to the guard but he could not see the ground beyond the leaders I was an outsider in the rear with the guard and tho much bruised was less hurt than other passengers the Coach fell over a raised road which had no fence, and the coachman fell among the horses and was seriously injured. Thus I managed to get home gradually viz. in about 2 days as my bruises were too painful to proceed faster.

His time at home, however, was to be short-lived as he needed to complete his education. His father decided to send him to the grammar school in Bury St Edmunds, Suffolk so that he could board with his paternal aunt, Mrs Hustler. Occasionally during the holidays William would visit his grandfather at his vicarage in the nearby village of Wickhambrook, recalling how he was once given a flogging by him for '*blowing his hen's eggs*, which *were set for hatching* – thus I plead to mischief like many other boys. My grandfather however was very indulgent and so reasoned me out of mischief so that I never felt inclined to repeat the same foolish trick.'

He remained in Bury for two years, and during this time met his cousin, Captain Hustler, an officer in the Engineers, and decided that he too wanted to embark upon a military career. The Peninsular Wars were at their height and the glamour associated with the uniform and these events must have appealed to him. His father, ever indulgent, gave his consent, and it was agreed that he should finish his education at the Royal Military Academy at Woolwich. In order to be received as a gentleman cadet, he needed to become proficient in mathematics. Fortunately his eldest cousin, James Hustler, was at hand to help. James, after being tutored by the Revd Nesfield, had become a Fellow of Trinity College, Cambridge, and he offered William tutorial assistance and free board in his rooms in the Library Court of the College. William 'felt in clover particularly as I dined at the Fellows table, not with the under-graduates – in fact I had a very jolly time at Cam for 2 terms.'

In 1809 he was enrolled as a candidate for a cadetship at the lower barracks in the Arsenal at Woolwich, and, having no difficulty passing his examination, he was immediately rigged out in uniform. He then moved to Great Marlow for six months' infantry drill. He complained that having to obtain two uniforms was a foolish custom and he was pleased that it was later abolished. The one for Great Marlowe was red with silver lace, whilst at Woolwich it was blue with red facings, as in the Artillery. William was in the second company at Marlowe under Captain Otter. The Commandant was Colonel Butler who, according to William, was 'a very strict old boy'. He enjoyed his time there but after only six months, as he had been so well taught at Cambridge, he was considered eligible for Woolwich much sooner than his contemporaries and was included in the next batch of intakes for training. Accompanied by a master he travelled to London, where he went into the lower cadet barracks, 'a miserable quarter compared to Marlow.' After a year he was advanced to the second Academy at the Upper Barracks, on the Common, where the quarters were much more comfortable, although there were four Cadets to a room: 'thus the change was a happy one and the officers very kind.' They had occasional holidays and in the winter would ramble over Shooter's Hill with guns for sparrow shooting:

> On one occasion, my chums, Richards and Stewart tempted me to poach over a preserved manor for *game* in their Company – this was near Eltham but we had not trespassed above ½ hour when a covey of partridge rose which of course caused all three guns to fire without a hit thus alarming a keeper who soon overtook us and demanded names. Richards answered first as Bill Brown, then Stewart as Harry Stokes, I was John Brown brother of Bill, all of Greenwich – thus the keeper *booked us* and *saw us off* the manor, but we never heard more of this exploit tho we shot an old hen near a farm without discovery and had a roast at midnight – taking good care to fix blankets against the windows for fear of lights being discovered – In fact 'boys will be boys' and so we were as tricky as those at other Schools.

He soon realised that promotion in both the Engineers and the Artillery was very slow: there was no purchase as in the lines. There was also a strict examination required for a commission in either corps in mathematics, fortification, or French and German. These difficulties he overcame by asking Lady Winchester if she would intercede on his behalf. She obligingly wrote to the Duke of York, whom apparently she knew well, and the result was that on the 10 July 1812 William was gazetted as 2nd Lieutenant in the 95th Rifle Brigade. He wrote: 'Thus I took my leave of many friends at Woolwich who now are old Generals or dead.'

Like most boys of William's social background he appears, after his initial period of homesickness at Winchester, to have taken for granted that he would be subjected to years of strict discipline and would spend a considerable amount of time away from home. The result of this deprivation, however, was that he gained a resourcefulness, self-confidence and self-reliance, which were all attributes that would stand him in good stead later in life.[1]

1 The above quotations are taken from William Nesfield's *Reminiscences*.

2.

Into the Army

After leaving Woolwich, William received a cheque from his father to enable him to go to London and buy the equipment and uniform he would need in his new appointment. His regulation sword was presented to him by Lady Winchester, with a Latin inscription written by another Hustler cousin, William Hustler, of Jesus College, Cambridge. He received an order to join the 95th depot at Shorncliffe near Hythe in Kent, where his commander was Captain Ewan; according to William, although very good natured, he was a desperate drinker:

> In those days a very sober fellow was considered a milk sop which somewhat applied to myself in as much as I nauseated all strong drinks from boyhood, although several efforts were made to conquer the singularity – the fact was that with the exception of Cyder and Perry I was nearly a teetotler, which eventually proved lucky for my Captain who on a stranger day at mess [i.e. when guests were invited] was taken off to his room reeling drunk, when shortly after Ewan's servant appeared in the mess room and told the butler in our hearing that he was much alarmed for his master who was black in the face and seemed choking. Thus I proposed to go to his room and several other officers followed (*all being screwed*) who merely expressed sorrow without attempting relief, when I (tho a junior) interfered by taking off the stiff stock from his neck and sluicing copiously with cold water and also remembering to send for Doctor Scott who not only pronounced my treatment as being judicious but that it was lucky for Ewan there was one sober man among his visitors.

William also noted, somewhat sceptically, that Ewan was a confirmed dipsomaniac, and therefore it was no surprise when he eventually died of delirium tremens.

A few months later William was ordered to Spain, which apparently caused much excitement at the rectory, tears being shed as hope and pride was mixed with apprehension that he might not return safe and sound. Unfortunately, his orders came through at such short notice that he was given little time to pack up and march to Portsmouth in order to take his place in a transport ship, which was ready to sail from Spit Head, on a journey that was to prove to be both crowded and uncomfortable. However, 'being fully aware that all hands must "rough it" there was no grumbling'. Soon after leaving the Isle of Wight a stiff, fair breeze took them across the Bay of Biscay. The wind changed suddenly to the east, however, so that instead of being opposite their given port (Passages in Asturias) they reached St Andrev, which was considerably west. It was dark, and by some blunder they ran aground in company with another vessel. Fortunately it contained a company of Life Guards, and as it became lighter they were able to hoist the horses overboard into the sea and swim half a mile to the shore, arriving without a single casualty. They paraded on the beach for roll call and marched up to Santander, where William was billeted with a doctor. Seeing the Latin inscription on his sword, he presumed that William was of noble birth and furnished him with a very comfortable room! William's good luck continued, for he wrote that he had: 'a jolly fortnight in Santander where there is a splendid Cathedral'. This delay had been caused by a lack of means to convey them to the front lines in the Pyrenees, but eventually they were moved to Passages, the nearest harbour to Wellington's army. They were quartered in a deserted convent in view of St Sebastian, which gave them the opportunity to examine the fortifications after the recent siege. This led William to observe that nearly every house was seriously damaged by shells, and although the Cathedral escaped it had been converted into a storehouse of goods for the army, such as biscuits, corn, chests of tea, barrels of rum, blankets and cavalry forage: 'The general ruin was terrific particularly in a large square near the Cathedral, which was strewn *with feathers* in consequence of the ripping up of every bed in search of hidden coin. We did not learn that much was discovered but as the system of pillage and every other wickedness seems a universal law after a siege with English as well as French, the destruction was not singular.' After a few days they received an order to join the light division, which consisted of the 43rd and 52nd light infantry, the 1st and 2nd Bn of the 95th and the Portuguese Caçadores. When they arrived in the mountains, William was pleased to find that they were quartered in a farm instead of in cold tents, but there was no mess, and they were on common rations with 'horrid sour wine.' Wellington's headquarters were at St Jean de Luz, where the Foot and Life Guards were also billeted, and when invited to the Guards Mess by one of his friends from Great Marlow, he enviously noted they were: 'as snug as tho in English Barracks'.

As the winter of 1813 closed in and the French retreated, there was little fighting until the French General Soult was able to gain reinforcements. However, unexpectedly:

> One morning the French made rather a large muster on the river Adour, which separated them from our side – A hint which Wellington thought advisable to act upon without further delay. The result was a general action extending several miles on 4th Dec which unremittingly continued night and day till the 8th when the French ran like sheep into the secure retreat of Bayonne. This was my 1st action as

> light infantry commence by skirmishing (which seldom lasts above a few hours). Our loss was not very serious. The line and cavalry after they advanced thro our open files afforded us an opportunity for boiling kettles for grub, taking rest and watching thro our telescopes how matters in advance were proceeding. Hundreds of wounded were brought to the rear every day and our cavalry took a great number of prisoners and scores of horses. After Dec 8th all was quiet for many weeks and sales of the kits of officers killed and captured soon occurred. When I bought a capital white steed belonging to a French trumpeter for 10 pounds this proved a great comfort for moving my baggage as well as, when on duty, to go to Head Qtrs.

His time in Spain proved to be short, as his father interceded on his behalf with Mrs Drummond, the daughter of William Russell, who owned Brancepeth Castle. Nesfield asked her to request her husband General Gordon Drummond (1772-1854), who commanded the North West army in Upper Canada, to appoint his son as his extra Aide de Camp. In this role, William would have been one of General Drummond's trusted personal assistants. His duties would have included preparing items for inspection and organizing lodgings. It is reputed that Colonel Drummond admired William's talent for drawing and hoped that he would make good use of it in Canada.[1]

William was promoted from 2nd Lieutenant of the 95th to full Lieutenant of the 76th and, having sold his horse, and accompanied by his servant, Antonio, he travelled back to Portsmouth in a large Bark, where he had a comfortable berth; the ship only held a few invalids and wounded. They had a stiff, fair breeze all the way to Portsmouth, and William spent two nights and two days in a lumbering coach to London. After a night's stay he was in time to catch the 'Highflyer' at 6 a.m. for Durham. Although he returned to London to be outfitted for the staff and appointed to the 89th Regiment, he was again able to return home for a few months, as no fleet could sail for Canada until the ice disappeared from the St Lawrence River and Newfoundland coast. When he returned to Brancepeth in his army uniform, with a Spanish servant, he must have been a figure of considerable interest to the villagers; and he was the hero of the hour as far as his family were concerned.

On the morning of Wednesday 5 May, 1814, William travelled to London on the Wellington stage coach. At Darlington he was joined by Squire Newbey Lowson (1773-1853) of Witton-le-Wear. Lowson was a neighbour of the Nesfield family in Brancepeth and also an acquaintance of the painter Joseph William Mallord Turner, a connection that would be very useful to William in the future. The two men spent time together in London, going to exhibitions at Somerset House and Spring Gardens and to view Cornelius Varley's improved Camera Lucida. They dined at the Marquess of Winchester's and with Miss Andrews (presumably William's maternal aunt and a lady-in-waiting at Court) at St James' Palace. The following week, he had an interview at the Admiralty with Lord Henry Paulet, the brother of the Marquess of Winchester, who

1 Eliza Anne Salvin, *Reminiscences*, *Ibid.*

directed him to proceed to Portsmouth without delay, where the fleet was under weigh in the next 24 hours. He lost no time in returning to his lodgings, giving instructions to Antonio for packing up, whilst he ran to the different military shops to equip himself. Unfortunately, when arriving at the inn to board the Portsmouth Mail, he was told that all his baggage would not be allowed to accompany him. On asking around he found that a heavy coach was leaving London the same evening, although it was not scheduled to arrive as early as the Mail. The coach eventually arrived in Portsmouth at eight o'clock the following morning, and he got his baggage down to the sally port just as his vessel, the *Leopard*, was getting ready to sail. An obliging lieutenant ran to the signal post on the ramparts, telegraphing the *Leopard* to lay to. William hired a boat and reached the ship in under an hour, but as the *Leopard* had by that time run aground a short distance from Spit Head, having little sea room, he need not have hurried. He was admitted to the officers' mess; but as the Ward Room was very crowded, with twenty-three men of the left wing of the 4th Bn of the Royals, and several ladies and children, he made for the lower deck where the number in the Gun Room was only eight: the Surgeon, Master, Purser, three Lieutenants and the Master's wife. He was able to procure a cot in a small cabin. The ship sailed for Ireland to pick up a convoy in Cork, and landed a few miles away in the harbour at Cove, which he described as a 'little, ugly, dirty village built on the cliffs of a blueish stone, there is a pretty chapel and a good sort of Inn. The shops were very bad.' The *Hebras* frigate was spotted at the mouth of the harbour, conveying the fleet to America, and, because it was intended that the convoy would sail together, this extended their stay by a further forty-eight hours as there was to be a court martial on board. Ever resourceful, William took the opportunity to see something of the area. Cork was ten miles from Cove, where they had landed, so he and the Purser hired a boat from Passages, two miles from Cove, an area for which he had nothing but praise, saying: 'It was well wooded with a number of gentlemen's seats, scattered about.' He also considered the city of Cork to be well built, and the Cathedral 'most beautiful, streets very wide with many good shops.' Whilst he was there he met a friend, Lieutenant Alderson of the Engineers, who was quartered at Spike Island, opposite the place the fleet lay. William decided to take the opportunity of staying there until the following morning, when the Blue Peter was hoisted and they set sail. There were seventy ships all trying to get out of Cove harbour at the same time and the inevitable happened: the unfortunate *Leopard* was run down by a large transport vessel. The encounter shivered its bowsprit to atoms, resulting in a new one having to be rigged out of spars once they were out at sea. From 20-26 May there was a fair wind and fair weather, but on the 27 this changed to a foul breeze and changeable weather.

The ship reached the Newfoundland Bank at the beginning of June, where those on board fished for immense numbers of cod. On 17 June the *Leopard* parted with the rest of the convoy, which set off for its different destinations. Overcast weather prevailed from 21 to 28 June, and on the 28 calamity struck off Cape Ray in the Gulf of St Lawrence, when the *Leopard* struck the rocks at the east point of the island of Anticosti in fog.

According to William they were all in bed at the time, awakening with the first thump and dressing in great haste. Great uproar and confusion resulted, with everyone being knocked off their legs, the women and children running on deck screaming and naked, and many of the men in little better condition. Although every effort was made to re-float the ship, it proved impossible. Eventually rafts were constructed, and the passengers made it to shore, just 1½ miles away. While they were packing up, dinner was cooking, which William and his companions ate in the doctor's cabin. The sailors in the meantime had placed rafts in the water. William jumped into one, with as many clothes and shirts as he could cram under his greatcoat. Although these rafts were far from comfortable, everyone was able to gain the shore: 'after which those sailors who were sober were employed in fishing up all the biscuit they possibly could with barrels of rum, pork, etc. from the Purser's store in the Cockpit.' The next day, three weeks of provisions for every hand were placed in one spot, with a guard constantly over it. The biscuit was dried in the sun on the rocks and there was an abundance of fish and wild fowl, and a considerable quantity of Anticostian produce was obtained daily. The men and officers, without breeches, waded through the breakers, each carrying a load of provisions on his back, and William managed to build himself a tolerable hut from wood and sails. This part of the island he described as being 'a plain with a fresh water lake close at hand, which was full of ducks and small fish.' There he was stranded until 2 July when a Halifax fishing boat, bound for the Labrador coast, was pressed into service. The Captain of the *Leopard* wrote dispatches for the commander of the forces and several senior naval officers, and an officer of the Royals embarked. William was given permission to accompany the officers, so at sunset they made sail in the little schooner for the St Lawrence River. The island of Anticosti is 90 miles long, and, because the schooner was becalmed, it took ten days to reach the western point of the island. As there was no compunction in those days about killing wild animals, they passed their time in attempting to kill wolves, seals and bears. When they eventually arrived at the St Lawrence River, they met a Merchantman bound for Quebec, and William was ordered on board. They arrived in Quebec on the 17 July, and on the 22 he took passage on a steam boat to Montreal, a distance of 170 miles, and landed on the 26. Of Montreal, he said it was 'a neat little town chiefly inhabited by French people, the churches are very handsome. In the interior there is a monument erected to the memory of Lord Nelson. The surrounding country is well settled, and the climate in winter not so severe as at Quebec.' However, he needed to make for Kingston, and some 9 miles from Montreal he acquired a small boat rowed by five Canadians. He later reflected that without them to pilot him he would have been completely lost amongst the hundreds of islands along the route. He explained that the Canadians commenced work at their oars at day-break and continued for about four hours, at which point they steered towards a house, and went ashore for breakfast. After a further four hours rowing, their work for the day was finished. However, in the middle of these four hours, they took an hour and a half for lunch. At night the boat was hauled up on the beach, the oars were fixed crossways, and a tarpaulin was thrown over the top,

The Dockyard, Kingston, Canada, sketch by William Nesfield.

which prevented the dew from falling on them. William reflected that: 'This was the sort of Robinson Crusoe life I led between Montreal and Kingston.' He arrived in Kingston on Sunday 7 August, where he met an old acquaintance who had been seriously ill with lake fever. Fortunately, he was able to stay with him, which was preferable to staying in a tavern filled with all kinds of people, merchants, Yankees, or anyone *en passant*: 'In the same room do all hands breakfast and dine, after which at about half past 9 o'clock p.m. the dirty mattresses and blankets are brought in for each person who chooses his corner, so that it has the appearance of a hospital instead of an Inn.'

When William enquired about the whereabouts of General Drummond, he was told that he had left Kingston and joined the army at Fort Erie, on the other side of the lake, in the Niagara district where he had been wounded. To get to Fort Erie from Kingston, where the General and the army were located, would take some twelve to eighteen days in the small boat in which he had travelled from Montreal, which only covered 12 to 18 miles a day. As there was no alternative, he left Kingston on 11 August with some ammunition for General Drummond's army, a change of clothing and his servant, via the Bay of Quinte on Lake Ontario. He described the country as the wildest-looking he had seen; there was nothing but wood, water and sky, and only a few scattered settlements between Kingston and York. The travellers experienced violent hurricanes which tore up hundreds of trees by their roots, making the roads impassable. In short, it was a very miserable journey. On 22 August he was twenty miles from York when he was nearly taken by the American fleet off York harbour, eventually arriving in York safely on 24 August, describing it as a little, paltry straggling town although it was the capital of northern Canada. He steered across the lake from York to Fort George, arriving at midnight, but as there was no possibility of getting any shelter in a house he rolled himself up in his cloak and slept in the boat. The next morning in torrents of rain, he and his kit being soaked to the skin, he reported to Major General Grant the commandant, who informed him that, as he was a newcomer, he must join a detachment of the 89th Regiment who in the fort about 1½ miles away. William objected strongly to this, but the General was adamant and would not let him proceed to join the army. His only recourse was to send Mrs Drummond's box by a despatch Dragoon and explain the reason for his delay. When the reply came he was able to gleefully remark:

> On 3rd September an order came by the express from the Dy Adjutant at Fort Eyre desiring General Grant positively to comply with what I had first requested. . . . This staggered old General Grant as he thought I was imposing on him. . . . However, in the hours after Gen'l Drummond had informed me of my route, I was in a boat with my large cargo of baggage which I could have almost crammed in my hat.

He arrived at Fort Erie the next day, 4 September, and immediately sent in his name. According to him, although the General had been injured in battle, he was making a good recovery and was very happy to see William and asked a thousand questions about Brancepeth and Spain. That night William was glad to find a corner in one of the wigwams with some straw, and, wrapped in his old cloak, he had his first sound sleep for weeks.

On 17 September there was a sortie by the Americans, who took one of the English batteries and destroyed it and its guns by setting fire to the magazine. After a battle of over two hours, 500 had been killed, wounded or taken prisoner. After this, a report came through that the American army was to be reinforced by 3000 men from Plattsburg. As General Drummond had no reason to doubt this, he decided to retreat and take up a more favourable position. Therefore, on 22 September the English army began retreating from Fort Erie and set up camp in Chippawa which, William noted, afforded one of the strongest positions in the Niagara district. There they were left undisturbed and with the approach of winter the American General Brown decided that the Niagara river could cut off his supplies, owing to floating ice, which was difficult to navigate. By 4 November, therefore, he had evacuated his troops to Blackrock and Buffalo, taking with him stores and guns and blowing up his works. This decision was to virtually end hostilities between America and Canada and the British were left in peace to rest and refresh themselves for the winter, after a most harassing and tedious campaign. During the above respite in the action, William wrote to his father a reassuring letter in which he said:

> You give me a hint in your No. 3 about Canadian ladies. I flatter myself Billie Nesfield is not quite such a fool he does not know what he's doing and that he will bear in mind no money no wife – I have seen enough of wives and botheration and the misery and inconvenience most wretchedly experienced by those who have unfortunately lost sight of their reasoning for the moment and tied the knot no no dear father you may assume that I have seen too much of the world within the last two years not to have gained and bought also a little experience.[1]

1 Reproduced by kind permission of the Trustees of Mrs Sheila Nesfield. Letter undated.

Niagara, watercolour by William Nesfield.

Reflecting on the Canadian winter, William said it could last for almost six months, with ice twelve to fourteen inches thick making a complete bridge across the St Lawrence River. Roads could only be travelled by means of sleighs and carioles and steamboats, and bateaux and ships were the only means of travel in summer throughout the country. He wrote that the roads could never be good until Canada was more thickly inhabited. He also noted how necessary the co-operation between the army and navy was for their mutual support:

> Off the mouth of the Niagara River we saw the British Squadron at anchor. Sir Jas Yeo had brought stores and provisions and reinforcements consisting of the 90th Regt., 37th and some detachments from England for the 6th and 82nd. The provisions were heartily welcomed for our army, tho small, in such an exhausted frontier could not have occupied it longer than 5 weeks, had not the fleet arrived. Appearances began long ago to look alarming, for the commissaries could get nothing not an ox, or a sheep or grain to be had nearer than Kingston.

Unfortunately, at that time he contacted 'lake fever' (perhaps malaria), and it was January 1815 before he started to mend. By 10 January he was sufficiently recovered to write home for shirts, a pair of sheets, three to four Durham newspapers, a box of Fothergills Heart Burn lozenges, a pair of short boots from Bell the Shoemaker and his green case of instruments. Although on 25 October the previous year he had written to his father that he was 'Perfectly reconciled and fixed firmly in my post under the General who certainly has behaved most handsomely to me on all occasions', nevertheless, he went on to say:

> I feel as much at home as if I was at the Rectory (but not of course as Happy) and I hope to go on in this way till we have a peace which people seem to think will be sometime during the Winter which in my humble opinion, is yet far distant – and then I have no doubt but that Gl D'm in this event will certainly steer across the Atlantic, I suppose I am ere this on ½ pay, so that when we have peace I rather think if nothing permanent or profitable or rather more a man's expectations stares me in the face you will see Master Billy taking up his corner once more at the Rectory fireside.

As President of the Province, on 1 February 1815 Colonel Drummond was to open Parliament in York, where he would hold a great dinner. Therefore, on 27 January, William was instructed to travel to York. For the journey sleighs were used, which he described as being like the body of a gig placed upon iron runners that slid over the snow as smoothly as a skate. By 18 March, when they returned to Kingston, Colonel Drummond was notified of his promotion to the position of Governor of Canada, and that he was to receive his Knighthood as K.C.B. In order to be sworn in he was required to travel to Quebec, and as his A.D.C., William was instructed to travel from Kingston to Quebec carrying Sir Gordon Drummond's private papers and baggage. He eventually arrived on 6 April after a miserable journey during which he was upset in a deep mud hole at Fort Wellington.

On 1 May 1815 he wrote to his father that, as an A.D.C., he received £70 a year in pay and had three rooms in the chateau at Quebec, the official residence of Sir Gordon Drummond, and was waited on by a groom and valet. In spite of these favourable circumstances, a mishap that occurred the following year further increased his disillusionment with Canada. Sir Gordon Drummond was in the habit of entertaining on a Saturday evening in the chateau. Unfortunately, on Saturday 3 February 1816, when William was in the middle of a rubber of bridge, he was told that his servants had lit a fire in their stove, resting it directly on the floor instead of on a metal pan. The flames had to be put out by tearing up the floor of their sleeping room and throwing snow and water on the beams. Unfortunately, the ballroom was just below and the ceiling fell in. The water from above deluged the whole chateau. William was blamed for this incident, although it was not his fault, and it was decided by his superiors that it would be a good idea if he took a trip to Upper Canada while everyone cooled off.

Apart from this unfortunate event, the rigours of the severely cold climate in Canada, and his bout of lake fever, he survived relatively unscathed and remained in Canada for

Weatley Farm, Brancepeth, County Durham, watercolour by William Nesfield.

almost two years carrying out his duties as A.D.C. to General Drummond and producing two large watercolours of the Niagara Falls, one from the American side and one from the Canadian side, together with a large map of the area.

His desire to return home, however, is reflected in the following letter to his father:

> I think you will say that Bill was born to be hung for neither Bullet or wave ever brought me low as yet, thank God! I am a tolerably lucky hand & can say that the idea of a Peace I am sure would restore me to health immediately how happy shall I be if ever I saw the day when the Gen'l & I start for dear old England once more. I vow and swear ardently that if ever my foot is safe on her shore, my bones shall never again desert her.

In May 1816, Sir Gordon Drummond left Canada. Ill health caused by neglect of the wound he sustained during the battle of Niagara led to this departure, and William sailed with him, arriving in England on 21 June 1816. His opinion of both the American General Brown and the settlers was recorded by him. He described Brown as a 'man of the meanest birth who from working his way into the Yankee world as a petty merchant of potash, made some money and then became a great but unlearned member of the United States Society.' His opinion of the settlers was no better:

> These noble *well bred* members of Parliament are the dregs of the world for tho people of the greatest landed property in Canada, they have been obliged to quit England to escape from an halter. This is positively the case with the major part of them and the idea of their being members of a House of Parliament is too ridiculous. However, they fancy themselves great statesmen and carry their heads not a little high.[1]

These views were ones that would have been shared by many of the English upper class of the day. However, before William returned to England, he met a Mr Vaughan, a master in the American navy, who 'behaved in a manner quite contrary to my expectations – in short we met with more civility than I fear they would have received on our side.' Hopefully, because of this encounter he came home with a more open-minded attitude towards difference than that possessed by some of the wealthy landowners who were later to be his clients.

The cold and homesickness William experienced in Canada meant that his father's well-intentioned efforts to get him transferred from Spain to Canada, in spite of the resultant promotion, had been a mixed blessing. Canada was perceived as a backwater; Europe was the only place to be. Here advancement, glory and the spoils of war were to be found, and it was the focus of the Nation's attention. On his return to England the war with France ended, and fewer soldiers, both officers and men, were needed. William was promptly placed on half pay, a situation that did not change. He did, however, secure a post in the Senior Department of the Royal Military College, Sandhurst for a spell, acquired, once again, with the help of Lady Winchester through her acquaintance with the Duke of York.[2]

On 25 December 1818 he resigned his commission, citing ill health brought on during his time in Canada.[3] This was not the real reason, however: by this time he was determined to become a professional painter. He returned to Brancepeth, where he was to spend the next three years painting and sketching the countryside around Brancepeth and further afield.

1 The expression 'escape from an halter' would have referred to individuals who wanted to escape from their life in England. This could be for a variety of reasons, perhaps they were in debt, wanted to flee from an unsatisfactory marriage or simply wanted a better life for themselves.

2 The above quotations are taken from William Nesfield, *Reminiscences*.

3 William Nesfield's Discharge Papers are held in the National Record Office, Kew.

3.

Medieval Influences

Brancepeth is situated in an area of County Durham, which even today is still very rural. The village remains a quiet backwater, the road terminating at the rectory, church and castle as it would have done in the early nineteenth century. It is not difficult, therefore, to visualize the Nesfield family carrying on their day-to-day life between these three social centres. Although in their paternalistic age they would have considered themselves to be a cut above the cap-doffing villagers, nevertheless they were all, squire, rector and villagers, part of a close-knit hierarchical community, with everyone knowing their allotted place in society –'the rich man in his castle the poor man at his gate'!

One of the ways the landed elite sought to put the profound changes undoubtedly taking place around them to the back of their minds was to indulge in a form of make-believe. William came to face-to-face with this 'fairytale world' when he returned home in 1818, although he was unaware of it at the time: the desire of the elites to return to what was considered a more acceptable past, before industrialization. During the three years he spent in Brancepeth, between 1818 and 1821, the great medieval castle, built at the same time as the church in the twelfth century, and which had originally belonged to the powerful Neville family, was undergoing restoration. This was a vast programme: one estimate suggests that more than three hundred men were employed at an approximate cost of £80,000 per year. It must, therefore, have been amazing, not only to the villagers but also the family in the rectory, to see and hear the activity going on around them.

Brancepeth Castle had been purchased in 1796 by William Russell, who had inherited a considerable fortune from his uncle. Russell was a self-made businessman who speculated in collieries, and had founded the banking firm of Russell & Wade and acquired the Wallsend Pit Company. By 1817, however, the castle had passed into the hands of his son, Matthew Russell, who was married to Elizabeth (née Tennyson), the aunt of Alfred, Lord Tennyson, the future Poet Laureate. Matthew apparently had few antiquarian interests, having been described as 'a large, amiable, pleasure-loving major in the Durham Militia.' However, the

Tennyson family had a strong romantic streak and a passionate interest in the Middle Ages, and because of their influence, Matthew Russell carried out the restoration programme in the true spirit of the Medieval Revival. The driving force behind the work was Elizabeth Russell's brother, Charles Tennyson, who engaged staff, assembled a collection of ancient armour, chose wallpapers, carpets and stained glass, and generally interfered with the work of the architect employed to carry out the restoration. Charles Tennyson had inherited Bayons Manor in Lincolnshire on the death of his father, and added d'Eyncourt to his name in the romantic belief that he was, through his mother's family, descended from the holders of the Barony of d'Eyncourt, formerly Lords of this Manor. The restoration at Brancepeth Castle was, therefore, the perfect outlet for his romantic vision.

The early nineteenth century had seen an upsurge in the restoration and building of castles of which Brancepeth castle is one example. There were a number of motives behind this interest. It has been suggested that 'Castles were picturesque, they were romantic, they stood for tradition, authority and military glory.'[1] As early as 1773 Richard Payne Knight (1750-1824) had built Downton Castle in Herefordshire, in what was described as a 'Picturesquely, irregular composition.'[2] James Wyatt designed a castle for George III on the banks of the Thames at Kew in 1802, whilst Robert Smirke was responsible for creating Lowther Castle in Westmorland in 1806 for Lord Lonsdale and, between 1801 and 1820, Eastnor Castle in Herefordshire for Lord Somers. Motivating these restorations was a growing desire to return to the perceived values and customs of the Middle Ages, as it was a time some members of the landed class believed to have been a golden age of stability and faith, which glorified war through a chivalric code. They felt a rapport with this romanticized view of the past, particularly with knights, who fought by a code of chivalry that ensured both sides would behave in a civilized and gallant manner. Popular figures were King Arthur and his knights and their mythological high standards of loyalty, bravery and heroism, and chivalrous behaviour towards damsels in distress. It was behaviour they perceived as being appropriate to the place in society that the landed class had occupied for generations, associated with traditional high standards of conduct which only they, through their exalted situation, could hope to understand! Therefore, by evoking a world of noblesse oblige, in which they could take pride in their ancient lineage, they aimed to gain a positive self-image based on a romanticized understanding of the processes that had helped shape their past. This intellectual play-acting was an indication of their unease at the unprecedented social and economic changes taking place around them, and was intended to insulate them from the slowly creeping tide of industrialization and population growth, which conceivably might lead to the end of their ordered way of life. A romantic vision of the Middle Ages was, therefore, a tool that the upper classes used to help them cope with these changes. The phenomenon was to manifest itself in every aspect of civilized life, in art and architecture, poetry, literature and county histories, in the work of the antiquarian and in garden design, and that escapist vision was one of the main reasons William's elaborate

1 Mark Girouard, *The Return to Camelot* (New Haven and London, Yale University Press, 1981), p. 44.
2 *Ibid.* p. 40.

Brancepeth Castle and St Brandon's Church
(with tree) and Brancepeth Park, watercolour by William Nesfield.

formal gardens were to become so popular in the 1830s. Horace Walpole's (1717-1797) seminal Gothic novel, *The Castle of Ortranto,* was published in 1764; Thomas Warton's *The History of English Poetry* in 1774; and Bishop Percy's medieval ballads and poetry, which included his *Reliques of Ancient English Poetry* of 1765 inspired Walter Scott (1717-1832) to bring the Middle Ages to life for a wider audience. Scott wrote his *Border Minstrelsy* in 1802, and in 1804 translated the medieval ballad *Sir Tristram.* Scott's down-to-earth, colourful heroes and their heroic deeds, in stories which covered a period from the twelfth to the fifteenth centuries, were so popular that when *Ivanhoe* was published in 1819 'twelve thousand copies were sold in the first weeks following its publication.'[1]

A group of enthusiastic antiquarians, including Thomas Hearne and William Byrne, sought out ancient remains in the countryside of the British Isles. Their series, *The Antiquities of Great Britain*, published between 1778 and 1786, and again in 1806, was mainly concerned with castles and monasteries. Rosemary Sweet has written that, 'Hearne's engravings were not simply exercises in picturesque composition, but showed meticulous attention to architectural detail and a high level of accuracy.'[2] There was a revival of old customs and traditions including organized pageantry and fancy dress. The most famous example of a Medieval revival pageant is probably the Eglinton Tournament, which took place in 1838 on the Scottish estate of Archibald, Earl of Eglinton and Winton. It was designed to represent, as authentically as possible, a medieval tournament

1 Joanna Banham, *William Morris and the Middle Ages* (Manchester University Press, 1984), p. 25.

2 Rosemary Sweet, *Antiquaries: The Discovery of the Past in Eighteenth Century Britain* (Continuum, 2004), p. 320.

with tented pavilions, knights in armour, medieval costumes, banners and jousting. Unfortunately, although the tournament cost an estimated £40,000 and received a great deal of publicity, it must be regarded as a failure, as it was accompanied by a torrential rain storm. Furthermore, it nearly bankrupted Lord Eglinton; his descendants were paying off his debts for years after the event.[1]

Alongside the historical interest in the Middle Ages, from the early years of the nineteenth century historic elements in gardening were also regarded as important.

For example, John Claudius Loudon's (1783-1843) *An Encyclopaedia of Gardening* of 1829 included a section on garden history, and George William Johnson (1802-1886) became the principal authority on the history of horticulture after his definitive *A History of English Gardening* was published in 1829.

It was against the background of the Medieval Revival that the Russells' restoration programme began. Their choice of architect was John Paterson of Edinburgh. Paterson, who was well respected, had a sound knowledge of building techniques, although according to Anthony Salvin, who was Paterson's pupil during the restoration, his knowledge of medieval architecture was minimal. As Salvin was Marianne Nesfield's nephew, it was arranged that he should live at the rectory during the three years it took to complete the restoration. The close proximity of the castle to the rectory and the fact that the Russells and Paterson dined regularly with the Nesfield family enabled them to keep up to date with day-to-day developments. It was Salvin's enthusiasm for historical accuracy that fuelled William's own desire to include historic detail in his work when he became a professional landscape gardener, and the two men became close friends and colleagues. The Salvins were an old and illustrious County Durham family, who could trace their ancestry back to the tenth century and the reign of King Stephen. It has been said of Salvin that his wish to re-establish the Salvins of Sunderland Bridge amongst the landed gentry 'at once fuelled his professional ambition and made "Old England" images come so naturally to him.'[2] William also took great pride in his family lineage, and this helped forge another link between the two men.

When Salvin took up architecture in 1818, his churches were built in the Norman, Early English or Decorated Gothic styles, and his meticulous research into medieval buildings earned him a reputation that led to restoration commissions at the Tower of London, Windsor Castle and Durham Cathedral. He collected prints and engravings of old buildings, his scrap-books were full of drawings of costumes, furniture and armour; and when he moved to London he was elected to the Society of Antiquarians.[3] His study of old texts and self-instruction in historic architectural detail was necessary at the time, when little had been published on the subject. One notable exception was Thomas Rickman's research into practical ways in which to define the stylistic development of Gothic architecture. This research was published in 1817 as *An attempt to discriminate the Styles of Architecture*

1 See Ian Anstruther, *The Knight and the Umbrella – An Account of the Eglinton Tournament 1839* (Geoffrey Bles, 1963).

2 Mark Girouard, *The Victorian Country House* (Clarendon Press, 1971), Foreword.

3 Salvin was elected member of the Society of Antiquarians on 4 March 1824.

in England. Minor, but increasing scholarly, studies of ecclesiastical buildings were also undertaken in this period, such as John Britton's research on cathedrals and other ancient buildings.[1] Salvin's domestic buildings, however, were, with few exceptions, Elizabethan or Jacobean Revival in style. For these he aimed to emulate the great prodigy houses built during the reign of the Tudors and early Stuarts, such as Wollaton Hall in Nottinghamshire, which was begun in 1580; Hatfield House in Hertfordshire (1607); and Blickling Hall in Suffolk, designed in 1616. New domestic buildings in the Gothic style had been few and far between in the eighteenth century, as classicism was the dominant style. A notable exception was Horace Walpole's 'Gothick' fantasy, Strawberry Hill in Twickenham, which was built in 1740. Walpole carried on the Gothic theme internally, adapting 'medieval tombs and screens to make chimney-pieces for living rooms and alcoves for bedrooms.'[2] Another early experiment in the style was undertaken by the wealthy aristocrat William Beckford (1760-1844) at Fonthill Abbey in Wiltshire between 1785 and 1812, which the architect James Wyatt designed for him in a 'synthesis of English and Portuguese Gothic.'[3] In the 1820s, Sir Walter Scott re-designed Abbotsford in Roxburgh in the Gothic style. The first major public building to be specifically commissioned, however, was not until 1837, when the Palace of Westminster was built by Charles Barry (1795-1860) and Augustus Welby Northmore Pugin (1812-1852). Salvin, together with a small group of architects, was to take a serious interest in authentic old buildings and their preservation in the early nineteenth century. The group included William Wilkins (1778-1839), who remodelled Tregothnan in Cornwall for Lord Falmouth, and in 1810 designed a new wing at Pentillie Castle in the same county; William Burn (1789-1870); and Edward Blore (1787-1879), who was responsible for twenty-two topographical works, and who published *Monumental Remains of Noble and Eminent Persons* in 1826.

Although William and Salvin shared similar ideologies, and Salvin's knowledge and understanding of historical precedents influenced William's thinking, this did not mean that either of the two men faithfully reproduced designs that would have existed in the eras of the Tudors and Stuarts. Salvin's architecture, for example, has been described as: 'a fusion of styles which came together to denote traditional values of Old English hospitality.'[4] And it was to be an amalgam of styles that would be seen in William's own designs: they included elements from the gardens of the early Tudors; those that accompanied the great Prodigy houses of Elizabeth I's reign; *parterres-de-broderie* derived from seventeenth-century French gardens; and reconstructions of the picturesque landscapes he painted and sketched throughout his life.

1 For John Britton's work see *Autobiography of John Britton* (2 vols., London, 1850); J. Mordaunt Crook; 'John Britton and the Genesis of the Gothic Revival', *Concerning Architecture: Essays on Architectural Writers and Writing*, ed. John Summerson (London, 1986), pp. 98-119; and P. Ferriday 'John Britton', *Architectural Review*, 77 (1957), p. 367.

2 Mark Girouard, *Return to Camelot*, p. 21.

3 *Gentleman's Magazine*, 1830, I, p. 541.

4 Mark Girouard's 'Foreword' in Jill Allibone's *Anthony Salvin – Pioneer of Gothic Revival Architecture* (Cambridge, The Lutterworth Press, 1987).

4.

Painting the Picturesque

Whilst the Brancepeth years were pivotal in introducing William to an idealized medieval past, they also enabled him to renew his friendship with Newbey Lowson, who introduced him to his circle of artistic and influential friends. As Lowson was already an important member of the Nesfield social circle, it could have been his influence that helped the younger man make up his mind to go to London and become a member of the Society of Watercolour Painters. Lowson was a wealthy bachelor, collector, antiquarian and amateur artist who enjoyed picturesque scenery and subscribed to topographical magazines. He was acquainted with Henry Vane, 1st Earl of Darlington, who lived at Raby Castle. The Earl was a patron of the painter Joseph Mallord William Turner (1775-1851) and Turner invariably stayed with him when visiting County Durham. William became a great admirer of Turner's work and copied his *Liber Studiorum,* which he collected in a small notebook of over one hundred drawings.[1] Indeed, so involved was he in the romantic associations of remote, wild places, he faced the real difficulties associated with landing on the remote island of Staffa off the Isle of Mull in Scotland in order to paint Fingal's Cave, as Turner had done before him. A comparison between the work of the two men was made by the critic and writer John Ruskin (1819-1900).[2] Newbey Lowson is reputed to have been Turner's travelling companion in 1802 when the painter visited the continent after the Peace of Amiens was signed in March of that year.[3] In 1820 William and Lowson followed in Turner's footsteps by visiting France and Switzerland.[4] William wrote that

1 This Sketch Book is in the Victoria & Albert Museum, Drawings and Paintings Collection.

2 That William Nesfield was acquainted with Turner is confirmed in Ruskin's diary entry of 6 July 1841 when he wrote that he had 'Dined with Turner, Jones and Nesfield in Griffin's yesterday'. Quoted in E. T. Cook, *The Life of John Ruskin* (Cambridge University Press, vol. 1, 1911) p. 121.

3 Cecilia Powell, 'Turner's Travelling Companion of 1802: A Mystery Resolved?' *Turner Society News*, no. 54, February 1990, pp. 12-15.

4 Shirley Evans, 'Following in Turner's Footsteps', *Turner Society News*, no. 67, August 1994, pp. 3-4.

Mamhead Lodge House, Devon, watercolour by William Nesfield.

they 'a pied with our rucksacks via Dover, Calais [no steamers then] Paris and then the Rhine up to Basle – thence to Neuchatel, Geneva, Lausanne, Val d'Costa, etc. returning by the weary Diligence to Paris and home – no railway.'[30]

In 1821, when the castle restoration was complete, and with his head full of medievalism, history and Picturesque landscapes, William went to live in London with Salvin, where they took rooms at 52 Newman Street off Oxford Street. William intended to pursue his desire to become a professional painter, and Salvin to further his career in architecture.

When the two men arrived in London, Salvin soon established himself as an architect. He designed Mamhead in Devon for Sir Robert William Newman, the senior partner in a prosperous firm of general merchants between 1825 and 1838. This property was described in 1830 as 'A splendid mansion of the Elizabethan character, the oriel windows, tower staircases and numerous chimnies, the gables crowning the attics, and the total absence of ecclesiastical architecture, are the characteristic features.'[1] William produced a watercolour of the garden at Mamhead showing a simple formal flowerbed and fountain, together with a sketch of Mamhead Park. There is, however, no evidence to suggest that at this early date he carried out any alterations to the landscape.

1 *Gentleman's Magazine*, 1, 1830, p. 541.

Tobermory, sketch by William Nesfield.

The Society of Watercolour Painters, whose galleries were then situated in Pall Mall East (now in Blackfriars), had been formed in November 1804 at the Stratford Coffee House in Oxford Street in direct response to the elitism of the Royal Academy and a desire on the part of its members to paint picturesque scenery in the remoter areas of the British Isles. The only evidence of any work of William's taking place indoors during this period was during his time in Brancepeth, when he painted his father at his easel in his study; the interior of his own Studio; and the Chancel in Brancepeth Church.

The desire amongst poets, artists and tourists to undertake on-the-spot sketches and paintings in romantic, remote locations, especially in the remoter areas of Scotland and Wales, had its roots in the early eighteenth century. It was part of the philosophy that emphasised man's insignificance in nature, and which was popularized in the writings of the poet and essayist Alexander Pope (1689-1744). Joseph Thomson's poem, 'The Seasons', was also very influential and demonstrated the author's sensitivity to his surroundings. These early eighteenth-century aesthetics did not, however, advocate painting outdoors from nature, but rather showcased classical iconography in landscape painting, demonstrated in the work of Nicolas Poussin (1594-1665) and Claude Lorrain (1600-1682). This school of art was later to develop into the Picturesque Movement, of which William and his fellow painters were members, and painting from nature was central to their work. One of William's first tasks when he arrived in London was to take lessons from Anthony Vandyke Copley Fielding (1787-1855), who also lived in Newman Street. It has been said of Fielding that he

Ross Castle on the Lower Lake, Killlarney, Ireland,
watercolour by William Nesfield.

Mill near Pembroke, watercolour by William Nesfield.

Horse, watercolour
by William Nesfield.

Deer and Cow, watercolours
by William Nesfield.

Castle and landscape.

Detail of a boat.

was limited in his subject matter, having only, 'one sea, one moor, one down, one lake, one misty gleam.'[1] However, he was an important member of the Society, its secretary in 1818, and its president from 1831. Fifteen of William's lecture notes survive and show that the syllabus covered basic painting skills including perspective, form of outline and colouring connected with the landscape.[2] These lessons reinforced those he had received whilst a gentleman cadet at the Royal Military Academy, where his drawing master had been Thomas Paul Sandby, a member of a family of talented painters. Thomas Paul's father, Paul Sandby R.A. (1731-1809) and his brother Thomas (1721-1798), were primarily topographers and architectural designers. They were skilled in the use of perspective, and innovators in the art of landscape painting, producing romantic, imaginative landscapes. It has been said of Paul Sandby that he was 'almost the first of the English artists to introduce his countrymen to the beauties and picturesque antiquities of Scotland and particularly of Wales.'[3]

Thomas Paul Sandby became a drawing master at Woolwich in 1797 and he continued the Sandby tradition of 'combining the art of watercolour with architectural design and perspective.'[4] This tradition was to be crucial to William's own philosophy when he became a professional painter and landscape designer, and can be seen in his work in Scotland, Wales and Ireland.

This interest in the wilder scenery of the British Isles can be traced back to the travels of the Revd William Gilpin (1724-1804), who publicized the results of the sketching and painting tours he undertook to the remoter areas of the British Isles between 1768 and 1776. These publications had great appeal for professionals and amateurs alike. The first publication, and the most popular, was in 1786, entitled *The Lake District Guide*. Gilpin's evaluation and analysis of the scenes he witnessed fired the imaginations of amateur painters from the leisured classes and professional artists. Painting in England was an occupation that could be undertaken by both sexes at a time when the Napoleonic wars prevented people from travelling on the continent, but it was also an interest that was to continue after the war ended in 1815. Watercolour materials were portable; there was a steady flow of literature demonstrating the techniques of the art; and they captured their subjects so well, at a time before the advent of photography. The more affluent members of society were able to travel with their paints, brushes and guide books to the remoter regions of the British Isles, looking to paint waterfalls, mountains, hills, old cottages, woods, lakes, crumbling ruins, medieval monasteries and abbeys.

His journey to the continent with Newbey Lowson meant that at the 1823 Annual Exhibition of the Society, William was able to exhibit a number of paintings from that tour. They included paintings of the Chateau di Jaro, near Aosta; Piedmont; the Bridge

---

1 Old Water-Colour Society's Club, Third Annual Volume, 1925. Courtesy of the Royal Watercolour Society.
2 Nesfield Archives.
3 Iolo Williams, *Early English Watercolours* (Bath, Kingsmead Reprints, 1970), p. 32.
4 John Harris, *The Artist and the Country House* (Sotheby's Publications, 1979), p. 309.

Watercolours by William Nesfield

Right, 'Innoculated' [sic] Beech.

Trees.

Details of foliage.

Sailing ship.

Group of trees.

Laundry ladies.

Man sitting.

Swiss milkmaid.

Man with fishing net.

Man reclining.

over the Reichenbach; and the Canton of Berne, in Switzerland. In total he was to exhibit ninety-one paintings at the Society's Annual Exhibitions over the years. Amongst his contemporaries were David Cox, William Harvell, John Varley, James Duffield Harding, Robert Hills and George Fennell Robson. It was their habit to travel around the British Isles painting and sketching as they went, and an incident on one of these trips was recorded: 'Nesfield was one of a party of painters, including David Cox at the Devonshire Arms, near Bolton Abbey, in September 1844. As was their wont, they were comparing their day's sketches in the inn parlour, when our artist signified his dissatisfaction with his own work by crumpling it up and throwing it towards the fire. Kindly old David, ever ready to encourage others, at once started up and saved it, declaring that it was a really fine work.'[1]

Although there are a number of William's paintings in museums and galleries, much of his work is still in private hands, including nearly 400 sketches and paintings, some unfinished, in the Nesfield family archive. That he was highly thought of by contemporaries is demonstrated by his election to full member of the Society of Watercolour Painters in June 1823, having only been made an Associate in April of that year. John Ruskin, who joined the Society at the age of sixteen, wrote in glowing terms of his ability, and his testimony is well worth quoting at length:

> Stand for half an hour beside the fall of Schaffhausen, on the north side where the rapids are long, and watch how the water first beds, unbroken in pure polished velocity . . . the dew feeding the lichens of the dark rocks of the shore and chequering them with purple and silver. . . . Probably you will not be much disposed to think of any mortal work at the time, but when you look back on what you have seen and are inclined to compare it with art, you will remember – or ought to remember – Nesfield. He is a man of extraordinary feeling, both for the management of the changeful veil of spray or mist, just in its curves or contours, and unequalled in colour except for Turner. None of our watercolour painters can approach him in the management of the variable hues of clear water over weeded rocks: but his feeling for it often leads him a little too far and, like Copley Fielding, he loses sight of simplicity and dignity for the sake of prettiness. His waterfalls are, however, unequalled in their way, and if he would remember that in all such scenes there is much gloom as well as much splendour, and relieve the lustre of his attractive passages of colour with more substance to the parts of his picture unaffected by spray, his work would be nearly perfect. His seas also are most instructive a little confused in chiaroscuro, but refined in form and admirable in colour.[2]

William's work ranged from monochromes to pencil sketches, pen and wash to watercolours. He painted mountain scenery, rivers flowing into deep valleys, storm clouds

1 J.L. Roget, *History of the Old Water-Colour Society*, (Society of Watercolour Painters, 1891), vols. 1-2, pp. 83-4. Taken from Solly's *Life of Cox*, p. 130.

2 John Ruskin, *Modern Painters*, vol. III, pp. 343-344. Completed in 5 vols., 1860.

and raging seas. He was also perfectly competent in drawing animals, ships, buildings and figures. However, his ability to paint landscapes is confirmed in a letter sent by Edwin Landseer to William's wife asking her to suggest that her husband 'slap a background; on to one of his animal paintings.'[1]

Salvin and William's relationship continued to be a close one, and after Salvin married Anne Nesfield in 1826, William made their home at 33 Somerset Street near Portman Square his base, until he himself married in 1833. This foothold in London was a useful one as it kept him in close touch with the Society, where he remained a member until 1852, as a Resolution dated 14 June that year testifies:[2]

> That members having heard read the Resignation of Geo. Cattermole Esq and W.A. Nesfield Esq deeply regret the loss of talent so admirable and so valuable to the interests of the Society with which they have been so long and so happily connected and that the Secretary be directed to forward the Resolution to both these Gentlemen.

Although William relinquished his connection with the Society, his commitment to the rural scenery of the British Isles never ceased and he continued to paint and draw throughout his long life.

1 Nesfield Archives.

2 Resolution passed 14 June 1852 at a meeting of the Society: See J.L. Roget, *History of the Old Water-Colour Society*, vol. 1-2, 1891 in *The Old Water-Colour Club,* vol. XXVVII, p. 29. Newspaper cuttings kept by the Revd Nesfield held in the Nesfield Archives confirm that his son was regarded as a valuable addition to the Society.

A seascape, watercolour by William Nesfield.

Harlech from the Peat Bog, watercolour by William Nesfield.

Barnard Castle, watercolour by William Nesfield, 1824.

On the Road to Harlech, watercolour by William Nesfield.

5.

Marriage and a Start in Landscape Gardening

In 1833, William's carefree bachelor existence ended when he married Emma Anne Mills. He met her when she was visiting her brother at Newton Hall near Durham, which he was tenanting from Matthew Russell of Brancepeth Castle. Emma was well connected; her mother was Alicia Harriet, the daughter of William Markham (1719-1807) Archbishop of York, Prebendary of Durham and chaplain to George II, and Emma's grandmother was Sarah (née Goddard), the daughter of a wealthy Rotterdam merchant. Emma's father was Henry Foster Mills of Helm Park, Chancellor of York Minster, and the brother of Marianne Nesfield. William addressed Emma as his 'Dear Pupil' when he wrote proposing marriage, as he had given her painting lessons during her stay at Newton Hall; although, if the watercolour shown below is anything to go by, she was already a competent amateur watercolour painter.[1]

Although at the bottom of the letter she wrote coyly: 'Oh no kind Sir this never will do "for me to wed myself with you?"',[2] they were married on Thursday 13 July 1833, at three o'clock, from Emma's family home at 35 Great Pulteney Street, Bath. William described the marriage in a letter to Salvin, sent whilst he and Emma were on their honeymoon, as having been conducted in 'a canny quiet way'.[3] Part of their honeymoon was spent in Brancepeth, from whence William sent the account of their honeymoon journey. He said they went firstly to the Clifton Downs near Bristol in 'a lent *300 guinea* carriage as flash as possible.' At the inn they were: 'amongst a host of dandies &c & a precious bill I had to pay for *wax candles* & other pieces of rascality.' However, after what he described as their 'aristocratic debut', they took 'to poor man's style', Emma fortunately being content to travel on the top of the coach. They continued

1 Nesfield Archives.
2 *Ibid.*
3 Letter from William Nesfield to Anthony Salvin, 29 July 1833, Durham University Library, Special Collections, Add. MS 1071/23.

their journey to Hereford via Chepstow up the River Wye, both of them no doubt enjoying the picturesque scenery of the area. They moved on to Shrewsbury, Liverpool and Manchester, and finally to Brancepeth.[1]

When the Revd Nesfield drew up his last Will and Testament, his money was left equally between his surviving children, apart from £200 a year to his wife for her lifetime, but with so many children the amount each received would not have been large. William was reliant on this bequest, plus his small army pension and what he made from the sale of his paintings. Although his income had been sufficient for his needs when he was a bachelor, after his marriage he needed to improve his financial situation. In his letter to Salvin he said he was: 'deficit in the way of coin', as he had only £10 left to last him until Christmas. Salvin did his best to bring him to the attention of his own clients. It helped that William's expertise as a surveyor and engineer made him competent to draw up the plans for the formal gardens to accompany the Elizabethan and Jacobean Revival mansions Salvin was designing, and to advise on how to improve their estates.

After their honeymoon, the couple went to live for a time with Emma's widowed mother in Great Pulteney Street in Bath, designed by Thomas Baldwin (1751-1820) in 1785, and linked to the city of Bath by the Florentine-style Pulteney Bridge, with its fashionable shops, designed by Robert Adam for William Pulteney between 1768-1774.[2] There, on 2 April 1835, their eldest son, William Eden, was born. Eden was destined to become an architect fascinated by decorative ornamentation and beautiful objects, and the city of Bath, thought by many to be one of the most elegant cities in England, was an appropriate birth place for him.[3] By 1835 Bath was already established as a spa town patronized by the wealthy for its therapeutic waters, concert halls, assembly rooms and medieval Abbey. Although the Roman Baths were not discovered until 1879, its planning in the middle years of the eighteenth century reflected the essence of the original Roman town. It became: 'an area of civilized urban life in which men and women of sufficient means could enjoy themselves and entertain one another in an agreeable setting.'[4] It was an ideal place for a widow of means to settle with her family, and so after her husband's death this is where Emma's mother took up residence.[5] By 1835 the great Palladian set-pieces associated with the city, the Circus, Crescents and Parades, had been constructed in one unifying material, oolite stone, by the Ralph Allens (father and son). In their midst was the great medieval Abbey church, one of England's major medieval monuments. When Mrs Mills resided in Bath the last major classical feature, the Royal Crescent, built between 1765 and 1775 was barely sixty years old; the soft Bath stone was still in pristine condition, making Bath an elegant and urbane city.

1 *Ibid.*

2 Mrs Mills was a welcome guest at the rectory. In his autobiographical notes, William Nesfield wrote: 'Alicia Mills a long time guest at Brancepeth on acct. of her *excellent music*'. Nesfield Archives.

3 Eden was baptised in Bath on 10 May 1835: Colin Johnston, Chief Archivist, Bath and N.E. Somerset.

4 Claire Tomalin, *Jane Austin: A Life* (Viking, 1997), p. 147.

5 Mrs Mills died aged 69 and was buried in Bath on 5 March 1840 Colin Johnston, Chief Archivist, Bath and N.E. Somerset.

Ilfracombe Harbour, watercolour by Emma Anne Nesfield, 1828, inscribed 'E.A.M.', lower right.

Our House, Fortis Green, North London, watercolour by William Nesfield.

The Office Yard, Methley Hall, Yorkshire, watercolour by William Nesfield.

Cows near Eton, watercolour by William Nesfield.

The time the Nesfields spent in Bath was always seen as a temporary arrangement until their home in Fortis Green in North London, which was being designed for them by Salvin, was ready for them. On 31 November 1833, Salvin bought twelve acres of land in Finchley from a Revd Haygarth and obtained a sixty-year lease on Elm House (renamed Elmhurst) in the East End Road, together with ten acres of paddock, stables and a farm. Nesfield purchased five acres for £500, and bought one of two Italianate-style villas designed by Salvin on the site, which the Nesfields named Coleshall House. The area was very rural in those days and the house was surrounded by farms and woodlands and had views towards Kenwood House and Highgate Church. There was easy access to the London omnibus, and the great coach routes to the north were becoming important to William as his landscape gardening business expanded. The family moved to Fortis Green sometime between 1836 and 1837 and William developed his own garden and that of his neighbour.[1]

By 1838 the land owned by the Nesfields and their neighbour, which covered 8¼ acres, with 4¼ acres belonging to the Nesfields, had attracted the attention of John Claudius Loudon (1783-1843). Loudon was an influential publicist, journalist and writer and he included the Fortis Green property in his series, *Suburban Gardens*, under the title of 'Descriptive Notices of select Suburban Residences, with Remarks on each intended to illustrate the Principles and Practice of Landscape Gardening' in his journal, *The Gardener's Magazine*. The plan showed the entrance gates of both properties and the boundary hedge, and how the Nesfields' land extended across both properties, whilst William's neighbour owned a grass field which gave him access to the public road. The division of the land longitudinally was part of the purchase agreement, as it enabled the budding landscape designer to create the illusion of more space. This he did by using a wire fence which was virtually undetectable from the villas. In the distance was woodland, which was part of the Earl of Mansfield's grounds at Kenwood House. This, together with the spire of Highgate Church, provided a fine view for both the Nesfields and their neighbour. The care taken to ensure that they would both benefit from the 'borrowed' landscape beyond their respective grounds showcases the skills William had learned as a professional painter of rural scenery, and reinforces his concern for the Renaissance principle of unity of all the parts.

Below the terrace of Nesfields' villa were peach trees, and nectarines and apricots adorned the greenhouse wall. The formal garden below the terrace consisted of simple beds containing scroll-like shapes in which he placed small flowers, surrounded by gravel and edged with box. These were early precursors to the later, much greater gardens he was to design for his wealthy clients. Below were herbaceous borders, beds and a lawn with trees on either side.

1 In the 'honeymoon' letter William remarked to Salvin, 'the ideal pleasure of being neighbours to *you* and *yours*, our happiness wd then in the reality be complete since Emma *truly* loves Anne, indeed she expresses the highest respect for you both.

The manner in which his work was regarded at the time, both as an artist and landscape gardener, was recorded by Loudon:

> Mr Nesfield has long been well-known as a landscape painter of eminence, and as connected with the Society of Painters in Water-Colours. He has lately directed his attention to landscape gardening, and that with so much success that his opinion is now sought for by gentlemen of taste in every part of the country.[1]

While Loudon was visiting Fortis Green in order to discuss his article, William provided him with at least one watercolour for his book, *The Trees and Shrubs of Britain*, which was published in 1838.

It is true that by the time of Loudon's visit William was a well-established landscape designer, but not all of his early commissions were successful. In 1834 he submitted a plan to redesign the grounds at Scotney Castle in Kent for Edward Hussey. However, as he was still very much a new boy, it was 74-year-old William Sawrey Gilpin (1762-1843), nephew of the Revd William Gilpin and the second son of the painter Sawrey Gilpin (1733-1807), whose romantically conceived design was chosen. Gilpin was already established as a Picturesque Improver, and this design was probably to be the last strictly romantic concept in England before the beginning of Queen Victoria's reign. It was also to prove to be Gilpin's last commission, and this left William with no serious rivals.

No-one had lived in the old moated castle at Scotney since the deaths of Hussey's sister, father and grandfather, which took place within one year. His mother, not surprisingly, became convinced that the low-set house was an unhealthy place to live, and moved away. However, when Hussey came of age he moved back to Scotney, and, the castle having fallen into disrepair, he decided to have a new house built on higher ground. Salvin was called in, and his work between 1835 and 1843 has been described as marking a very important stage in his architectural development, from 'confectionery' Gothic to correct Elizabethan. The new mansion overlooked the fourteenth-century castle and its seventeenth-century wing, which was deliberately ruined so that it could be used as an 'eye-catcher'. Between the new mansion and the old castle Gilpin planted up an old quarry, so the viewer could look across the valley taking in both the quarry and the romantic ruin in the distance. The differences between the garden principles of William and those of Gilpin become obvious at Scotney. William would never have submitted a design that was completely asymmetrical, informal, and placed between one architectural feature and another. His own picturesque interpretation called for strict formality in the environs of the house, as they needed to reflect its architecture. This should gradually merge into informality beyond. The unexecuted plan he had submitted for Scotney was for formal *parterres* in the environs of the new mansion. William did, however, secure one successful commission in 1834. This

1 John Claudius Loudon, 'Fortis Green, Muswell Hill, The Villa of W.A. Nesfield, Esq', *The Gardeners' Magazine*, (February 1840), pp. 53-58.

was at North Runcton Hall in Norfolk for the banker David Gurney, again through Salvin's recommendation as he was engaged in restoring the old Tudor manor at North Runcton between 1833 and 1836, adding new reception rooms and offices. William mentioned in his report to David Gurney that his intention was to incorporate a *parterre* in the area adjoining the house, and the similarity between his design at North Runcton and the one at Fortis Green is striking (a very simple affair compared with the sophisticated designs he was to achieve later, however). It was the work he secured for the 3rd Earl of Mexborough at Methley Hall in Yorkshire that was to be the turning point for him, making him less reliant on Salvin's help. Lord Mexborough had come into his estates in the West Riding of Yorkshire in 1830, and Salvin spent six years between 1830 and 1836 carrying out improvements to the Hall, parts of which dated back to the fifteenth century. William said that Lord Mexborough was one of 'the jolliest, kindest fellows I ever knew and through his recommendations my employment became very extensive and enabled me to have a clerk James Howe who was an excellent surveyor & therefore very useful.'[1]

After a few years at Fortis Green the Nesfields moved to Eton so that Eden could be educated there. Their move was recorded:

> & so I sold the place thro an Agent at Highgate who humbugged me dreadfully – on leaving however for Eton there happened to be no vacant house, tho one was expected occupied by Selwyn Curate of Windsor – Thus I waited patiently. . . . When Selwyn was appointed Bp of New Zealand we moved to the house occupied by him at Eton.[2]

William was no stranger to Eton, for he had stayed there on many occasions with his friend and colleague at the Society of Watercolour Painters, William Evans, who was a drawing master at Eton College and held property in Keate's Lane, where between 1835 and 1837 Nesfield had rented a cottage.[3] Whilst the Nesfields were waiting for the Eton house they rented property 'on the north side of the Lower Ward or Court at Windsor Castle in one of the houses or apartments that housed the Dean, canons, minor canons, clerks, vergers and other officers of the foundation.'[4] In the Nesfields' case, it was one of the Canons'. Whilst at Eton a further four children were born to the couple: a daughter, who died soon after birth and was buried in the Chapel yard; Arthur Markham, in April 1841, who was christened by his uncle, the Revd David Markham in Eton Chapel; and two sons, David William and Henry William.[5]

1 William Nesfield's *Reminiscences*, Nesfield Archives.
2 *Ibid.*
3 Gambier-Parry, *Annals of an Eton House (J. Murray 1907)*, pp. 28-37. I am grateful to Timothy Connor for this information.
4 The Royal Windsor Website and Halhed Genealogy Family Trees .
5 William Andrews Nesfield, *Reminiscences*,

6.

Concerning the Landscape

Formal gardens in the vicinity of his clients' mansions, with their accompanying *parterres-de-broderie*, were very important elements of William's schemes, and they were what his clients expected him to deliver. He did not disappoint them. His ability to design and build these gardens made him, thanks to the prevailing fashions, the right man in the right place at the right time. However, during the early years it was his advice regarding the landscape further beyond the house that was eagerly sought by his clients. One early example of his interest in an area beyond the immediate environs of the house is from Clumber Park in Nottinghamshire, where in 1838 he submitted his *Explanation of Improvements for an Arboretum* for Henry Pelham-Clinton, 4th Duke of Newcastle (1785-1851). His scheme was intended to produce a unity between the house and the lower end of the pleasure ground at Clumber Park, 'Thus creating a new and highly interesting feature which will not only counter balance the perpetual parallelism between the pleasure ground and the lake but will heighten the effect of extent and produce variety.' The entrance to the Arboretum was to be through a wire trellis, which William intended to arch over the walk and gradually lead down to the lake, where he proposed to site a hexagonal rustic hut or temple. In front of this was to be 'a mass of various shaped beds for the genus *Rosa* which should be principally of the dwarf species having a few high plants in the middle.' He also prepared a list of scattered plants that could be used in a rosarium. They included a variety of Cotoneaster; *Crataegus* (hawthorn); *Pinus*; *Pyrus* (Pear); *Amelanchier* (Service Tree); *Mespilus smithii* (Medlar) and *Prunus* (Cherry). William commented that all plants 'which belong to the same order whether trees, low trees, grafted dwarfs or shrubs should be planted as contiguous to one another (i.e. in families) as the broken outlines of the design will admit thus avoiding as much as possible a mixed character.' He also pointed out that: 'as the spaces between the trees in mass will be wide for several years, they be occupied by duplicates and as the low trees and shrubs must be placed on or near the margins it will be necessary to thicken them with common undergrowth, such as laurels, Portugal laurels, green holly, privet and box but it should be all evergreen to produce a quiet background, as a contrast to the flowering exotics.' As an artist William had drawn and painted waterfalls, and this is probably the reason why he was asked to make suggestions regarding the siting of a Cascade at Clumber which he discussed in a letter to the Duke:

> With reference to the cascade which I criticised at Clumber, I suggested improvements upon what was an evident failure from beginning to end – Your Grace's remark that 'there are few who have sufficient of the artist in them to execute a work of this kind,' is perfectly correct – As a painter I have studied from Nature for the last 18 years & have drawn the character of torrents & cascades, perhaps with as much assiduity as any Artist in England, which assertion may be borne out by my works in the Watercolour Exhibition Pall Mall East, I much regret, though at the same time am not surprised, from my estimation of your Grace's just taste, at the disappointment you have experienced in finding that it, belongs to, the Painter alone, to see, that, put into execution, which his feelings & impression received from Nature, could alone have designed & have carried into effect.[1]

William also mentioned a 'French' garden he was to design, but unfortunately there is apparently little information relating to this, although an aerial photograph of 13 July 1949 shows the outline of formal beds and walls in the area immediately adjoining the mansion.

Although William was to design formal gardens to satisfy his clients, his commitment to picturesque scenery meant that whenever he could he made sure that the estate lands beyond the immediate environs of the house were included in his overall schemes. He particularly admired the writings of the landowner Sir Uvedale Price (1747-1829), who put his theories into print in his publication *Essays on the Picturesque*, which went into a number of editions. Price's tenacity of purpose in developing his estate at Foxley in Herefordshire; the Picturesque manner in which he enhanced his landscape, whilst bearing in mind the naturalistic contours of the ground; his dedication and single-mindedness, led to his work being regarded by many as the epitome of the perfect landscape. The way he opened up distant views, planted, pruned and shaped, his good husbandry in ensuring that carriage-ways, roads, woodland and pasture were well maintained, and his belief that landscape design should be seen as one of the fine arts (that he was practising picture making with the materials of nature) was completely to William's taste. Indeed, he described Price in glowing terms to at least one of his clients. Herefordshire was a county William knew well: he painted there and had a number of commissions in the area. It is inconceivable, therefore, that he would not have taken the time to visit Foxley when he was in the county, especially as the Garnstone estate where he worked was adjacent to Foxley.

1 Letter from William Nesfield to the Duke of Newcastle, 8 June 1838, Nottingham University MSS. Ne C 8969/1-3. William Nesfield was paid £39 6s. for his work in 1837.

It was also in his best interests to applaud Price's disapproval of Lancelot Brown, whose designs, Price maintained, impoverished and disfigured the English landscape, destroying harmonious connections, intricacy and variety, three essential qualities in producing the perfect scene.

In order to achieve cohesion between the formal garden and the landscape beyond, William applied the concepts of harmony and unity associated with the Renaissance. He could never have hoped to emulate what André le Nôtre accomplished at Versailles in the seventeenth century for Louis XIV, when 'the army drained 37,000 acres of land and diverted an entire river thirty miles to supply water for the fountains, which eventually numbered 1400.'[1] Nevertheless, he was as much a practical engineer as an artist, for all gentlemen cadets at the Royal Military Academy needed to be proficient in 'Copying from drawings, which qualified them for Drawing from nature, teaches them the effect of Light and Shade, and makes them acquainted also with Aerial Perspective – Taking views about Woolwich and other places.'[2] These skills enabled William to carry out excavations of large areas of ground.[3]

One of his first tasks when he visited an estate was to assess its potential, and he spent a considerable amount of time walking the grounds, noting the approaches to the house and the view from it; the siting of any lodge houses and the positioning of avenues, water and trees. At the Crewe estate in Cheshire his contribution included creating a new access road, the enlargement of the western end of the park and possibly a tunnel beyond the northern *parterre* running under the lake to allow cattle to pass.[4]

The Positioning of the House

The house was the pivotal and focal point in William's schemes, and its situation in the landscape was always an important consideration for him. At Barham Court in Kent he had nothing but praise for the estate and situation:

> With reference to the house which a landscape painter would pronounce a picture because in his language it is complete as a composition and the reason why this is thus complete is because in the foreground the lawn is furnished with some remarkably fine detached trees which happen to be grouped as to form a

1 Marian Moffatt, Michael Fazio, Laurence Wodehouse, *A World History of Architecture* (Laurence King Publishing, London, 2003), p. 385.

2 Buchanan-Dunlop, Lieutenant Colonel H.D., Records of the Royal Military Academy, 1741-1892; second edition (F.J. Cattermole, Woolwich 1892).

3 Ralph Sneyd of Keele Hall, Staffordshire, mentioned that he spent the whole day at Trentham Hall in Staffordshire: 'staking out an Approach from the Whitworth side with Messrs Nesfield, Barry and Locke'. (Keele University Library, Sneyd Papers, S3707, within the diary of Ralph Sneyd, 1844-45).

4 Report on the Crewe estate prepared by Adrian Wikeley for the Land Use Consultants, London, 1998.

> beautiful balance to each side of the picture thus at once directing the eye in a combination of interesting features viz. the flat meadows the bending course of the Medway Teston Bridge which is an old and picturesque structure, the Farleigh Road which winds so agreeably up the first hill with its hanging wood down to the water and the distant hill varied by masses of wood, hop grounds, etc.

William criticized the siting of a number of houses for failing to command a strategic position, which prevented them achieving a view towards the middle and far distant ground. For instance, he said of Offchurch Bury in Warwickshire: 'the house stands on the lowest ground which evil is aggravated by the general floorline being on the same level 1' below the surface.' He advised on the siting of new mansions: at Mentmore in Buckinghamshire he had the option of two sites, and shelter, not only from the elements but from intrusion from outsiders, together with good drainage, were the important considerations when deciding on where the house should be placed. However, his main emphasis was on the necessity of a good platform on which to position it in order to facilitate the architectural alignment of the house with the formal garden.

Positioning of Trees

Although William never claimed to be a 'plants person', he had painted, measured and drawn trees from his youth, and justifiably felt he knew a great deal about them. It was an affinity he shared with Price, who said: 'It is in the arrangement and management of trees, that the great art of improvement consists . . . they alone form a canopy over us, and a varied frame to all other objects, which they admit, exclude and group. . . . Without them the most varied inequality of ground is uninteresting.'[1] William maintained that a favourable first impression was essential, with approaches that were varied and well-wooded with mature trees, but that these should not be too dense. Trees were essential as objects that would interest the eye, enhancing and opening up the landscape. His advice at Dorfold in Cheshire was that: 'the removal of a few unimportant Trees on the west belt would loosen the present hard lines, improve the forms of the fine groups & give more diagonal extent.' Broad masses and broad openings were to be encouraged and confusion of foliage should be avoided, for the primary aim was to loosen hard and artificial lines. A contrast in shape and texture was also important. At Peper Harow in Surrey he suggested that: 'cedars and round headed trees eliminated monotony and provided variety.' He disliked the belts and clumps of trees favoured by Lancelot Brown, as is obvious from his remarks relating to Alton

1 Uvedale Price, An *Essay on the Picturesque* (Farnborough, 1971), vol. 1, p. 259. Although William Nesfield rarely contributed to gardening journals he did write an article, which related to tree planting, entitled 'A Slight Sketch of a visit to Allanton'. This was the seat in Lanarkshire of the late Sir Henry Steuart an authority on tree planting. *Gardeners' Magazine*, 1838, 14, pp. 14-18.

Hereford, sketch by William Nesfield.

Worcester, sketch by William Nesfield.

Buttas Farm, near Garnstone, Herefordshire, watercolour by William Nesfield, 7 May 1847.

Kirkham Priory, near Castle Howard, Yorkshire, sepia by William Nesfield, 1828.

Towers in Staffordshire: 'they did not allow the eye to rest on anything interesting, they constricted the views and discounted largeness and space.'[1] His image of the Picturesque landscape, therefore, was that trees should not interfere and obscure the views to the distant horizon, an error of which Brown had been accused with his belts and clumps. He therefore had no hesitation at all in advising the axing of trees if he felt they either obscured or confused the visual enjoyment of the scene, and this is very obvious in a letter he sent to Rowland Egerton-Warburton of Arley Hall in Cheshire:

> I now think my visit to Cheshire very doubtful in Feby because some ignoramus has been frightening Lord Crewe about opening out the views I had suggested, w'h necessarily must condemn many hundred trees w'h can never be missed & his Ldship has so little judgement that it is useless to argue the point – believe me.[2]

William told Warburton that he got too much of his own way with Lord Crewe, which was not good for him, and it does appear that Lord Crewe had an unrealistic faith in his abilities. However, he had trees cut down at Crewe only where they over-shadowed the house, obscured the lake banks or where plantations could be thinned. When necessary he also planted trees, for example to hide the North Staffordshire railway line and the growing railway colony of Crewe from Lord Crewe's view.

Railways

Many landowners were opposed to the phenomenon known as 'railway mania', a term often applied to the rush to purchase shares in the burgeoning Railway Companies that were relatively free from Government legislation. This was at its height by 1846, when the Liverpool & Manchester Railway produced high profit margins and even the smallest investors were confident enough to risk their savings in the venture. 'Lines routed along river valleys to ensure gentle gradients almost inevitably coincided with landscaped parks.'[3] However, some landowners were actually to gain financially from these unwanted changes, as they were able to negotiate for railway halts to be sited near to their estates, for their own and their guests' convenience. Stations: 'often came to be seen as simply another estate building, with landowners treating them as additional entrance lodges.'[4]

William compiled a number of reports for landowners to enable them to receive recompense if they felt the railway impinged on their privacy. For example, at Crewe, Lord Crewe was concerned about the encroachment of the railway on his estate. The Grand Junction Act of 1833 gave Parliamentary sanction to the cutting of a railway line through the outlying hamlets adjacent to the area now known as Crewe. The population of the town had risen from 295 in 1831 to over 2000 in 1846 and still continued to grow,

1 Nesfield Archives.

2 Letter from William Nesfield to Rowland Egerton-Warburton, 27 December 1842, Arley Hall Archives.

3 Tim Warner, 'Line of Least Resistance', *Country Life,* April 1991, pp. 86-87.

4 *Ibid.*

as did the railway complex.[1] In 1849 the Turnpike Trustees, in conjunction with the Grand Junction Railway Company, borrowed £2,000 from Lord Crewe to build a new road. It has been said that the reason he lent the money was so that he could close, and then provide an alternative, to the right of way through Home Farm, which led past the front of Crewe Hall.[2]

Rivers and Lakes

The artistic principles which William employed in his paintings of seascapes, waterfalls and rivers could be transferred to the rivers and lakes on his clients' estates. He asserted that a stretch of water should either be natural or artificial, not a mixture of the two. His criticism at Peper Harow in Surrey was that: 'The river which, from its reflecting nature, cannot escape observation, appears neither natural nor artificial and is therefore totally out of harmony with its landscape, at least in its present condition. It ought to exhibit its character as a river, and should not evince the hand of art at all.' The ultimate criteria when attempting to reproduce a naturalistic stretch of water, he considered, was that it should blend into the scenery around it so that in time it would appear to have been the work of nature and not of man. This was his intention at Bourne Park in Kent; here he advised his client, Mr Bell, that: 'Art in the present case can only propose that which time and growth must furnish, such as the feathering and picturesque growing of trees, broken banks, gravel beds, dots of thorn, gorse and rushes in fact anything that will conduce in the concealment of art.' On the suggestion of Mr Bell he also submitted proposals for an island, which he suggested should be modelled after an accident in nature. To be probable, the accident should have some relation to the undulatory character of its neighbourhood. Mr Bell objected that the island proposed was too large in circumference and height, but William disagreed, using his knowledge as a painter to reinforce his argument. He explained that in natural lakes and sea lochs there were quantities of examples of abrupt islands even higher than the mainland, and consequently there was nothing to fear. He said he only regretted that there was no rock in the vicinity to cause a still greater abruptness, as on the lake at Trentham, where he made a peninsula almost perpendicular from the models in Loch Fyne. He maintained that Mr Bell's objection was hardly tenable, as a sketch in his possession of a remarkably picturesque rocky island in the middle of the River Tummel, six miles from Loch Rannoch and surrounded by comparatively low ground, supported his argument.

An interesting glimpse into the way William approached improvements to the landscape can be seen in his annotated copy of William Sawrey Gilpin's publication, *Practical Hints upon Landscape Gardening*, published in 1835. Both men were in agreement regarding what constituted the perfect landscape, Gilpin writing that:

1 W.H. Challinor, *Social and Economic History of Crewe 1780–1923* (Manchester University Press, 1950), p. 5.

2 *Ibid.*

'Composition in landscape embraced three distinct parts, the distant, the middle distant and the foreground.' William's sentiments precisely. The two men had a number of things in common, for example, both were painters of picturesque scenery and turned to landscape design later in life. Gilpin was a founder member of the Society of Watercolour Painters and third drawing master at Great Marlowe between 1806 and 1820. Both men objected to the work of Brown and his removal of cottages and even villages because they offended the eye of his clients. Gilpin criticised an example of his work as follows:

> At the mouth of the gorge stands a picturesque cottage, as if placed by the hand of taste itself. The improver, conceiving this cottage an improper appendage, has removed a large portion of earth from a situation to which it was essential to raise a mound on this foreground, for the purpose of excluding it: this he has completely effected, and, with the cottage, has shut out the valley, the gorge, the river, and buried behind his mound the boles of the foreground trees, thus contriving to render abortive the judicious selection of the architect. A more glaring example of perverted taste cannot exist.

William replied: 'unfortunately there are many such who would rather be smothered with trees than that a farm house three miles off should be visible in a grand open space – I never allow such puerile reasons to thwart any schemes of operating but argue it out & set to work.' Both men objected to the 'ha-ha', or sunken fence, a device used in order to give the impression of a landscape which flowed seamlessly from the environs of the house into the landscape, and which was a popular accompaniment to the landscapes of eighteenth-century England. Gilpin's comment was: 'I cannot but think that (with the exception of Sir Uvedale) the different writers upon the improvement of scenery connected with residences have, as far as I am acquainted with them, altogether mistaken the question of a separating fence. They think it is essential that no visible interruption should exist between the smooth and decorated lawn and the scenery. . . . To effect the junction they have recourse as the happiest expedient, to a sunk fence, they recommend various modes of hiding this fence, in effect they are likely to raise a far more objectionable line of separation than the rudest fence would be.' William's reply leaves no doubt as to his opinion regarding contrivance: he disliked all forms of it, considering that if an object was man-made it should be shown to be so and not masquerade as something it was not. However concealed a sunk fence might be, the contrast in colour between a mown lawn on one side and a pasture on the other, he considered, was bound to indicate the line of separation. He said: 'sunk fences are abominations . . . the question is why should there be such a fuss about fences by prejudiced people whatever is useful or indispensable is reconcilable. Therefore why not make a virtue of necessity & exhibit the truth by making fences ornate.' When it came to the placing of trees near to the house, William disagreed with Gilpin. The balance of the composition being of the utmost importance, William

Near Mount Alexander on the Tummel, watercolour by William Nesfield.

expressed his disapproval with the use of a sketch when Gilpin condoned the placing of some Lombardy Poplars and a group of deciduous trees in the immediate vicinity of the house: These (the trees) being too near the House take the scale out of it & everything else.'[1]

> The siting of lodges was also a topic of interest to William and Gilpin, who wrote: 'A gate between pillars, if upon a large scale, seems to require a lodge for each flank; but such an arrangement, appearing as a sacrifice of comfort for display, is not, perhaps, in the best taste.' William replied: 'a pair of Lodges under any circumstances (grandeur out of the question because no excuse) is a vile perpetration!! Gilpin's remarks on this are very sensible – make a Gate & fence as grand as you like but stick to common sense & have but one lodge for the common comfort of the Lodge Keeper.'

An example of a case in which the two men were not in agreement related to formality in the environs of the House. William asked why Gilpin: 'did not study the Old Masters and restore the barbarism he deprecates – He never aimed at anything beyond a terrace and that generally in the wrong place – but geometric gardens he never attempted.'

1 Taken from William Nesfield's copy of W.S. Gilpin's *Practical Hints upon Landscape Gardening* (T. Cadell, Strand and W. Blackwood, Edinburgh, 1835), p.44, Nesfield Archives.

Also amongst these annotated notes were William's comments regarding Humphry Repton (1752-1818), and it is enlightening to consider the class prejudices that were at play in his opinions of Repton and Joseph Paxton. He said of Repton that he was: 'a very clever fellow & worked well to eradicate the mischief of Brown & Co although he could draw landscape in a very humble manner, yet if he had been a first rater he would have been the greatest Lands Gardn that ever appeared.'[1] Repton was born in Bury St Edmunds in Suffolk, a stronghold of the Nesfield clan; William's father had been born there and his sister lived in the town. Both Repton and William had been educated at Bury St Edmunds Grammar School, and Eden and William had a number of commissions in the County. For instance, William worked on the landscape and gardens at Bradfield Combust for Arthur Young, the writer and agriculturalist, where later Eden was to build a house for him. Repton's background was somewhat similar to William's: his father was a Collector of Excise whilst his mother Martha (née Fitch) had lived at Moor Hall in Suffolk and had inherited property in the county. William would have regarded Repton as a 'gentleman', unlike Paxton, whose family background was a humble one. This fact, combined with what must have been a certain amount of professional jealousy on William's, part clouded his judgment and prejudiced him against Paxton.

In 1880, a year before his death, William wrote an article which gives an insight into his philosophy, specifically when he felt it was appropriate to apply strictly geometric treatment to the ground and when it was not. The article related to what he considered to be the gradual urbanization of Regent's Park, which he could observe from his home in York Terrace. 'Tree mania' was what he said had descended on the Park, because trees were being planted with little thought for aesthetics. For although 'one principle seems to govern the very desirable introduction of trees, viz. the "geometric" or formal manner, which although most fitting in some localities . . . (because the "genius loci" respectively deems such treatment) it does not follow that alike modus operandi consistently applies to Regent's Park, the general feature of which being "picturesque" requires that this character should be most scrupulously conserved to insure harmony in a pictorial sense.'[2] On the other hand, in order to justify his formal treatment of the Avenue Gardens in the Park, which was strictly geometrical, his argument would have been that formality was acceptable for a walkway designed to carry people from one area of the Park to another. Art and Nature, as far as William was concerned, should always be judged on very different criteria.

---

1 William Sawrey Gilpin, *Practical Hints*, *Ibid.*

2 William Andrews Nesfield, *An Important Question Regarding Regent's Park 1880,* Nesfield Archives.

7.

The Return to Formality

William's training at the Royal Military Academy meant that he was a practical man in many ways. However, he also sought inspiration from the ideals of the Renaissance, which had occupied the minds of artists, philosophers, writers and scholars for generations. Specifically, he was inspired by classical horticultural concepts that had originated in the hillside gardens of Imperial Rome, where paths and avenues were aligned with the windows and doors of the main façade of the villa, with long vistas leading to a piece of statuary as a focal point. These principles had been adopted by the fifteenth-century Italian architect and humanist scholar Leon Battista Alberti (1404-1472). Alberti maintained that beauty came from a harmony of all the parts of the whole. In his Treatise *De Re Aedificatoria Libra*, book five, written in 1452, he wrote that gardens should occupy the foreground overlooking the owner's land, but they should also take in the hills and mountains beyond. The concept of leading the eye towards the middle and distant landscape became central to William's landscape design principles and enabled him to reconcile strictly formal pleasure grounds in the immediate area around the house with the landscape beyond. Although picturesque landscapes were his first love, and he was always concerned to include them in his designs as the social and economic changes in England in the nineteenth century led to a gradual return to formality in the garden. It was his formal gardens, and especially French seventeenth-century *parterre-de-broderie,* which his clients wanted, with their associations with power, control and order. In order to appreciate the reasons underlying the move away from the English Landscape School associated with Lancelot Brown and his followers, an understanding of social change is important. Although social historians have noted that the real challenges to the power of the landed classes did not take place until after the First World War of 1914-1918, changes were being felt long before that date. As early as the 1830s the pace of life William would have known as a boy and young man was disappearing. Ian Anstruther has described how the changes brought about by the power of steam led to a revolution in travel, reflecting that: 'the homely plod of hoof and sail and the ancient limits of a day's journey started to crumble and disappear.'[1] Old social certainties were also crumbling, leading to a growing nostalgia amongst the old landed classes for the paternalistic, hierarchical system of society which had been in place for generations and a way of life they would have considered to be strictly English. Elite attitudes to industrialisation were somewhat confused for, aligned to their dislike for the growing industrial towns, where dirt and squalor were inevitably the result of over-crowding and unsanitary conditions, there was a fascination with the new innovations that industry brought. Some landowners undoubtedly benefited from these changes as, for example, valuable minerals were discovered on their land, and their commercial investments in industry flourished. These were conundrums which they endeavoured to mitigate by metaphorically 'pulling up their drawbridges' as they sought to reconcile themselves to events which, they perceived, could damage their power bases as landowning oligarchs at the apex of society. The struggle between the aristocracy, a growing middle class and the working class in the late eighteenth and nineteenth centuries has been described as a 'friction of interests.'[2] The changes which led to this 'friction of interests' were complex and protracted, but ultimately they were to seriously challenge the position of the landed elites.

To counter social instability, various elites proposed reinforcing the bond between master and man as the country gradually shifted from a rural to an industrial nation. This solution, combined with an attachment to the rural scenery of the British Isles, was the philosophy not only of Sir Uvedale Price, but the statesman Edmund Burke (1728-1787) and the writer on picturesque scenery, the Revd William Gilpin. They considered that a contented workforce was less likely to revolt, as it had in France. For both Price and Gilpin, absentee landlords were a threat to the welfare of the people and social stability, and: 'the ancient country seats of the nobility have an essential part to play in the landscape of dignified images that sustained tradition, property and the capacity for self-respect, grace and manners, taste and elegance.'[3]

From his vicarage at Boldre in Hampshire, the Revd Gilpin wrote a series of articles and sermons that demonstrated that he regarded the ownership of land as a trust, and the landowner as a central and unifying figure in the small community of servants, tenants and labourers. The landowners' role was to protect his 'inferiors' and secure their comfort in a life which would be spent on his estate, spending his income to improve and maintain that estate for the benefit not only of himself and his dependents but also for the comfort of his employees. Neither Price, Burke nor Gilpin could have had any knowledge of how the growth of the industrial towns would divide man from master, but their conviction that the whole system of society would change once men were divorced from their roots proved to be correct.

1 Ian Anstruther, *The Knight and the Umbrella* (Geoffrey Bles, 1963), p.3.

2 Eric Evans, *The Forging of the Modern State: Early Industrial Britain 1783-1870* (Longmans, 1989), p. 171.

3 Nigel Everett, *The Tory View of Landscape* (New Haven and London, Yale University Press 1994), p. 101.

England was ruled from 1760 to 1820 by George III (1738-1820), a monarch who, it has been said, 'instinctively revered ancient institutions, above all the Church and the monarchy. He disliked and distrusted change.'[1] These were views that would have automatically endeared him to the aristocracy and gentry. William had been born into this Georgian society and his family background ensured that he was very much part of the paternalistic system, the standards of which were advocated by Gilpin, Burke and Price. A patriotic zeal for king and country was the predominant ethos of his childhood, whilst he was pursuing his classical studies at Winchester and the grammar school in Bury St Edmunds, and the French Revolution was still uppermost in the memories of the landed class. The Napoleonic wars still had a decade to run. It was this patriotic atmosphere that contributed to his decision to give up the idea of following his father and paternal grandfather into the Church and join the army instead. His patriotism was re-ignited when he returned to the quiet backwater of Brancepeth in 1818, fuelled by dreams of Britain's romantic past.

The ideal of romantic past was to play a defining role in the nineteenth century, and its relevance to William's philosophy can be discerned in the remarks he made to Lord North of Wroxton Abbey in Oxfordshire. At Wroxton the old abbey buildings had been rebuilt in the reign of Henry VIII, but nothing remained of the Tudor garden, something he was anxious to rectify, as he explained to Lord North:

> For many years having studied our old English architecture I cannot help expressing a patriotic veneration for it (if I may use the term) & am therefore naturally zealous in rescuing places really worthy of restoration from their debased condition.[2]

A property he would have been familiar with was Harlaxton Manor in Lincolnshire, the estate of Gregory Gregory (1786-1854). Between 1831 and 1837, Salvin was commissioned to improve the house in the late sixteenth and early seventeenth-century style. The work was one of Salvin's most impressive undertakings, and William must have gained much inspiration from the grounds at Harlaxton at a time when he was considering taking up landscape gardening. The grandeur of the gardens was recorded in four watercolour perspectives produced by Salvin's office in 1834. They were reported on by John Claudius Loudon in his *Gardener's Magazine*, after a visit he made to the property whilst on a tour of Staffordshire and Lincolnshire in May 1840. Loudon wrote: 'The terraced gardens will be on seven different levels, communicated by flights of steps, ornamented with vases, figures and numerous other suitable objects, and in appropriate places, there will be canals, basins, and fountains, summer-houses, shrubs clipped into

1 Mark Girouard, *The Return to Camelot: Chivalry and the English Gentleman* (Yale University Press, 1981), p. 22.

2 Plans and drawings, eighteenth-nineteenth centuries, including (fols. 1-100) plans by W.A. Nesfield for the gardens at Wroxton, Oxon., with a letter from him to J.S. North, 1846 (dated 6 March '46 and addressed from Eton Coll., Windsor). MS. North a 17[R] fols 1-2. Bodleian Libraries, University of Oxford.

artificial forms, &c.'[1] However, although the rich decoration and four-way perspective associated with the Jacobean period were central to William's overall designs, he was not averse to mixing a number of historical styles, including elements from English Tudor. On at least two estates he included a maze, popular in the Tudor period, both of which still exist at Somerleyton Hall in Suffolk and Worden Hall in Lancashire.

He incorporated ornamentation from the reign of Henry VIII, and in particular the heraldic devices of the Earls of Scarborough who owned Lumley Castle in County Durham, on whose estate he had been born, and where his father was perpetual curate in nearby Chester-le-Street. He would presumably, therefore, have known of the great pride the Earls of Scarborough took in their lineage. Lumley Castle contained sculpture, inscriptions and heraldic devices, 'lauding the family and its achievements over the centuries.'[2] Their ancestor, John, Lord Lumley, had inherited Henry VIII's great Tudor palace of Nonsuch in 1578, from his father-in-law Henry FitzAlan, 12th Earl of Arundel. John's main obsession was his family's genealogy, and under his auspices Lumley Castle was gradually transformed into a shrine devoted to the family's achievements.[3] The Lumley Inventory of 1590 survives in the possession of his descendants. It is a unique document listing not only the contents of his collections and containing his pedigree, but also including watercolours of the furniture, tombs and sculpture he had commissioned.[4] In the gardens at Nonsuch he replaced Henry VIII's heraldry with his own, which included two marble columns flanking a central fountain. The columns were referred to in 1650 as 'the Fawlcon perches', a misreading of the Lumley popinjays.[5] There is a drawing in the Lumley collection which matches this description exactly, and although there is no evidence that William ever saw this drawing, his interest in this type of historical detail is apparent on at least one estate where he designed a similar device on a gateway. The heraldic symbols, monograms and family crests that were prevalent in the Elizabethan period in England were devices that had also been used in France to announce 'the status of the owner from at least the beginning of the sixteenth century.'[6] One example was at Anet, where in 1547 Diane de Poitiers had a large DH emblazoned on the *parterre*.

William also incorporated monograms in a number of his *parterres-de-broderie;* examples can be found at Stoke Rochford in Lincolnshire, Brodick on the Isle-of-Arran, Drayton House in Northamptonshire, Alton Towers in Staffordshire and Eaton Hall in Cheshire. There are sundials at Crewe Hall in Cheshire, Stoke Edith

1 Priscilla Boniface, ed., *In Search of English Gardens: The Travels of John Claudius Loudon and his Wife Jane* (Guild Publishing, 1987), pp. 189-202.

2 Roy Strong, *The Renaissance Garden in England* (Thames & Hudson, London, 1998), p. 63.

3 John, Lord Lumley devoted his time to his family genealogy after being excluded from office and court life as a result of his involvement in the Ridolfi Plot to assassinate Elizabeth I.

4 Roy Strong, The Renaissance Garden in England (Thames & Hudson, London, 1998), p. 64

5 *Ibid.*

6 Kenneth Woodbridge, *Princely Gardens: The Origins and Development of the French Formal Style* (Thames & Hudson, 1986), p. 197.

Parterre design for Stoke Edith, Herefordshire.

in Herefordshire and Stoneleigh Abbey in Warwickshire. William referred to the engravings of country seats in the 1707 *Britannia illustrata*, a publication that contained over seventy-seven bird's-eye views, drawn over a period of eight years by Leonard Knyff (1650-1722) and then engraved on copper by Johannes Kip (1653-1722) for inspiration.[1] He also studied the garden statuary from a Dutch publication of 1730, the translation of which reads: 'Jewels of Parks Existing in many kinds of dry and wet bowls, *parterres*, lawns and fountains to serve all lovers of country estates, Henrik and Daniel Van Damme'. Evergreens were important features around a *parterre*, and box was used to edge the plant-like shapes within the *parterre* itself, as well as to edge the perimeter of the whole *parterre*. Clipped box was known to have been used in Roman gardens, although John Parkinson (1567-1650), in his *Paradisi in Sole Paradisus Terrestris* of 1629, said that in England at the time of writing box was a novelty. On 19 November and 28 December 1848 in letters to Sir William Hooker, the director of the Royal Botanic Gardens at Kew, William explained that evergreens should be: 'clipped into various artificial shapes i.e. to be orthodox – therefore any natural forms which are most quaint & formal of course will answer best . . . the more you ring the changes on the spiral – the round or the pyramid the better they should be.'[2]

A move towards artifice in gardening towards the end of the eighteenth-century, and again with the Jacobean Revival of the mid-nineteenth century, can be partly explained by the abandonment of certain theories about nature. The upper classes became disillusioned with the open spaces advocated by Lancelot Brown, perhaps in part because nature was no longer glorified as being the unmarred work of God. Older schools of thought about the divinity of nature were largely superseded by the latter years of the seventeenth century; for example Thomas Burnet's (c. 1635-1715) metaphysical theories were abandoned. He had postulated that: 'the earth originally was a paradise with a

1 William Nesfield referred to the importance of Kip's folio works in his Plan 1; 'Gd. Plan of Details of *Parterre*, Entrance Court at Wroxton Abbey', Oxfordshire, March 1846 (Nesfield Archives).

2 Royal Botanic Gardens, Kew, English Letters.

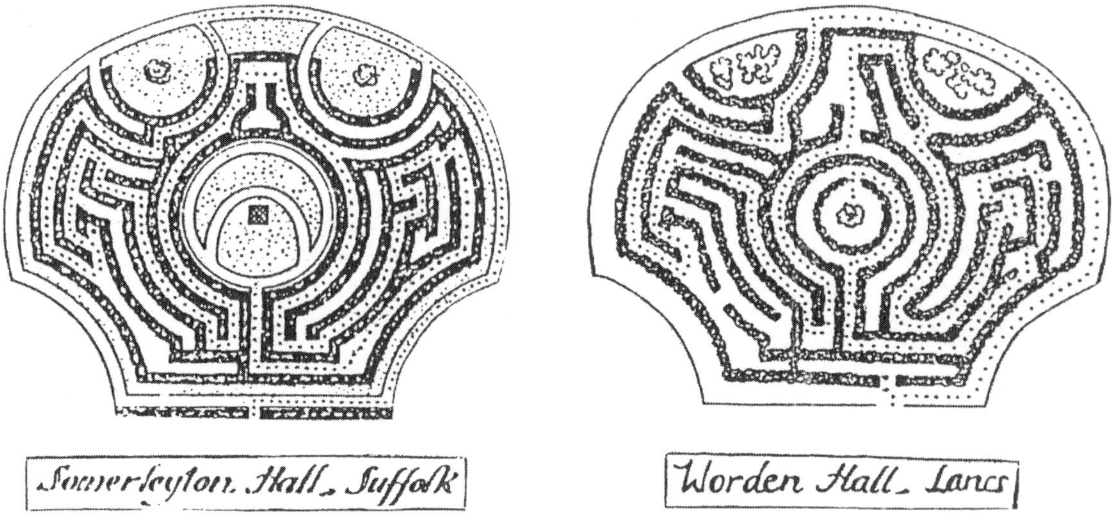

Comparison between the mazes at Somerleyton Hall, Suffolk and Worden Hall, Lancashire.
The dotted line indicates path to the centre of the maze in each case.

smooth and unobjectionable skin marred by neither Mountains nor oceans',[1] a theory that had been accepted for generations and had been set down in his *Sacred Theory of the Earth* of 1681. A more radical philosophy had emerged by the early eighteenth-century: men were self-determining and shaped their own environments. It was recognised that there was nothing natural about the English landscape, as it had been altered and cultivated by man for generations. By the latter years of the eighteenth century, therefore, the proposition could be developed that if the landscape did not derive from unaided nature, why pretend otherwise?

The gradual re-emergence of the geometrical gardens (which were to be produced by William from the late 1830s) began with the creation of a formal flowerbed at Nuneham Courtenay in Oxfordshire. The second Earl of Harcourt commissioned the services of landscape gardener and poet George Mason (1725-1792), who transferred to the garden his interpretation of a scene laid out by Jacques Rousseau's novel of 1761, *La Nouvelle Heloise*, which Paul Sandby Snr painted in 1772.

These early flowerbeds were still, however, informal picturesque creations in keeping with the landscape in which they were placed. They were not situated below the main façade of the house as they would be in the nineteenth century. An exception to the rule, however, occurred at Hartwell in Buckinghamshire, the seat of Sir William Lee and his wife Elizabeth, both enthusiastic gardeners. Mark Laird cites a sketch planting plan in the Bodleian Library, Oxford depicting sixteen

1 Marjorie Hope Nicolson, Mountain Gloom and Mountain Glory (University of Washington Press, 1959), p. 71.

flowerbeds which were circular, elliptical and kidney-shaped and suggests that: 'The disposition of flowers in 10 of the beds suggests residual elements of the grid of quincunx arrangements that had dominated the plat-bands and straight border since the time of London and Wise – an astonishing degree of continuity.'[1] The gradual awakening of interest in colour and formality, as a relief from Brown's bland landscapes was reinforced by Uvedale Price and Henry Holland (1745-1806) who declared that old, venerable avenues should be preserved, a notion that grew in popularity. As has been observed, 'thereafter it became a consistent theme that venerable avenues ought not to be destroyed, even when the writers opposed the planting of new ones'.[2] The introduction of the terrace as an architectural platform and transitional zone between the house and the park was a crucial element in ensuring that the symmetrical formal garden could be aligned on the most important rooms of the house. As Price explained in 1794:

> Nothing, I think, can be more natural, or more pleasing than to discover that intense design has been at work in the immediate environs of a house . . . any sudden transition from the manifest design which must necessarily be found in untamed nature, must always be harsh and unpleasing. Straight terraces, terraced walks, statues, fountains, flights of steps, balustrades, vases, architectural seats, and formal *parterres*, knots and flower beds, are therefore most naturally the more immediate accompaniments of a mansion. They are employed for the purpose of softening off art into nature, and thus removing the harsh effect of sudden transmission, in the same way that an artist softens off hardness of outline in his picture.[3]

Price bitterly regretted destroying the flower garden on his estate at Foxley in Herefordshire: 'not from disliking it: on the contrary it was a sacrifice I made against my own sensation to the prevailing opinion I doomed it, and all its embellishments with which I had found such an early connection to sudden and total destruction.'[4]

These opinions developed alongside the growing interest in historical accuracy, which John Claudius Loudon's *Encyclopaedia of Gardening* helped to promote. Examples of random serpentine flowerbeds featured in Maria Jackson's *Florist's Manual* of 1823. By the time George Johnson wrote his *A History of English Gardening* in 1829, the move towards history and artifice in the garden was well under way. Johnson was amongst a number of writers, journalists and gardeners who recommended a certain artificiality in gardens close to the house, in keeping with the architectural structure it was intended to complement. Johnson condemned 'the more easy mode Brown and his corrupt imitators

1 Mark Laird, *The Flowering of the Landscape Garden: English Pleasure Gardens 1720-1800* (Philadelphia, University of Pennsylvania Press 1990), p. 363.
2 Brent Elliott, *Victorian Gardens* (B.T. Batsford Limited, 1987), p. 57.
3 Uvedale Price, *Essays on the Picturesque*, 1842, p. 162.
4 Charles McIntosh, *The Flower Garden* (S. Orr & Company Limited, 1838), p. 4.

adopted.'[1] He wrote that their designs were: 'so palpable and ignorantly unvarying that it soon roused the satire of better judges.'[2] Johnson traced the changes in garden style from the Romans through to the time in which he was writing, regarding the close of the eighteenth century as a time of great improvement in gardening. Humphry Repton's (1752-1818) gardens were becoming increasingly antiquarian in nature, even taking the form of geometric *parterres*, as at Beaudesert in Staffordshire. Here, in 1813, he placed a *parterre* across the façade of the house. At Ashridge in Hertfordshire he emphasised the necessity of returning 'to those ancient trim Gardens, which formerly enlightened the venerable inhabitants of this curious spot.'[3] Repton is credited with laying out flowerbeds in the environs of the house, and there are examples of isolated island beds designed by him in 1808 for the Royal Pavilion, Brighton for the Prince Regent, where he used French-style basketware containing flowers. Mark Laird has remarked on Repton's use of French motifs such as *parterres*, *treillages* and *corbeilles*. The circular *corbeilles* (flowerpots or large nosegays) demonstrate Repton's familiarity with the French garden.

Repton's visual standards and sources differed from William's, as his formal designs were largely set in a framework of the picturesque garden. Nevertheless, both had a desire to do away with hard lines and open up wide vistas and incorporate well-disposed trees into the landscape. That William was in accord with Repton's interpretation of what constituted a Picturesque scene is not in doubt, and there is evidence to suggest that Repton's work was the catalyst that prompted him to install the French *parterre* as the central feature of his designs. He undoubtedly admired Repton above all other landscape gardeners that would have influenced him at the start of his landscape design career. For example, he would have been in agreement with Repton's 'Appropriation' theory, which proposed that an estate should display a united and uninterrupted appearance. Repton had a commonsense attitude regarding the laying out of gardens so that the domestic fronts were in alliance with the House: 'The intimate connexion between the kitchen garden, for produce, and between the stables and the garden, for its manure, is so obvious that everyone must see the propriety of bringing them as nearly together as possible, consistent with the views from the house.' This commonsense view also applied to Repton's opinion that the garden:

> Is an artificial object, and has no other pretence to be natural, than what it derives from the growth of the plants which adorn it, their selection, their disposition, their culture, must all be the work of art, and instead of that invisible line, or hidden fence – which separates the mown lawn from the lawn fed by cattle it is more rational to

1 George William Johnson, *A History of English Gardening* (Baldwin & Cradock and Longman & Company, 1829), p. 267.

2 For information regarding Brown's introduction of colour, floral display and formality in his gardens, see Mark Laird, *The Flowering of the Landscape Garden*, p. 382 and Jane Brown, *The Omnipotent Magician: Lancelot 'Capability' Brown 1716-1783* (Chatto & Windus, 2011).

3 Humphry Repton, *Fragments on the theory and Practice of Landscape Gardening* (T. Bensley & Son for J. Taylor, London, 1816).

> shew that the two objects are separated, if the fence is not unsightly – otherwise, we must either suppose that cattle are admitted to crop the flowers and shrubs or that flowers and shrubs are absurdly planted in a pasture exposed to cattle, or which is more frequently the case, we must banish flowers entirely from the windows of a house, and suppose it to stand on a naked grass field.[1]

Renaissance theories advocating both unity and variety in both the landscape and the garden, which were consistent themes by the time William took up landscape gardening in the late 1830s, were expressed by a number of garden writers. For example in 1839 Charles McIntosh (1794-1864), the head gardener at Claremont in Surrey and later Dalkeith in Edinburgh, wrote *The Flower Garden,* in which he observed: 'We cannot see why the smaller beauties of the flower garden should not require attention, as well as the larger beauties of the lawn, vista and the approach.'[2] McIntosh was a practical gardener with a wide experience in the gardening world and he contributed to the gardening magazines of the day, founding the *Cottage Gardener* in 1848, which, in 1861, was to become the *Journal of Horticulture*. He was also a barrister and garden historian and, therefore, was interested in the move towards history and artifice in the garden and the argument that because gardens were made by man they should complement the architecture of the house. McIntosh was influenced by the French philosopher Victor Cousin (1792-1867) and his book *The Philosophy of the Beautiful,* which had been translated by Jesse Cato Daniel in 1848. Cousin wrote on what he considered constituted Beauty, maintaining that: 'in order that an object may be beautiful it must express an idea, second it must present unity which manifests the idea, third it must be composed of different, and determined parts; in other words, the three conditions of Beauty are, the moral idea, unity and variety.'[3] This is a theme that was also taken up by Shirley Hibberd in his publication *Rustic Adornments for Homes of Taste,* which was published in 1856, 1857 and reissued in 1870. Hibberd observed that it was necessary to:

> Subordinate every detail to the production of a complete effect. Every contrast should help to conserve and strengthen the harmony of the whole, the details should assist each other in creating a succession of pleasing, cares, anxieties, and occupations, and a varied scene of ever changing delight. It should be borne in mind by every cultivator of taste in gardening, that a garden is an artificial contrivance, it is not a piece scooped out of a wood, but in some sense a continuation of the house. Since it is a creation of art not a patch of wild nature, so it should everywhere show the evidence of artistic taste in every one of its graduations, from the vase on the terrace to the 'lovers' walk in the distant shrubbery.[4]

1 John Claudius Loudon, *The Landscape Gardening and the Landscape Architecture of the late Humphry Repton, Esq.* (Cambridge University Press, 2013).
2 Charles McIntosh, *The Flower Garden* (William S. Orr Company Limited, London, 1838).
3 Victor Cousin, *The Philosophy of the Beautiful,* translated with notes and an introduction by Jesse Daniel (William Pickering, 1848), pp. 133-134.
4 Shirley Hibberd, *Rustic Adornments for Homes of Taste* (Groombridge & Sons Limited, 1870).

A number of garden writers attempted to classify the various garden styles, and amongst them was McIntosh. Although his publication *The Flower Garden* was largely devoted to the practical area of gardening, giving advice on, for example, rock work, water basins, seed sowing, the growing of bulbs and the preparation of soil, his interests went much further. He endeavoured to place the various styles into categories: 'Like all the fine arts, gardening has at different periods been practical in particular styles – all, markedly distinguished for their several peculiarities as the Egyptian, Grecian, Roman, and Gothic styles of architecture, or the Italian or Flemish styles of painting and every such style must, more or less, have had its foundation in human nature, having the prevalent acquired taste grafted upon and intermingled with the innate principles of taste.'[1]

McIntosh listed what he considered to be the main characteristics in these gardens and categorized them accordingly:

> ITALIAN Characterised by one or more terraces, sometimes supported by parapet walls, on the coping of which vases of different forms are occasionally placed, either as ornaments, or for the purpose of containing plants. Where the ground slopes much, and commands a supply of water from above, jets d'eau and fountains are introduced with good effect.
>
> FRENCH The French partially adopt the Italian style close to their chateaux and houses, and, beyond the terraces, lay out *parterres*, sometimes in very complicated figures.
>
> DUTCH The leading character of the Dutch style is rectangular formality, and what may sometimes be termed clumsy artifice, such as yew trees cut out in the form of statues, though they require a label to inform the observer what they mean to represent.
>
> ENGLISH It is generally understood that the style termed English in gardening consists in an artful imitation of nature, and is consequently much dependent on aspect and accessories. In the true English style, accordingly, we have neither the Italian terrace, the French *parterre*, nor the Dutch clipped evergreens.[2]

There was still uncertainty, however, throughout the 1830s regarding the appropriate style to adopt in the flower garden. For example, in 1834, although the editor of the *Gardener's Magazine* proclaimed that to be a work of art the landscape garden has to be artificial, he apparently was unable to decide on what form this return to artificiality should take, indiscriminately labelling designs 'Classical', 'Gothic', 'Elizabethan', 'Dutch' and 'French'.

By the early 1840s the subtle changes in garden design that had taken place from the Tudor to the Stuart period was better understood. Covered walks, bowling greens, bowers, mazes, mounts, knot gardens containing herbs and native flowers, topiary, small

1 Charles McIntosh, *The Flower Garden* (William S. Orr Company Limited, London, 1838).

2 *Ibid.*, pp. 9-23.

fountains, canals and heraldic decoration on painted wooden poles were attributed to the Tudor period. By contrast, during the reign of James I a distinctly Italianate style prevailed, the house aligned with the garden, and featuring hydraulics, straight approach roads, stone steps, balustrades and long straight avenues.

When William began to develop his formal gardens the foremost garden writer was Loudon, but he was not always in agreement with Loudon's theories. For example, he would not have approved when, in 1832, Loudon promoted what he termed the 'Gardenesque', a term which meant the isolation of trees and flowers as individual specimens. William's opinion was that it was necessary to subordinate detail to the overall effect as a way of achieving variety and harmony. However, in the early years of his landscape design career he was anxious that his clients should appreciate that such an influential writer and publicist approved of his work and he would have appreciated Loudon's interpretation of what constituted a Picturesque landscape which was: 'the imitation of nature in a wild state, such as the painter delights to copy.'[1] When Loudon visited Fortis Green in order to discuss the article he was writing in the *Gardener's Magazine*, William took the opportunity to impress his influential client the Duke of Newcastle, who owned Clumber Park in Nottinghamshire. In a letter to the Duke he wrote: 'At the time I was drawing the plans for Arboretum & French garden, Mr Loudon happened to call – and I showed him the designs which he highly approved of – the latter was especially admired in as much as he begged for a tracing of it for his publication.'[2]

By the early years of the nineteenth century the tentative return to artifice in the garden, and the rejection of the landscape park associated with Brown, was complete. Brown's destruction of the terraces, steps and statuary associated with the Jacobean period was now considered as something to be regretted, as was his: 'destruction of villages and even towns if they were in line of sight of the landowner's mansion.'[3] There was a need for more controlled gardens close to the house. There are isolated instances of *parterres* being introduced in the 1830s, for example at Audley End by instructions of the 3rd Baron Braybrooke. The design is reputed to have been taken from an eighteenth-century pattern book, and included plants such as geraniums, fuchsias, old rose varieties, and eschscholzias, with evergreen trees providing a backdrop around the outer edges. The criticism levelled at this *parterre* design was that 'it ought to have been sunk to have done it justice, and so viewed from a terrace, but in consequence of the low position of the house that idea was no doubt found to be impracticable.'[4] Later in the century, at Oxburgh Hall in Norfolk, a *parterre-de-broderie* was laid out to the

1 John Claudius Loudon, *Gardener and Villa Companion* (Longman, Orr, Brown, Green and Longmans and A.C. Black, Edinburgh 1838), pp. 164-166.
2 Correspondence between William Nesfield and Henry Pelham, Clinton, 4th Duke of Newcastle, 8 June 1838, MSS Ne C7 302/21, Manuscripts and Special Collections, Nottingham University.
3 David Watkins, *The English Vision – The Picturesque in Architecture, Landscape and Garden Design* (John Murray, 1982), p. 181.
4 *The Garden*, 21 July, 1877, p. 57.

east of the Hall. It was almost identical to one of the designs illustrated in *La Théorie et la Pratique du Jardinages* by Antoine-Joseph Dezallier d'Argenville (1680-1765), which was published in 1709. The design had been used in a garden near Paris, where it was seen in 1845 by a member of the Bedingfeld family, who had owned Oxburgh Hall since the fifteenth century. However, instead of dwarf box hedges surrounding the plant-like shapes that made up the pattern and gravels, cotton lavender (*Santolina chamaecyparissus),* Rue (*Ruta graveolens)* 'Jackman's Blue') with panels of French marigolds (*Tagetes patula* and *Ageratum houstonianum)* were planted. It was not until William became a landscape gardener that the *parterre-de-broderie,* based on the ones at Versailles, was widely re-introduced. Although it was impossible for him to recreate the vast and wide sweeping vistas to be found at Versailles, which had been constructed on a monumental scale that could only have been afforded by someone with the power of an absolute monarch, such as Louis XIV, nevertheless, the principles embodied in the Versailles design were aspired to by William. This brings us to his contribution to the retention of strict formality in the garden, but, before looking in detail at his clients and their estates, the following chapter will consider the origins of the *parterre-de-broderie* which was such a central component within his work, together with the artist designers he chose to emulate.

8.

The *Parterre-de-Broderie*

Although *parterres* in one form or another have a long history, they were not introduced into England until Charles I came to the throne in 1625. They can be traced back to the Italian Renaissance garden, whose influences reached France in the sixteenth century when the two countries were brought closer together through dynastic marriages between French kings and members of the Medici family of Florence, wealthy bankers and patrons of the arts. Catherine de' Medici (1519-1589) married Henri II, who was responsible for the initial designs for the Jardin des Tuileries in Paris; and Marie de' Medici (1573-1642), the wife of Henri IV, instigated the building and gardens at the Luxembourg Palace in Paris. The inspiration for these gardens came from the Pitti Palace and the Boboli Gardens in Florence, both dating from the fifteenth and sixteenth centuries. They brought to perfection the visual representation of control, through iconography and symbolism, thus empathizing the absolute power of their owners. The Medici villa in Fiesole near Florence, which looks across to the palaces and domes of the city and the distant hills, was built between 1458 and 1461 by Michelozzo Michelozzi for Cosimo de' Medici (1389-1464). It has been described as the first true Renaissance villa, as it embodied the new principles of symmetry and mathematical arrangement then in vogue in Florence due to the influence of Filippo Brunelleschi and his work on the dome of Florence Cathedral. It is completely classical in concept, and demonstrates classical proportions. Height is carefully calculated in relation to width, and round arches are featured, carried on columns with triangular pediments.[1]

Although the French adopted Italian designs, they adapted them to suit their flatter terrain, and their designs became less rigidly geometrical than the Italian model. They had a unity and harmony that was completely their own. The French gardens were, however, still laid out on a symmetrical, longitudinal axis leading the eye down to an

1 Peter Murray, *The Architecture of the Italian Renaissance* (Thames and Hudson, 1981) pp. 68-69.

architectural feature, with a side axis running parallel. The narrow alleys in between were still marked out in low box, infilled with coloured gravels. However, the strictly geometrical designs within the pattern disappeared to be replaced by flowing curvilinear designs of plant-like shapes (scrolls, florets and rays).

The Baroque garden attained perfection in France at Vaux-le-Vicomte, which was built, and its gardens laid out, by André le Nôtre between 1656 and 1661 for Nicolas Fouquet (1615-1680). The primary purpose for the building at Vaux was to create a backdrop for lavish entertainments and to advertise the power of its owner. This was a conceit which ultimately led to Fouquet's downfall: when Louis XIV saw its magnificence he craved it for his own. Fouquet was thrown into prison soon after the completion of Vaux in 1661, where he languished until his death. With its double water theatre and sculptures of river gods and their attendants, Vaux was the forerunner of the superb gardens at Versailles designed for Louis by André le Nôtre after 1660. Apart from the services of le Nôtre, Louis also acquired from Vaux those of the architect Louis le Vau (1612-1670) and the painter Charles Le Brun (1619-1690), who were put to work on a scheme at Versailles which was to be the envy of all who witnessed it. The scheme was a song of praise to Apollo, whom Louis wished to emulate in his role as 'Sun King'. An interest in the arts, combined with the need to establish a power base were abiding principles of the Renaissance monarchy. The most prestigious gardens were, therefore, designed during the reign of Louis XIV, and his reign marked an era of extraordinary blossoming of the arts. Versailles at the end of the seventeenth century was inspired by a 'drive towards artistic perfection.'[1]

The first *parterre-de-broderie* is reputed to have been laid out on the instructions of Étienne Dupérac for the Duc d'Aumale, St Germaine-en-Laye, between 1582-1595. [2] It was designed by Claude Mollet, a member of a great French gardening dynasty, who is reputed to have introduced *Boxus* (box) into Italy from France.

These early attempts were the forerunners of the later, much more elaborate designs created by his son, André (d. c. 1665), who formulated the archetypical French garden plan of rectangular beds divided by paths into a regular grid arranged symmetrically about a central axis.

Charles I and his queen, Henrietta Maria, employed André Mollet to lay out the royal gardens in England. The most significant ones were at Wimbledon House and St James' Palace. The *parterres-de-broderie* he devised preceded the Baroque gardens of Charles II's reign. However, the Civil War meant that gardening patronized by royalty disappeared until the Restoration of 1660, when the French style once again

1 Jacques Girard, *Versailles Gardens – Sculpture and Mythology* (Sotheby's Publications Limited, 1985), p. 98. See also John Dixon Hunt, *Greater Perfections – the Practice of Garden Theory* (Thames & Hudson, 2000), p. 98: 'all great European gardens of the seventeenth and eighteenth centuries were developed as expressions of their owner's status and position in the world, we know, because the gardens made it their business to alert visitors to this fact.'

2 George and Susan Jellicoe (eds), *The Oxford Companion to Gardens* (Oxford University Press, 1986), p. 378.

dominated. Charles II, having spent his years of exile in France and Holland, had the opportunity to see the great French gardens, and when he returned to power a number of French gardeners were attracted to England. André Mollet and his brother Gabriel had remained in England throughout the war. Within two years of his restoration, Charles sent for André le Nôtre, who is reputed to have redesigned the parks at Whitehall and Greenwich.[1]

Two English royal gardeners, John Rose (1629-1677) and George London (d. 1714) both visited France, Rose having been sent by the Earl of Essex to study at Versailles under le Nôtre early in his career. They became gardeners to Charles II, who was consequently able to take advantage of the skills of men trained in the French tradition. However, this style was virtually lost in England with the onset of the eighteenth century: landscapes, featuring the mythological statues and follies associated with Classical allegory, followed by the landscaped parks of Lancelot Brown and his school of design, held central stage for most of the rest of the eighteenth century.

It was William who was instrumental in returning the *parterre-de-broderie,* the grandest and most complicated garden device, to a central place within the formal garden. Its purpose is explained to one of his clients:

> The *parterre* was rendered as conspicuous as possible by being centrally placed on a public room or garden front, indeed the old Masters were so fastidious regarding the design of a *Parterre* that it was as conformable to the rules of art as the composition of a Picture on canvas, their aim was concentration & such a combination of accessories as conduced to richness without confusion but more especially to variety *altho symmetry* was invariably adopted.[2]

William invariably aligned his *parterres-de-broderie* with the most important rooms of the mansion, usually in the form of a sunken panel so that they could be viewed from an elevated position, often a raised terrace. They would be placed on a wide, longitudinal axis running parallel to the main rooms of the house, and enclosed so that they resembled a picture in a frame. They would invariably be enclosed by solid balustrades or open grille-work panels to echo the parapet on the outside of the house. William expanded upon the elements to be used within the scheme to his client, John Manners Sutton:

> The area of a *parterre* was regulated according to the size of the house and dealt with as artificially as art could desire by means of grass slopes, terraces, panels, verges, sculpture, fountains, box embroidery, flowers and other exotics. The details should invariably be worked into rich compartments, the main and flanking centres of which should be formed upon the most important windows or doors according to

1 Helen M. Fox, *André le Nôtre: Garden Architect to Kings* (B.T. Batsford, 1962). For sources relating to le Nôtre's visit to England see 'Warrant from Treasurer', (October 15, 1662) book x, p. 137. 'To permit le Nôtre, the King's Architect, to transport six horses to France custom free as by royal warrant recited.'

2 Report to Lord Howe, Gopsall Hall, Leicestershire Nesfield Archives.

circumstances. The business then of an artist is to create an agreeable combination of the aforesaid materials in such a manner as to produce a concentration of effect upon the said principles as he would enhance the focus of a picture on canvas i.e. by keeping accessories subordinate thus there would be a gradation from the highly artificial to the neutral character.[1]

Finial for Swillington Hall, sketch by William Nesfield.

Low-growing clipped box plants were used to edge the plant-like shapes within the *parterre*, and evergreens were symmetrically placed around the perimeter. To give height to the sunken panels, William used a large architectural feature, such as an armillary sphere.[2] Tazzas, vases and finials were placed around the *parterre* interspersed with clipped evergreens. Their purpose was to achieve complete symmetry by complementing each other across the *parterre*.

Plants were never key components in the original *parterres-de-broderie*, bedding plants of course being unavailable in the seventeenth century, and *parterres* in this period always conformed to the image we have of them: of military precision associated with the pristine look of clipped evergreens and well-raked gravel. Before the *parterre-de-broderie* was introduced to England from France during the reign of King Charles I, simple designs known as Knot Gardens were used in the immediate vicinity of the manor house. The history behind these devices can be traced back to a book entitled *Hypnerotomachia Poliphili*, which was published in Venice in 1499. Flowerbeds in this volume were filled with flowers and herbs to represent Eastern-style carpets. They were simple in form and geometric in shape, unlike the curved, plant-like scrolls associated with the *parterre-de-broderie*. As William's own horticultural knowledge was limited, as he freely admitted, a restricted colour palette suited him. He used a small, predictable range of low-growing plants, graded in blocks of one colour, with lighter colours at the front. Keeping the plants and box low in the *parterre* meant they could be viewed from the house whilst carrying the eye beyond. Reduced

1 Correspondence between William Nesfield and John Manners-Sutton of Kelham Hall, Nottinghamshire Nesfield Archives.

2 The armillary sphere or equatorial sundial is French in origin. The rings represent the great circles of the heavens, put together in their relative positions as symbols of eternity. The time is indicated by the shadow cast by the shaft, which passes centrally through the sphere.

colour towards the end of the *parterre* with the use of compartments of grass enabled the *parterre* to blend into the parkland. His awareness, acquired through his artistic training, of the subtle blending and grading of colours is highlighted in his suggestions for Stoke Edith in Herefordshire:[1]

> All plants nearest the house should be as low as possible & pegged – those for the subdivision at the North end of Compartment may be as high as the most dwarf Geraniums. The foliated beds must have particularly low flowers or their forms will be confused – The endeavour must be to make gradations of one colour in the same bed, where the deepest scarlet commences at the circle A & blends imperceptibly towards B into orangy red & thence towards C into salmon red. At D the gradations are from deep yellow to very brilliant pale yellow at E & so on throughout to the purples, blues &c.
>
> The darkest & most sober colours should be in the North beds to advance the more positive Colours at the South end – The foliated Beds Nos. 1, 2, 3 should gradate in colour from light rose No. 1 to the deepest rose or maroon.
>
> No. 3 The flank foliated Beds
>
> No. 4 should contain the deepest blue possible.
>
> The Scallop to be prismatic by means of light colours, yet gradating at the south ends from darker, shading to very pale & by way of enhancing the dark introduce white spots of verbena –
>
> No. 5 Yellowish white such as Mignionette
>
> 6 very bright bluey white
>
> 7 Real white
>
> 8 pale blue.

William would have studied the colour theories in current use, whilst bringing his own artistic skills to his designs. One gardener whose colour theories were close to his own was John Caie (1811-1879). Caie was head gardener to the Duke of Bedford at Bedford Lodge, Kensington, and in 1838 he produced an article for the *Gardeners' Magazine* setting out his scheme for Bedford Lodge, principles which were to be repeated in William's work. They included the notion that colours should be presented in solid masses and not mixed together, for solid masses allow the eye to rest instead of continually agitating it by small juxtapositions; furthermore, the eye's first impression ought to be one of dignity and greatness of expression. Caie also maintained that the height of plants should be in proportion to the size of beds and arranged for contrast. Colour should be clean, simple and intelligible: 'Order, he maintained, was the source of peace and this could only be achieved by balance and proportion.' [2] The impact of Caie's ideas on the bedding-out system was discussed by the gardener David Taylor Fish (1824-1901): 'Take, for example,

1 Herefordshire Record Office, Hereford, Foley Collection.

2 See Brent Elliott, Victorian Gardens (B.T. Batsford Limited, London, 1986), p. 88. for Caie's influence on garden design.

Proposed tazza for Holkham Hall, sketch by William Nesfield.

the bedding-out system, of which in its best form he was undoubtedly the originator. He was possessed with, lost in it, for years.'[1] William was also to make use of bedding plants, a valuable horticultural source that had not been available to designers in seventeenth-century France, whose *parterres were* formed solely of low box and different coloured gravels. Between the 1830s and 1840s, a range of plants was introduced to England from South Africa and North America, which could be bedded out each summer and discarded when they became untidy. They included pelargoniums, lobelias, verbenas, petunias, calceolarias and salvia *splendens*. The plants were to be intensely hybridized, and by 1850 the bedding range covered six colour groups, yellow, purple, scarlet, blue, pink and white.[2] By careful juxtapositioning of one shade against another, William rescued these plants from becoming garish, as bedding-schemes in the late Victorian period could easily become, especially in public parks. By the 1850s the zonal hybrids of pelargoniums were frequently used, together with the Regal and scented-leaved varieties.

William maintained that only an artist could appreciate the qualities of beauty and aestheticism necessary to produce a *parterre-de-broderie*. Therefore, when he decided to make the *parterre-de-broderie* the centre-piece of his formal gardens, he turned to some of the most talented French artist-designers active in the seventeenth century for inspiration. These he referred to as the 'old Masters of Gardening'. He brought together in a large scrapbook the *parterre* patterns of six of these artists, together with twenty-four pages of thirty designs that he did not attribute to any particular artist, and used them as inspiration for his designs. It has not been possible to ascertain for certain where he obtained these designs; one source could have been the British Museum, as the Prints and Drawings department there holds a number of patterns by these artists. These were collated by the museum into one volume in 1850, and the only notable designer whose work is missing from the collection is Jean Bérain. However, the Bibliothèque Nationale de France in Paris holds three large volumes of his work, which include designs for interiors and theatre sets. In one of these books are a number of *parterre-de-broderie* designs. William was always anxious to assure his clients that garden design was as important an art form as architecture and painting, and therefore, at least two of the designers who inspired him were architects.

1 *Gardeners Chronicle*, 1879, pp. 442, 489, 534.
2 Brent Elliott, *Ibid.* p. 89.

Three Examples of Jacques Boyceau's Designs, taken from William Nesfield's Pattern Book.

These designers were: Jacques Boyceau de La Barauderie (d. 1633), of whom it has been said: 'The whole tenor of his landscape design doctrine bespeaks a true worship of aesthetic beauty. By enveloping the practice of gardening in an aesthetic atmosphere, he thereby establishes landscape design as an Art.'[1] By collaborating closely with architects, Boyceau was to establish landscape gardening as an honoured profession and ensure that the French garden was seen for the first time as important an art form as architecture, sculpture and painting. Boyceau was the first to differentiate between the mere tiller of the soil (*Jardinière du Roi*) and the knowledgeable designer who understood the artistic requirements necessary to produce historic gardens (*Intendant des Jardinière du Roi*). This distinction was reiterated in the remarks of the Vicomte Amédée de Viart, who owned and created the park of Brunehaut in Essonne, and who in 1819 published *Le Jardiniste Moderne* in which he coined two new terms, '*jardinise*' and '*jardiniste*', to differentiate between the recognised artist who designs gardens and the workman who cultivates them. These definitions were important to William, who considered himself to be very much the artist behind the plan. Boyceau has also been credited as being the first to site the *parterre-de-broderie* in close proximity to the palace.[2] This was at the Palais du Luxembourg in Paris, which was built between 1615 and 1630 for Marie de' Medici.

By establishing landscape design as an honoured profession, the principles established during these early gardening dynasties laid the foundation for the aesthetic and intellectual theories which were to be fully realized during the reign of Louis XIV. Jacques Boyceau was attached to the powerful

1 Franklin Hamilton Hazelhurst, *Jacques Boyceau and The French Formal Garden* (University of Georgia Press, 1966), p. vii.
2 Robert W. Berger, *Antoine Le Pautre: A French Architect of the Era of Louis XIV* (New York University Press, 1969).

An example of Le Blond's Patterns, taken from William Nesfield's Pattern Book.

household of Charles de Gontaut, duc de Biron, and has been described as a soldier, philosopher, scientist, botanist and poet. He lived in an age when it was not considered incongruous for a soldier to be an artist, diversity and versatility being seen as a virtue. He was a favourite at the French court, coming to prominence during the reigns of Henry IV, Marie de' Medici and Louis XIII. By 1610, the year of Henri IV's assassination, he was already recognised as an outstanding designer.

Jean Le Pautre (1618-1682) was a designer and printmaker. He came, as many artists did in the seventeenth century, from a dynasty of designers and artists. They included architects, a draughtsman, a surveyor and a sculptor. He produced designs for the interior at Versailles and also statuary for the park and the *parterre-de-broderie* for the *Bassin de Latone*.

André le Nôtre (1613-1700) is probably the best known of the six designers, especially for his grand siècle designs at Versailles for Louis XIV, where only the best sculptors and craftsmen were employed to enhance and beautify the estate. Le Nôtre is considered to be a near genius due to the enormous unified and sweeping vistas he devised at Versailles, with their unimpeded central vistas to the horizon.

Jean-Baptiste Alexandre Le Blond (1679-1719) was a pupil of Le Nôtre's. He later became architect general to Peter the Great of Russia, for whom he designed the Peterhof gardens in St Petersburg. He also designed the Hôtel de Vendôme and the Hotel de Clermont in Paris, and his augmented edition of Claude-Louis d'Aviler's *Cours d'Architecture* of 1710 was an important book on architectural work. Le Blond engraved the plates for *La Théorie et la Pratique du Jardinages*, written in 1712 by Antoine-Joseph Dezallier d'Argenville, who was a man of quality, a lover of the fine arts and a scholar, having gathered together and catalogued all the available material on the subject of classical garden design at that time. This book became the principal reference on the subject in the early eighteenth century, and went into a fourth edition in Paris in 1747.

One of the designs from the above book was reproduced by William for use at Worsley Hall in Lancashire for the Earl of Ellesmere. This is the only known case where it has been possible to verify that he replicated, in its entirety, a design from one of the six designers.

An Example of Le Pautre's Patterns, taken from William Nesfield's Pattern Book.

An Example of Le Nôtre's Patterns, taken from William Nesfield's Pattern Book.

An example of Bérain's patterns, taken from William Nesfield's Pattern Book.

He usually selected elements from different designs and adapted and altered them to suit his purpose. The same design had been published by Loudon as early as 1812, and a similar design had been used at Syon Park and Oxburgh Hall in the mid nineteenth-century.[1]

Sieur Bouticourt (1618-1682) was a designer and printmaker and was known to have been the Director of the gardens at the Palais Royale in 1790.

Jean Berain (1640-1711) was a versatile artist, being both an ornamentalist and engraver. He was the chief designer of scenery and stage machinery for the Paris Opera. In 1702 he designed the stage sets for Antoine Watteau's interpretation of the operas *The Triumph of Venus* and *Les Bohémiens*. Both sets show gardens leading towards a palace along a single axis of perfect symmetry, an important concept in the seventeenth-century French garden. In 1670, through the influence and support of Charles Le Brun (1619-1690), who had been a fellow student of Le Nôtre's at the studios of Simon Vouet, Bérain became *Premier Peintre du Roi* and was given control of the direction of the gardens at Versailles. In 1674 he succeeded Henri de Gissey (1621-1673) as *Dessinateur de la Chambre et du Cabinet du Roi* and became one of the principal artists of the court, working for the *Batiments du Roi* and the *Menuss-Plaisirs du Roi*. In 1677 he was appointed *Dessinateur des Jardins* and designed a number of *parterres*. He was attached to the household of the Dauphin in 1680 and again in 1681.

The importance William attached to Bérain's designs is reflected in the number he included in his book. Bérain's skill in designing theatrical scenery is reflected in the way he visualised the garden as a concave stage set and a magical place:

> Of dreams and illusions but also as the practical realisation of these dreams. By its very conception, by the efforts created within it, the fabrique placed in it, the vistas contrived, it becomes more or less dramatic, more or less charming. Nature is evoked and used according to the required effect.[2]

1 Brent Elliott, *Ibid*, p. 71.

2 Michel in Mosser, Monique and Teysott, (eds), *Garden Design – The Western Tradition from Renaissance to the Present Day* (Thames & Hudson, 1991), p. 9. When a contemporary asked Nesfield how he could continue making so many fresh plans each with a different design, he said: 'Look here, friend – producing a very large book which was designs from end to end – when I have exhausted and adapted all these to suit my purposes I should by that time be a very old man': Taken from a lecture on Landscape Gardening given by William Miller at the Athletic Institution, John Bright Street, Birmingham, 4 November 1901.

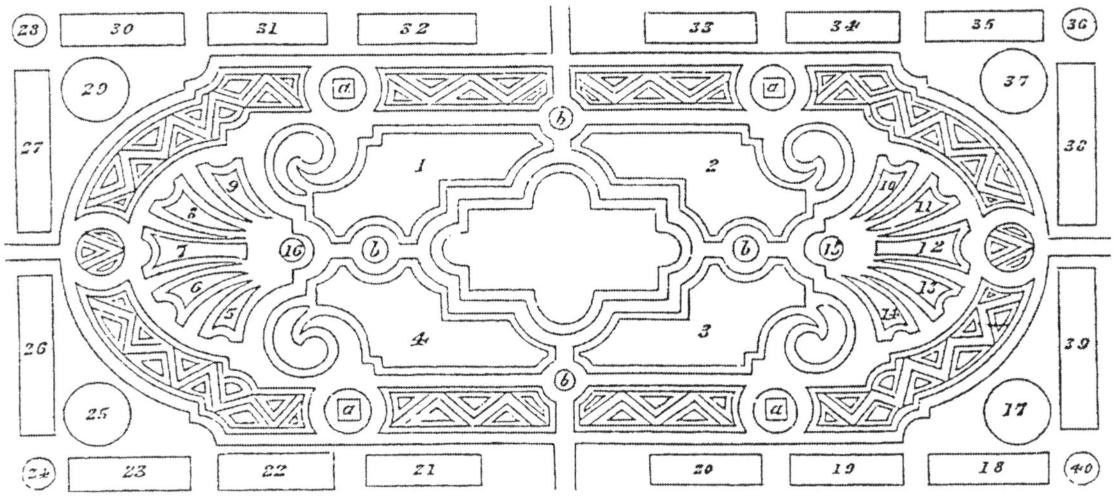

Parterre design for Worsley Hall, Lancashire.

Left: An Example of Bouticourt's Patterns, taken from William Nesfield's Pattern Book.
Right: An example of Bérain's patterns, taken from William Nesfield's Pattern Book.

9.

Painted Gardens

During the 1840s, the pace of William's landscape gardening career increased considerably, and he was beginning to find it increasingly inconvenient to be so far from London. Consequently:

> After about 2 years at Eton Emma looked about for a London House & at last hit upon 3 York Terrace under a Mr Olive who lived at No. 4 at whose death his nephew the Rev. John Olive became my landlord as well as an excellent neighbour. He had an only Daughter who when marriageable to Lord Kilcoursey, wanted to raise cash for her & so sold his 3 houses for that purpose i.e. Nos. 2, 3 & 4 – but as my lease had 2 yrs to run No. 3 sold for only £500 to me. On becoming firmly established my new profession flourished rapidly but I did not for several years resign at the W.C. Socy. – i.e. till it was impossible to devote even a small amount of time for the brush.[1]

By this time William he had few business rivals: Humphry Repton and William Sawrey Gilpin were dead. However, two other important garden designers were active during this period, Sir Joseph Paxton (1803-1865) and Sir Charles Barry (1795-1860). Paxton was head gardener to the 6th Duke of Devonshire at Chatsworth, where he carried out many improvements to the gardens. His main claim to fame, however, was the vast Conservatory, better known as the Crystal Palace, which he designed for The Great Exhibition of 1850 in Hyde Park, London, and for which he received his Knighthood. Paxton's interests and capacity for hard work were impressive, but he was primarily a designer of public parks and cemeteries, as opposed to private domestic estates – apart from Chatsworth. A Member of Parliament for Coventry, a publicist and railway magnate, he founded and edited a number of horticultural magazines, including the *Horticultural Register* and *Paxton's Magazine of Botany*. He also wrote a practical treatise

1 Nesfield Archives.

on the cultivation of dahlias, a pocket *Botanical Dictionary* and *Paxton's Flower Garden*. William did not have a high opinion of Paxton, and the root of this antagonism lay in a combination of professional jealousy and snobbery: Paxton originally worked with his hands as a humble gardener.[1] He considered John Fleming, the Duke of Sutherland's head gardener, very able; however, Charles Barry was the architect who designed the new Houses of Parliament, formally completed in 1852. Barry received a number of commissions from the Duke of Sutherland at Trentham in Staffordshire, Dunrobin in Scotland and Shrublands in Suffolk. However, this could have been because William was dismissed by the Duke from his estate at Cliveden in Buckinghamshire – the grand *parterre* at Cliveden ultimately being designed by John Fleming. The reason for the rejection was recorded by his second son, Arthur Markham Nesfield in his diary:

> At the Duke of Sutherland's was a wood on the hill – which my Lady was not fond of – add to it said my father – you must not take it away – So some hanging woods were staked out to get some antirustic lines – it was done but with deer in the park they were obliged to enclose all the new plantations with large hurdles – when the bill came in the duke kicked up a thundering row with the Duchess about the expense – and after explanation my father got his congé and has never been there since.[2]

This rejection was, however, an isolated circumstance for William, who usually had no difficulty in gaining commissions, sometimes resulting in his working on an estate for decades. His charges were not modest, as can be appreciated from the comments made by Ralph Sneyd of Keele Hall in Staffordshire, when he grumbled to a contemporary that he had had: 'Nesfield here for a very few hours, at a great many guineas an hour.'[3]

Nesfield's Table of Charges read as follows:

> In consequence of Mr Nesfield being frequently requested to explain his Terms for professional services in Landscape Gardening he deemed it expedient to state them in detail thus:
>
> For personal attendance a visit 5 Guineas per diem. For time on a journey 5 G's per diem exclusive of travelling expenses.
>
> For ground Plans, Sections, Reports, Working Drawings, Tracings, Landscape and other sketches to illustrate proposed Improvements, and special appointments in London for conferences according to the Time occupied at the rate of 5 G's per Diem.

1 I am grateful to the late Robert Markham Nesfield for this information. William Nesfield wrote to one of his contemporaries that there were a number of 'professional pretenders to landscape Gardening from whom it is feared not much original design can be expected because there is not a man among them a real Artist'.

2 Arthur Markham Nesfield's Notebook, Nesfield Archives.

3 Keele University Library, Sneyd Papers S[HWV/RS], 120, Spring 1844: Ralph Sneyd to H.W. Vincent.

In some cases it is necessary by way of avoiding a prolonged visit on the part of Mr Nesfield to take with him or send his Assistant to survey, take Levels, transfer Designs to Ground or instruct Gardeners or Clerks of Works in carrying out proposed operations, for which the charge is One Guinea per Diem, exclusive of travelling expenses by second class and also his Time on a Journey.[1]

As William's workload increased he was sometimes required to travel great distances in order to fulfil his landscape design commitments, often in the most uncomfortable circumstances. In the winter of 1842, for example, he wrote from Haverland Hall, Norwich to Rowland Egerton-Warburton, his client at Arley Hall in Cheshire:

I came here this morning for the first time across a cold country in an open carriage dreadfully petrified, after w'h I had to explore & walk all day w'h has so knocked me up that I feel totally incapable of reconsidering my own misdoings & yr ideas with any degree of unfatiqued judgement as I find her even a more difficult & intricate case to contend with than yr's my time tomorrow will be stretched almost beyond concert pitch especially as I must travel in the ev'g 28 miles to Flixton Hall (not per comfortable rail) – at all events on Satyd ev'g I will steal off to my bedroom & thus be enabled to digest y'r scheme.[2]

He did, however, have one advantage that was not available to his predecessors: the railway network, which, by the 1840s, was steadily creeping across the countryside. In 1845 Parliament authorized the building of over 2000 miles of track and William took full advantage of it. His working method was to make a preliminary visit to the site, and, after he or his surveyor had walked the grounds, to provide a written report setting out his recommendations and criticisms. If his comments met with his clients' approval, he would draw up detailed plans for their consideration, which could be changed many times before a satisfactory scheme was arrived at. By this time he had refined and shaped a formal garden plan which could be readapted for different gardens. It was situated on the principal front of the house in question and the design was to prove extremely successful; he never really needed to deviate from it. The centrepiece was the *parterre-de-broderie,* with its flowing, plant-like shapes, giving the impression of a piece of embroidery or a colourful carpet thrown over the ground, but using coloured gravels and low-growing, brightly-coloured plants in blocks of one colour instead of fabric. He emphases that it was a device that had been used by the old 'Masters of Gardening', and therefore a concept which only the most cultivated of minds could appreciate, with the result that he rarely had any trouble in winning his clients over to his schemes. The formal garden with its *parterre-de-broderie* was, however important, only one element in William's plans which were intended to enfold the house on which he was working in a four-way, symmetric design. He explained this typical Nesfieldian layout to his client Sir John Guest:

1 Keele University Library, Sneyd Papers S80/91 (Box 38).

2 Correspondence between William Nesfield and Rowland Egerton-Warburton, 8 December 1842, Arley Hall Archives.

The Broad Walk, Crewe Hall, Cheshire.

> Every house of pretension had its outworks, which formed essential component parts thereof, consequently without such adjuncts a mansion was incomplete as whole outworks were comprehended within a line of circumvallation and consisted of from one to three fronts – one devoted to Entrance Court their object was twofold viz. a fence against cattle and in an artistic sense to act as a line between Art and Nature.[1]

Single-point perspective, which was a device for carrying the eye towards a central vanishing point, was an important element within the four-way system, and the person responsible for bringing it to England was the painter and architect Inigo Jones (1573-1652). In January 1614 he returned from Italy, where he had been travelling in the entourage of the Earl of Arundel. He had made Roman antique sculpture and classical architecture and he would have seen how classical elements were incorporated into the Italian Renaissance garden, which also emphasized unity and harmonious organization of space. Jones was responsible for designing the elaborate stage sets for the masques and entertainments of the Stuart court. He made use of the proscenium arch, the purpose of which was to direct the eye to a focal point, a feature he had observed in Italy. Similar

1 Report from William Nesfield to Sir John Guest, Canford Manor, Dorset, Nesfield Archives.

tricks of perspective were used in garden design, helping to link gardens axially to the building of which they were a part, so that gardens were no longer isolated enclosures. This resulted in 'the architectural alignment of house and garden, the use of monocular perspective in planning and a preoccupation with hydraulics in the form of highly symbolic fountains.'[1] William also linked the formal garden and the distant landscape into one cohesive whole, with an Entrance Court aligned on the central axis of the main façade of the House to give the design harmony and order. The Crewe estate in Cheshire is an excellent example of this. At Crewe, his sole purpose was to restore and enhance the original character of the Jacobean mansion. Adjacent to the public road at Crewe were a set of elaborate gates leading to the front of the house by means of a straight drive flanked by sweet chestnut trees.

> The drive still leads to the southern entrance to the Entrance Court of the Hall, which has low balustraded walls and is aligned with the main façade of the house. William's preliminary report of February 1842 demonstrates his desire to produce a scheme for the Entrance Court which would reflect the Jacobean period in which the Hall was built: 'The area within the proposed walls are furnished in geometric or artificial manner the character of which is deduced from authorities of the olden time – thus a whole will be created in harmony with the Building.[2]

On the west front at Crewe was a kitchen garden, and on the east two large lion statues surrounded by a low balustrade. On a lower level was a broad walk, flanked by two small *parterres* containing statues and evergreens. On the north face of the house, overlooked by the most important rooms, he designed his most prestigious garden, which included a *parterre-de-broderie*. His intentions for the garden were explained in his preliminary report:

> As this front of the House is Northern & overshadows the ground, this portion of the *Parterre* will not be congenial to herbaceous plants therefore various devices will be adopted in grass & box upon gravel & with the addition of architectural objects such as Statues, Vases &c much rich and appropriate variety will be gained. Embroidery consists of symmetrical or other figures formed with outlines of low box – the old Masters filled the intervals with different coloured sands but small light coloured pebbles will do better set in Musgrave cement.[3]

The purpose of the *parterre* garden was to be viewed from the Long Gallery and to form a striking foreground to the lake, which had been designed by Repton. The *parterre-de-broderie* itself was a large, rectangular sunken panel with broad pathways on either side, which led to a central path at the northern end. On each side of the central path were two reflecting *guilloches* or cable friezes, culminating in a statue of the Sea God,

1 Roy Strong, *The Renaissance Garden in England* (Thames & Hudson Limited, 1998), p. 168.
2 Cheshire Record Office, Chester, DCR/15/2.
3 *Ibid.*

Neptune. The *parterre-de-broderie* was infilled with red and blue gravel, to reflect the diapered red-and-blue brickwork of the Hall. Box cut to three inches high by two inches wide provided a solid outline to the central motif of the *parterre*, which was a large floret. Plant-like arabesque shapes derived from French *parterres* surrounded this central motif. This led to an armillary sphere which formed the centre of a quincunx at the southern end of the *parterre*, the purpose of which was to give height and lead the eye down to the lake. The whole was framed by a border containing low-growing flowers, surrounded by clipped evergreens, interspersed with tazzas, and enclosed by a low balustrade.

William's success at Crewe was highlighted by the remarks made by one of Lord Crewe's kinsmen, the Revd Edward Hinchliffe, vicar of St Bertoline's Church in the nearby village of Barthomley. Hinchliffe had seen William's plans, which he anticipated would return Crewe Hall, which had been built in 1633, to its former glory. In 1856 he published a book in which he gave an interesting insight into his views regarding previous garden restorations at Crewe, and his nostalgic desire for a return to formality:

> Time came when national taste as to buildings, and the laying out of grounds, experienced a wretched change and retrograded, and languished almost to extinction. Some aspiring landscape-gardeners resolved to introduce what they were pleased to designate, English scenery, and in order to do this, they deemed it necessary to demolish all terraces, balustrades, straight walks, box embroidery, beds, cut out in lace-like patterns, &c, &c. To them a Dutch garden was an abomination; an Italian one a heresy; let England have its own style; and let this be formed in walks through shrubberies, imitating nature, and dotted about on grass plots, let everything architectural and avowedly artificial be carefully eschewed. Bring your approach sideways to the house, and not at right angles to the front: separate the two by an invisible iron fence, so that your house will appear to stand in simple majesty in the midst of its park, and our oxen, and deer, and sheep, may enjoy the privilege of peeping in at the windows of your well-furnished rooms. Now a gentleman adopting these tenets came unluckily to Crewe Hall. He drew his lines, erected his batteries, and nature laid siege to art. What Royalists and Parliamentarians did not – that did he down went garden walls, and garden houses, and *parterres* and avenues.[1]

Wilbraham Spencer Tollemache was the son of Admiral John Tollemache, who owned the nearby Peckforton Castle. Although Admiral Tollemache was a rich man, Wilbraham Tollemache was a younger son, and, therefore, although accepted in elite society and aspiring to compete with his wealthier neighbours, he himself was not wealthy. He had married Anne Tomkinson, whose family owned the Dorfold Estate; but unfortunately for Wilbraham, Anne's mother held the purse strings. Although he had invited William to advise on extensive alterations to the grounds at Dorfold in 1848, old Mrs Tomkinson did not approve of the scheme; neither did Anne or her sister, and the project was abandoned until Mrs

1 Edward Hinchcliffe, *Barthomley*, (Longman, Brown, Green & Longmans, 1856), pp. 328-9.

The design for the Northern *Parterre* Garden at Crewe Hall.

Tomkinson's death in the 1860s. Anne was still opposed to the scheme, especially to the cutting down of trees including a favourite elm, which William christened 'the pet'. He tried to reconcile her to the idea by pointing out: 'how merciful he was over cutting timber, knowing how ladies loved to be smothered in foliage.'[1] However, she was unimpressed, especially when he said that 'the alterations and a lodge would make a 1,000 look very ugly' (by which he meant there would be little change from £1,000). [2] She also objected to William's suggestion that the pool, where she and her sister bathed, should be made smaller and moved away from the new drive he proposed. This exasperated him enough for him to remark that: 'If the water were even limpid . . . but it was stagnant, and a receptacle for sewerage and decaying vegetable matter, and its situation right in front of the house was a propos to nothing.'[3] When the suggestion was put forward by Tollemache for an island, William's reply was it would produce: 'a cockneyfied effect.'[4] To accompany this Jacobean manor house, William instead recommended that additions be tightly-structured and formal, as at Crewe and elsewhere, consisting of an Entrance Court with a carriage sweep, and a Pleasure Ground aligned with the most important rooms in the Hall in which he would site his grand *parterre*. The scheme was finally put in place whilst Anne was travelling in France. William removed trees, installed elaborate wrought iron gates surmounted with lions bearing shields (to which he claimed Tollemache was not entitled!) He straightened the avenue up to the front of the Hall, drained and altered the course of the pond, advised on the building of a lodge, coach-house and clock tower, and paved the forecourt, which included a carriage sweep. In the middle of the forecourt was placed a grass circle and a bronze statue of a mastiff and her pups similar to that at Tregrehan in Cornwall (but at Tregrehan the statue was a recumbent lion). At the back of the house he built a small

1 Horatia Durrant, 'The Trials and Tribulations of a Landscape Gardener', *Cheshire Life*, 1954, pp. 18-19.
2 *Ibid.*
3 *Ibid.*
4 *Ibid.*

The Northern *Parterre* Garden at Crewe Hall.

parterre, with liminal scrolls. When Anne returned, she was horrified. However, there was little she could do; unfortunately, although technically she owned Dorfold, she lived before the passing of the Married Women's Property Act, and she had no control over her own possessions. Interestingly, a codicil in her Will stated that when she died she wished her body to be carried to the Church, not down the hated new drive, but over unspoilt fields!

Arley Hall in Cheshire has been the principal seat of the Warburton family since 1469, and is still lived in by descendants of the family. In 1826 Rowland Egerton-Warburton (1804-1891) came into his inheritance and after his marriage in 1831 he and his wife Mary embarked on the re-building the Hall. Both Rowland and his wife were amateur artists, enthusiastic garden designers and antiquarians, and it is therefore no surprise that when Salvin built a private Chapel for them between 1842 and 1845, it was requested to be in the Gothic style. A concern for accuracy was evident on Warburton's part when he asked that the ornamental angels in the Chapel 'should be in the fashion of the time in which the Chapel may be supposed to have been built.'[1] William was aware of Warburton's interest in historic detail, and that he was 'proud of the history and Antiquity of his inheritance. Influenced by the "Romantic" movement he wished to escape from neo-classical architecture, and, as an enthusiast for religious revival, he wanted his new house to suggest something of the piety of the Middle Ages as well as the grandeur of Elizabethan England.'[2] Rowland

1 Letter from Anthony Salvin to John Lewis, 23 December 1842, Arley Hall Archives.
2 Charles Foster, *Arley Hall, Cheshire*, 1982, p. 4.

was doubtful about the use of a *parterre-de-broderie* in the vicinity of a Gothic chapel. In order to reconcile Rowland to the scheme, William used all his persuasive powers to convince him that the addition was a good idea. He suggested that he and Rowland should meet at Crewe Hall in order to persuade him of the superiority of the *parterre-de-broderie*, compared with an old design that Rowland had seen at Crewe. This design resembled a Knot Garden, a simple pattern of geometric designs often containing herbs. According to William, this meeting was for the 'sake of criticism & information to us both, since I want someone like yourself to tell me when I am wrong having too much of my own way at Crewe . . . I quite subscribe to the old adage that "two heads are better than one" i.e. provided they come from the same school.' He also wrote that:

> I ought to observe that my chief aim has been to provide for *Winter* effect & that I tried geometric forms (as you call them) for the beds, against my conscience, but they were so insufferably commonplace that you must excuse me if I differ from you – indeed I candidly confess that I should be shy of owning such a design as that to which you alluded in the Crewe picture, although it was old – first because in the works of former days, we have sufficient evidence that there existed 2nd as well as 1st rate Art, which many *hundred* prints in my possession will prove – I regret being unable now to give you a long yarn on the subject, therefore must be content to state that to the best of my judgement, you advocate the refinement of elaboration *internally*, so should you be governed in a minor & yet an harmonious degree *externally* – be it further remembered that this quaint but good old manner of gardening is bona vide architecturally & that a *Parterre* professes to be a component part of the great artificial mass of the Building.[1]

William's desire to impress upon his clients that his designs were superior to the 'insufferably commonplace' ones of an earlier era is reflected in this letter. Unfortunately, it also demonstrates that he was closing his eyes to the probability that the earlier design, seen by Rowland at Crewe Hall, would have been much more suitable for an area that adjoined a small Gothic building, rather than an elaborate *parterre-de-broderie,* which required a much grander setting. However, his *parterre* was eventually put in place at Arley, as an adjunct to Salvin's Chapel. However, it was a much simpler affair than the one at Crewe, and the main garden at Arley was designed by the Warburtons.

In the latter part of the decade, William was engaged at Eaton Hall near Chester by the Marquess of Westminster, where he was asked to 'extend the garden over part of the area covered by the garden in the 18th century.'[2] New plantations were formed and shaped to enhance the middle distance view from the main rooms of the house, which enjoyed a framed view of the ancient Beeston Castle, seven miles distant. This was a view which would have given him great satisfaction as it incorporated both the formal garden in the vicinity of the mansion and the informal landscape beyond.

1 Letter dated 5 November 1846, Arley Hall Archives.

2 *Gardeners' Chronicle*, 1871.

Parterre in Conservatory Garden, Alton Towers.

Parterres at Broughton Hall, Yorkshire.

Parterres at Broughton Hall, Yorkshire, from above.

The *Parterre* Garden at Keele Hall, Staffordshire, watercolour, c. 1870.

The *Parterre* Garden at Keele Hall, Staffordshire after it was redesigned in 1985.

A number of mansions had been erected on the site over the years, but the Eaton Hall that William's design accompanied was completed around 1825. It had been designed in the Gothic style by William Porden, but was substantially altered by William Burn in the 1840s. By the 1850s new woodland approaches and parkland had been introduced, and although there is no suggestion that William was responsible for these alterations, he did lay out two large, impressive reflecting *parterres-de-broderie* in sunken panels to the east of the Hall. They contained scrolls and rays outlined in box and in each compartment he incorporated large monogrammed 'Ws'. This symbol commemorated Robert, 2nd Earl Grosvenor (1767-1845), who was created Marquess of Westminster in 1831. The title passed to William's client Hugh Lupus (1825-1899), 2nd Marquess (created 1st Duke of Westminster in 1874). The *parterres* were situated on each side of a central avenue, which contained reflecting guilloches. These are oblong borders, sometimes described as ribbon borders or friezes. They are often edged with low box and used to divide one area of the garden from another. There is an example of a guilloche at Witley Court in Worcestershire. The avenue led down to a small artificial lake, which in turn led fed into the River Dee.

The approach to the *parterre* was from a raised terrace via a central double flight of steps, dropping down to a further four. A matching pair of steps were placed at the far end of the *parterres*. Two large groups of statuary, sculpted in 1852 by Charles Raymond Smith, and depicting the 'Great Hunter', added variety to the garden. Smith was well known to both William and Salvin, for he had been responsible for carving a series of life-sized statues at Mamhead Park in Devon, and a small fountain to accompany the *parterre* designed by Nesfield at Keele Hall in Staffordshire.

From the two main *parterres*, steps led down to two smaller panels with scrolls, reflecting the same planting material used in the main *parterres*, which included:

> A: Purple Verbena; B: Alyssum; C: Scarlet Pelargonium; D: Pink Pelargonium; E: Scarlet Verbena; M: Yellow Calceolaria; I: Tropaecolums; J: Box; K: Heliotrope; N: Lobelia.

The *parterres* were surrounded by topiarized evergreens, shaped into cones and pyramids, and six large vases were used to mark the cross-axis, placed on either terrace. In 1857 the following description of the gardens appeared:

> box edged elegantly scrolled flower beds are planted with verbena, calceolarias, geraniums and various sorts of gay flowering character whose rich tints harmonize so well with the several features of the place. Lines of lavish yews and others of the same order, with box trees cut in spherical form are interspersed at regular intervals. The whole being surrounded by a stone balustrade, thickly studded with shields bearing the numerous heraldic devices of the family.[1]

Also during the 1840s, William received a commission to design a *parterre-de-broderie* at Alton Towers in Staffordshire, in the Countess of Shrewsbury's private garden. Due to its position, sandwiched between the armoury, the house conservatory and the

1 E. Aveno Brooke, *The Gardens of England*, (T. McLean, London 1857).

chapel, it was known as the Conservatory Court, and it had no open vistas. This was a departure from William's usual sites, where the *parterre* could be viewed from the most important rooms of the house before opening up to the open vistas beyond. His scheme in this case incorporated two *parterres*. In one were planted rose, shamrock and thistle emblems, infilled with coloured gravels, and featuring a small fountain standing on carved lion's paws, flanked with three tazzas. In the other was a large monogrammed 'S' in box embroidery, representing the family name of Shrewsbury. In 1857 the garden was described as containing 'some fine specimens of sculpture by Nys, who flourished in Rome in 1721 . . . a copy of the Warwick Vase in marble, on a tripod stand of the same material, a David strangling the lion, and a Flora in white marble.'[1]

The commission William undertook at Broughton Hall, near Skipton in Yorkshire, for Sir Charles Tempest, was also in a restricted area. In this case, the problems he had to contend with related to the steeply-sloping contours of the ground around the Hall, as well as the limited space available. To add to William's troubles a Conservatory was to be built, which also restricted the space available to him. He was, however, able to reassure Sir Charles that 'you have certainly given me the most difficult job I have experienced, but I am one of those who cannot endure to be beaten, hence my endeavours shall be untiring.'[2] Due to the restricted space his solution was to design a small *parterre*, with supporting walls and steps. He also provided a basin with shells and dolphins, and reshaped the curving shrubs above the high ground. To the east he designed a *parterre* on a steep slope, into which he introduced a scroll and feather design. This was situated within two lines of box, on coloured gravels, with yellow spar around the outside and crushed tile and spar in red, white and blue to fill the interstices of the box.

On the north corner William placed a gazebo, whilst above on the high ground, where space was at a premium, he introduced statues of a Piping Shepherd, Shepherdess, Haymakers and three figures known as Faith, Hope and Charity. From the gazebo a path led into the woodland walk to Broughton Brook, where William placed a stone statue of a boy with a dog.

The manor of Keele in Staffordshire dates from the sixteenth century, and was purchased in 1544 by William Sneyd. For the next 400 years, 'the village was dominated economically and to a large extent socially and politically by the Sneyd family', until the Hall and park were sold in 1948. Subsequently it formed the new University College of North Staffordshire, later the University of Keele.[3] William's client, Ralph Sneyd, was a bachelor and had inherited the property on the death of his father in 1829. He launched an extensive landscaping campaign; William Sawrey Gilpin was called in and continued to offer advice on the landscape at Keele for several years. By the early 1840s, Sneyd must have been aware of William's commissions in Cheshire, especially his involvement on the Crewe estate, which lies only a few miles away over the Cheshire border. Consequently, in

1 *Ibid.*

2 Letter from William Nesfield to Sir Charles Tempest, 12 January 1855, Broughton Hall Archives.

3 Christopher Harrison, ed., *The History of Keele University of Keele* 1988), p. 23.

1842, William was asked to advise on the landscape at Keele, Sneyd presumably wishing to emulate his wealthy neighbours. In 1842 William submitted a plan headed *References & Remarks on Plan for an Arboretum & alterations of the Bowling Green at Keele Hall.* He also submitted a list of evergreen trees for a Pinetum, as a contrast to the mainly deciduous portion of the Arboretum. In November 1845 he submitted details for a Pomarium Nursery, which contained Apple and Pear Standards, Cherries, Plums, Dwarf Medlars, Apple half-Standards, Filberts, Cobnuts and Hazels. Unfortunately, it is not thought that these schemes were implemented. His scheme for the Bowling Green was adapted into an Italianate Garden. During these years he recommended that a terrace should be formed on the south-east front of the Hall, overlooking the lake, where he advised flowerbeds 'in a botanical scene' should be installed, alternated with segmented stone seats surmounted by urns at either end. In 1854 Sneyd decided to alter to the Hall itself, and called in Anthony Salvin to undertake the task. However, the old Hall proved to be so derelict that it was rebuilt between 1854-1860 at a cost of £31,635 6s. 8d. Eden Nesfield had at this time commenced his career as an architect, and was working in his uncle's office. He was sent to Keele to receive instructions under the Clerk of Works, Thomas Lewis. After the rebuilding, William recommended that Sneyd make 'the most of the south-west front in a botanical sense.' As a result of this communication, he designed a sunken *parterre* and fountain for this front.

William's close relationship with his clients is revealed by his willingness to offer advice completely unrelated to his professional commitments to Ralph Sneyd. In the following instance, the advice related to a remedy for Sneyd's nervous condition. What Ralph thought about Nesfield's extreme remedy is unfortunately not recorded!

> I am truly sorry to learn that you have been so severely dealt with by the worse of all enemies, viz. Nerves in bad humour – having formally suffered considerably myself, I know how to feel for you – perhaps it may not be credited, but I found unremitting cold bathing (winter & summer) with plenty of exercise a complete remedy.[1]

In 1846 William travelled to East Anglia to undertake a commission for Sir Samuel Morton Peto (1809-1889). This time his client was not a member of the old landed class, but a railway speculator and builder. At his house, Somerleyton Hall, William designed a large formal garden to the west of the house, adjacent to the park with its ancient lime avenue. He incorporated a terrace with balustrades which overlooked an elaborate *parterre-de-broderie,* the central motif of which, it had been suggested, was based on an old church hinge.[2] It was outlined in box and infilled with glittering white chippings, and featured an equatorial sundial on a richly carved marble pedestal. It was surrounded by vases and topiarized evergreens, culminating in a low balustrade that separated it from the Park. Sixteen symmetrically-placed green and golden topiarized Irish Yews enclosed it and isolated it from the rest of the garden.

1 Keele University Library, Sneyd Papers, S.2768. Correspondence from William Andrews Nesfield to Ralph Sneyd from Eton College, Windsor.

2 This is mentioned in the Sales Particulars for the estate in 1861. Suffolk Record Office, Ipswich. 749-2-165.

'A.A.' initials representing Anstruther in a *parterre* at Balcaskie, Fife, Scotland.

The gardening journals of the day were complimentary about William's contribution at Somerleyton, particularly about how he had managed to link the west garden with the flower, winter and kitchen gardens. The *parterre* was maintained until the onset of World War II, when it was grassed over to prevent the white chippings, which formed the base of the *parterre*, being seen by enemy aircraft. His maze at Somerleyton has survived, together with one he executed at Worden Hall in Lancashire.

In 1847 William was summoned to Pittenweem in Scotland by Sir Ralph Anstruther. After their initial meeting in May he had submitted a plan for a flower garden, but apparently Sir Ralph was not happy about the use of coloured gravels within the design. Consequently, on 3 June 1948, William hastened to reassure him regarding their use:

> Harmonious variety is the most essential ingredient in every work of art (having any pretension) whether relating to form, expression, or colour, the adoption therefore of different coloured gravels is not only in accordance with the maxim, but with that of the old Masters in gardening, who carried refinement far beyond what our ideas of the expense of good keeping are accustomed to – the term 'fantastu' however as applied to the subject in question, is I conceive hardly admissible unless decoration generally by means of colour is irrational such as the varieties in the Marble Hall at Versailles etc. Innumerable examples of illuminated ceilings and wall panels in England as well as abroad, also external walls constructed of variously coloured bricks with stone dressings, stone and flint – combinations of different granites etc. Why should such textures be advocated but to avoid monotony and insipidity? Suffice it to observe that in the olden time changes of colour were rung in every manner Art could devise.[1]

The design for the *parterre* at Balcaskie included the initials AA to represent his client's name, Anstruther, and included the following suggestions:

1 Nesfield Archives.

No. 1 Plan of proposed details for a *parterre* on the Terrace at Balcaskie May 1848 (on sides) frieze compartments which are rendered simple in order to enhance the richness of the main centre.

SP. Very elaborate centre: Scroll of AA – box edged, coloured gravel, Verbena of different colours etc: *Prunus laurocerasus* and *Phillyrea* at ends, plus standard roses.

NB. Steps on East end of Terrace only.[1]

Today the flowerbeds have been eliminated to minimise upkeep, and two trees at the west end of the design have gone. However, the *parterre* in the terrace garden remains. The only change is that a large cedar tree was lost in the gale of 1968.

In early 1846, William was asked to advise on the landscape at Holkham Hall in Norfolk by Thomas William Coke, 2nd Earl of Leicester (1822-1909). He was initially to discuss alterations to estate buildings, particularly the stables, and a proposed island in the lake. However, by November of that year, work was under way on a series of terraces around the Hall designed by William. On the west front there was to be a *parterre* featuring the Earl of Leicester's initials in box, and on the south a pair of sunken panels with coloured gravel and a fountain, which today survive virtually unchanged and pristine.

Between 1846 and 1847, Salvin was employed in designing a mansion in the French Empire style, with a mansard dome over the centre bay, at Oxon Hoath in Kent for Sir William Geary. This was a deviation from Salvin's usual Elizabethan/Jacobean style, but Sir William was a Francophile. In May 1847 William submitted a plan for a *parterre* and rosarium to accompany the new house. He produced his usual layout, which included two reflecting *parterres* on each side of the central avenue, surrounded by topiarized yews, similar to the ones he had introduced at Somerleyton. He suggested the use of stone kerb edgings instead of the usual box to surround the *parterres*. This was a feature he recommended to his clients as, although initially it was a more expensive option than box, it saved time and labour in the long run as it did not need constant clipping. In the subsidiary garden to the side of the House he designed a rosarium, which was destroyed in the Edwardian period to make way for a Billiard Room. The plants he used in this small garden reflected those in the main garden; they included the conifer *Juniperus excelsa*, whose sward-like, dark-green leaves contrasted well with *Quercus ilex* (Holm Oak), a red-headed evergreen, and a *Yucca gloriosa*, whose architectural form was used in a border with miniature roses infilled with white gravel to give contrast.[2]

In the mid-1840s, and again in the following decade, William was in Cornwall. In 1845 he worked at Tregrehan for Edward Carlyon, designing a small formal garden to the south of the house. The garden included two reflecting *parterres-de-broderie* intersected by a central path, and contained the traditional arabesque scrolls outlined in

1 Sir Ralph H. Anstruther Bart., Balcaskie Archives. Professor Michael Tooley and Sophieke Piebenga provided additional information (unfortunately this particular design was not implemented).

2 Oxon Hoath Archives.

The Gardens surrounding Holkham Hall, designed by William Nesfield.

coloured gravel. As a terminus he provided a small fountain and statues depicting 'The Seasons'. The *parterre* has fallen into disrepair, but the fountain and statues remain, as does the fabulous view towards St Austell's Bay. To the west of the house he provided a small subsidiary garden which contained succulents. A small fountain was installed in the Kitchen Garden, similar to the one at Worden Hall in Lancashire. At the front of the house William designed an avenue with an entrance court surrounded by stone balustrades and with a carriage sweep with a stone lion was placed in its centre, a play on his client's surname.

Whilst he was employed at Tregrehan, William was asked by Christopher Henry Thomas Hawkins of Trewithen, near Truro, to prepare a plan for an approach to and site for a lodge. The plan, dated 10 May 1845, does not appear to have been implemented, and there is no evidence of a formal garden at Trewithen. However, in the latter years of the 1850s, William returned to Cornwall to effect improvements to the grounds at Tregothnan, owned by Evelyn Boscawen, 6th Viscount Falmouth (1809-1889) and his brother, the Honourable and Reverend John Townsend Boscawen of Lamorran. His design included a pleasure ground to the south and south east of the house. The estate at Tregothnan is five kilometres from the village of St Michael Penkevil, and was acquired by John Boscawen in 1334. Although damaged in the Civil War, it was rebuilt in 1650. The house was again rebuilt on the original site by the architect William Wilkins in the

Left: a Pedestal for Tregothnan, designed by William Nesfield.
Right: *parterre* in West Compartment, Tregothnan, Cornwall. ½ inches = 10 ft.

Gothic style in 1816-1818. Whilst the architect Lewis Vulliamy has been credited with designing the forecourt railings which lead from the main drive, there is evidence to suggest that William was responsible, and there are plans at Tregothnan that appear to confirm this. The drive is enclosed from the north east and south east by wrought iron gates, which stand on a low stone wall, supported by elaborate octagonal stone piers set on square bases, and surmounted by crowned sea lions holding the Falmouth Arms.[1]

The *parterres-de-broderie* no longer exist at Tregothnan, but a faint outline of two formal *parterre*s can still be seen in dry weather to the south of the house. Although the outline shapes of these *parterres* and the corner bastions are the same as the design proposed by William, the complicated scrolls and rays had been simplified. This is not an unusual occurrence, as they were very costly to maintain.

1 Report on Tregothnan by the Register of Parks and Gardens of Special Historic Interest, October 2000.

10.

The Royal Botanic Gardens at Kew and Buckingham Palace

William received a number of prestigious public commissions over the years, the majority of which came to him through the patronage of Prince Albert (1819-1861). William admired the prince greatly and said of him:

> This clear headed working man is one who can never be replaced. Few know his real worth, except those with whom he has so assiduously conducted business. I could fill a quire in his praise, no doubt history will tell his character honestly.[1]

William would have empathized with Prince Albert's interest in the arts and sciences, his methodical attention to detail, his tenacity of purpose and his strong work ethic. Amongst the Prince's wide range of interests was gardening, as a letter he wrote to his eldest daughter, the Princess Royal, on 18 May 1859 confirms: 'the artist who lays out the work and devises a garment for a piece of ground has the delight of seeing his work live and grow hour by hour; and whilst it is growing, he is able to polish, to cut and care, to fill up here and there, to hope and to love.'[2] The first public commission that brought William's name to the attention to the Prince was probably at the Royal Botanic Gardens, Kew.

The Earl of Lincoln (1811-1864), the first Commissioner of Woods and Forests 1841-1846, invited William to submit plans for the Royal Botanic Gardens at Kew in 1844. He also introduced him to Sir William Jackson Hooker, who was appointed the first Director of the Royal Botanic Gardens in 1841 when it ceased to be the property of the Crown and was transferred to the Commissioners of Woods and Forests. The Earl of Lincoln was the son of Henry Pelham-Clinton, 4th Duke of Newcastle-under-Lyme, William's client at Clumber Park in Nottinghamshire.[3]

1 Correspondence between William Nesfield and Wilbraham Spencer Tollemache of Dorfold Hall, Cheshire. In Horatia Durrant, *Cheshire Life*, 1954, p. 19.

2 John Matson, *Dear Osborne* (Hamish Hamilton Limited reprinted 2000), p.3.

3 Another connection was Salvin, for although he was not personally involved at Clumber, the Earl was interested in the authentic restoration of medieval buildings and aware of the damage caused

Initially William was requested to design an Arboretum at Kew and on 26 January 1844 he wrote to Sir William to inform him that he had: 'received instructions from Lord Lincoln to prepare a design for an Arboretum at Kew & to confer with you on the subject – Will it be convenient for you to spare me a few hours on an early day next week?'[1] The report was not submitted until June 1845, and it was not popular with everyone. When William proposed grading trees by height in the vistas and abandoning rigorous botanical order, the gardener and writer Robert Glendinning (1805-1862) accused him of 'sacrificing the object of an arboretum for the sake of appearance.'[2] William's anxiety to place art above botany did not impress Sir William; the whole purpose of an Arboretum is to facilitate the study of specific species, so related species are grouped together irrespective of size. Sir William, therefore, was far from convinced that William was the man for the job, his own preference being for Glendinning. He had written to Lord Lincoln expressing his concern:

> I am no less obliged to your Lordship for instructing Mr Nesfield to call here. I was all over the ground with him yesterday and much gratified with his intelligence and with the nature of his enquiries and he was much struck with the beauty and capability of the grounds. So far as I can judge from the little I have yet seen of him I should think him well qualified for what is expected of him. He perhaps favours too much the formal or what he called the 'geometrical' arrangements which to a certain extent with so noble a piece of ground may be desirable but I trust he has too much good sense to carry it too far.[3]

Sir William had two main concerns: William's desire to place a formal garden in the vicinity of the Palm House, and his lack of botanical knowledge. It would appear, therefore, that it was William's connections that won him the commission. By 2 February 1846, William informed Sir William that he had discussed the cost of the Arboretum, which was to be £1,290, with Lord Lincoln:

> I have written to Lord Lincoln with whom I shall go systematically thro' the whole affair – and the moment there is aught to communicate you shall hear from me and when Lord L. gives me his [?] with reference to general propositions – a fair copy of the survey shall be made forthwith, the one now done being private for revision and correction.[4]

The instructions that accompanied the Plan were intended to explain the position of the Pinetum in relation to the Arboretum, but they also demonstrate William's overall proposals for the area in the vicinity of the Palm House. The three radiating avenues

---

by: 'misjudged *reconstruction* under the name of restorations *and repair*.' Jill Allibone, *Anthony Salvin: Pioneer of Gothic Revival Architecture*, (The Lutterworth Press, Cambridge, 1988), p.7.

1 Director's Correspondence, vol. 22, English Letters, K-Z, 1844, folios xx-xx, Royal Botanic Gardens, Kew.

2 Brent Elliott, *Victorian Gardens* (B.T. Batsford Limited, 1986), p. 118.

3 Sir William Hooker to Lord Newcastle, MSS Ne C, 8969/103, Manuscripts and Special Collections, Nottingham University.

4 *Ibid.*

he indicated on the Plan are still in place, one leading to the Pagoda, designed by Sir William Chambers between 1761 and 1762; another to the south-east, terminating in a large cedar; and a third, the 'Syon Vista', leading from the main gate at Kew past the Orangery, also designed by William Chambers in 1761, where William planted Deodora conifers. A watercolour shows the formalized lake to the north of the Palm House, which was rendered geometrical according to his instructions.

The Palm House, which was built between 1844 and 1848 by the architect Decimus Burton in association with the engineer Richard Turner, became the architectural focal point of William's scheme for Kew. As far as William was concerned, it took the place of the mansions of his private clients in his plan. In 1848 he designed six *parterres* for the terrace facing the pond, and to the west his circular beds contained specimens of *Araucara araucana* (Monkey Puzzle).

This part of the design was an important one as it was seen by large numbers of visitors on the daily basis. William Eden was later to design a lodge house in the Queen Anne Revival style in this section of the garden. It still stands in the vicinity of the Temperate House.

The next public commission William planned should have resulted in his name and work becoming not only nationally, but internationally recognized, and ensured that his reputation would have endured beyond his lifetime. If it had been implemented, his design would have been situated on the east front of Buckingham Palace, where the statue of Queen Victoria now stands. Situated at the top of the Mall, Buckingham Palace acts as a magnet, drawing vast crowds to it on all great national occasions.

In May 1846, six commissioners were appointed by Prince Albert to oversee the enlargement of Buckingham Palace. They included the Prime Minister, the Chancellor of the Exchequer, the Chief Commissioner of Woods and Works (Lord Lincoln), Earl de Grey and Frances Egerton (one of William's future clients). It was intended that gardens should complement the new east façade, completed in 1847 by Edward Blore, which had been built to enclose the east courtyard. On 31 December 1848, William submitted iconographical designs for the space and his report to the Commissioners. The designs consisted of:

> Ground Plan of Architectural Gardens to occupy portions of St James's and the Green Parks east and contiguous to Buckingham Palace [Pen and Coloured washes, 720 x 1000 mm] A perspective of a fountain for the part of the garden lying to the S. of the principle approach to the palace Britannia on the apex of a rock directing Plenty to diffuse her gifts over the globe, which rests on the shoulders of Atlas attended by Commerce and Neptune and termination of basin and labelled Watercolour with White Pen and watercolour with white highlights, on linen-backed cartridge paper 295 x 695.
>
> Perspective showing same fountain as in No. 3 to a larger scale, St George and the Dragon on the apex of a rock. Father Thames at the base with Fame and Victory on either side of him. [Watercolour with white highlights on line-backed cartridge paper 490 x 613.][1]

1 Plan, Royal Institute of British Architects, Victoria & Albert Museum, London (PA 91/111-4).

The Palm House at Kew with the lake and *parterres*. The caption reads: 'Punt a little out of perspective and going uphill'.

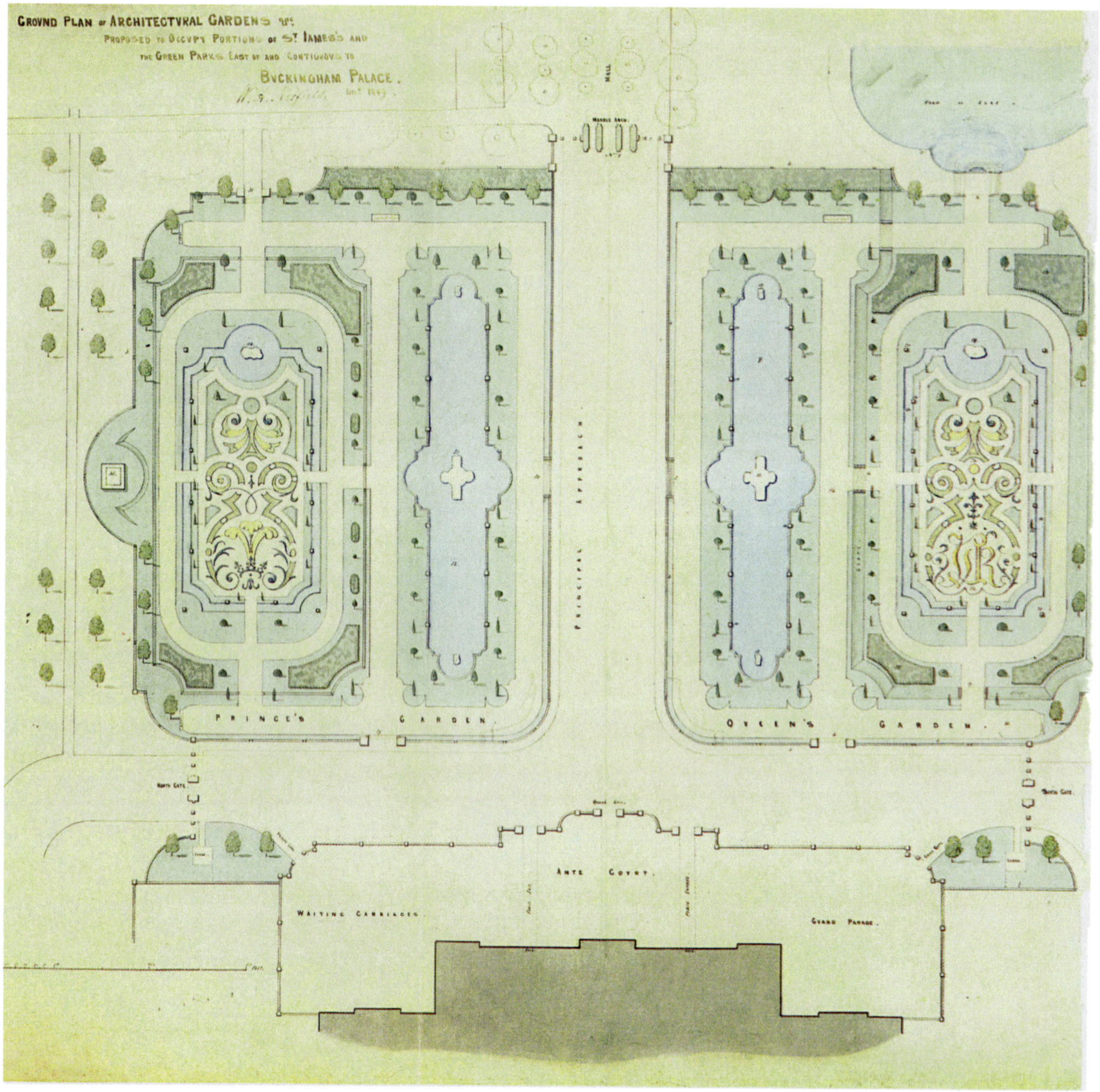

Ground Plans for Buckingham Palace Gardens.

The intention was that the formal garden would be viewed from the central ante-court of the palace. This would be in alignment with the avenue which was to run centrally between the two *parterres*. William intended to place two reflecting *parterres*, the one on the left representing the Prince, and the one on the right the Queen. They were symmetrical and identical, apart from the Prince of Wales' feathers in the left-hand *parterres* and the monogrammed letters V.R. on the right. They both contained central scrolls terminated by rays, surrounded by topiarized evergreens.

By 2 February 1850 William was able to write to the Right Honourable the Earl of Carlisle setting out the cost of his proposals, which amounted to approximately £4, 5195 4s. 4d. Unfortunately, the gardens were never created, although William's beautifully-drawn designs still exist. The high cost of the design could have been one reason for their rejection, for, unlike at Osborne House on the Isle-of-Wight and Balmoral in Scotland, the privately-owned homes of the royal couple, the improvements to Buckingham Palace had to be paid for by Parliamentary grant. Although William was asked to undertake the re-erection of the Marble Arch to its present site north of Park Lane, with the architect Sir James Pennethorne (1801-1871), this must have been small compensation for the loss of the prestigious Buckingham Palace commission.[1] It is tempting to speculate that the designs for the Buckingham Palace fountains were adapted by William for his great fountain at Castle Howard in Yorkshire, which depicts Atlas carrying a Globe on his shoulders, and at Witley Court in Worcestershire, where he proposed a statue of Britannia on a Rock (although in this case another of his designs was used).

Prince Albert did not forget William's efforts at the Royal Botanic Gardens, Kew and Buckingham Palace, as he was to gain two future prestigious commissions through the Prince's recommendation.

1 Writing to Holkham Hall in Norfolk on 11 February 1850, William said: 'I beg you to have the goodness to give me three or four months notice, because I have lately been employed by the Queen which will be a death blow to any usual space time'. Holkham Archives.

11.

Enter William Eden

William Eden Nesfield was educated at Eton College between 1846 and 1849, and, at twelve years old, was the youngest boy to enter the school.[1] He and his brothers, who followed him to Eton, would have rubbed shoulders with some of the wealthiest in the land and the connections he made at this time undoubtedly helped his future career. Eden was always conscious that he came from an old and illustrious family and he considered himself the equal of any of his contemporaries at Eton. The atmosphere of the Nesfield household, once the family had moved to 3 York Terrace, Regent's Park, must have been a heady one for an impressionable youth with romantic ideals, as Eden was. He would have witnessed his father and his father's surveyor, James Howe, drawing up the elaborate plans and reports to present to William's clients. These would have included the drawings necessary for the installation of the magnificent *parterres-de-broderie* that were William's trademark, and for the creation of which a thorough understanding of architectural drawing, surveying and draughtsmanship was needed. The comings and goings of William's friends from the Royal Watercolour Society were also part of the fabric of the house during Eden's early years. By the time he was ten years old, Eden had learnt enough to produce a *parterre* design and a planting plan for his father's friend, Major Jebb of the Royal Engineers. Proud of his efforts, his mother wrote on the design: 'Willey's first tracing Jany.'46, 10 years 3 months.'[2]

Even before he left Eton in 1849, Eden's sketch books demonstrate that he was already producing many pencil drawings and watercolours – some original and some copied. For example, there is a drawing from the summer of 1848 of the Summer House at Krate's Lane in Eton. William, always anxious to foster his son's undoubted talent, asked James Duffield Harding, who lived nearby at 6 Waverley Place, St John's Wood, to give him drawing lessons. Harding was a close family friend and fellow member of the Royal

1 William Nesfield, *Reminiscences*, Nesfield Archives.
2 This plan and planting scheme is in the Nesfield Archives.

Watercolour Society where he was elected an Associate on 5 July 1820 and a Member on 11 June 1821. On 24 August 1848 Eden received his first lesson from Harding, whose method of teaching was to make a drawing that Eden then copied. One of his first drawings was a sketch of a branch of a tree on 29 August 1848, this first attempt being once again recorded by his mother. Eden must have enjoyed these lessons, for on one of his drawings he wrote: 'One of J. D. Harding's lessons, most loveable and cherished.' On 2 September there is a drawing containing two hearts labelled J.D. Harding and W.E.N.[1] In 1848 the pair spent two months in North Wales, where they sketched at Beaumaris Castle.

Eden and his younger brother, Arthur Markham, would sometimes accompany their father on painting trips, sometimes to the great estates where William was working; painting from nature, therefore, came naturally to Eden. What he wanted to do was to follow in Salvin's footsteps and become an architect, so after a short spell with a tutor in Berne, Switzerland, he gave up all thoughts of going on to university, and in 1850 he took his first steps in realizing his dream.[2] However, unlike Salvin, it was ornamental detail that became his obsession. Why he did not go into Salvin's office at this time is unknown; perhaps there was no vacancy, or perhaps it was felt that Eden would benefit from the experience of working in the office of someone who was not so closely connected with the family. Whatever the reason, William looked elsewhere for a mentor for his son.

Eden was considered to be a youth whose 'confidence and impetuosity of character already lent him dynamism, charm and the independence, of early maturity.'[3] He was also impulsive and over-confident and therefore what he needed was a safe and steady pair of hands to teach him the rudiments of his craft. When he was sixteen he was placed with William Burn (1789-1870), who was well-known to both William and Salvin. The son of an Edinburgh builder, Burn had begun his practice in 1812, and in 1843 had moved to London and set up in Stratton Street, Piccadilly, where he ran a busy and successful architectural practice. He has been described as a master of the baronial style, but he was an aging, predictable and prosaic individual. This did not bode well, for Eden, young and impetuous, who was in thrall to High Victorian Gothic as advocated by Augustus Welby Northmore Pugin (1812-1852), the decorative and ecclesiastical Gothic details of which he loved. Pugin was a Roman Catholic convert who believed fervently that Gothic was the only true style that a Christian country should adopt.

Pugin had an early triumph at The Great Exhibition of 1851, when he was chosen as the chief designer of the Medieval Court. His output included wallpapers, hangings, china, jewellery, vestments and stained glass. His craftsmen were John Gregory Crace, who supplied decoration including wallpaper and paints, and Herbert Minton, who designed the ceramic tiles. Minton's encaustic flooring was a speciality. He had 'followed

1 *Ibid.*
2 Whilst in Berne Eden took the opportunity of visiting Italy, as he wrote in 1850: 'My first visit to Italy went in canoe across Lake [Lucerne] by myself'.
3 Andrew Saint, *Richard Norman Shaw* (Yale University Press, 1976), p.2.

recent excavations of medieval kilns and been able to overcome the principal difficulty of encaustic, which is to make the different coloured clays, which fire at different temperatures, bond in the kiln.'[1] John Hardman, whose ecclesiastical metalwork included candlesticks and hanging lamps, and George Myers, who was Pugin's right-hand man and a master builder, also made their own contributions. But although all these craftsmen played their part in making the Medieval Court a success, it was Pugin's inventiveness that supplied the overall effect. His aim was 'to promote his belief in Gothic as a style suitable for domestic as well as church use and affordable by the "middleing sort" as well as the upper ten thousand.'[2] The *Illustrated London News* wrote: 'To Mr Pugin . . . who furnished the design for this gorgeous combination, is the highest honour due, and he has marvellously fulfilled his own intention of demonstrating the applicability of Medieval art in all its richness and variety to the uses of the present day.'[3] Today Pugin is probably best remembered creating sumptuous medieval details, both inside and outside the Houses of Parliament, which was been built between 1837 and 1860 by Charles Barry.[4] In Eden's eyes, Pugin stood for traditional honesty and the highest standards in architecture, and these interiors were a treasure-trove for aspiring Gothic architects such as Eden and his future partner Richard Norman Shaw (1831-1912).

After his schooling it was decided that Eden would not formally sign any articles with Burn for a year, as it was considered that he needed additional grounding in architectural drawing, and would benefit from instruction from a practising draughtsman. Burn, therefore, sent him to study with James Kellaway Colling, who was an excellent architectural draughtsman and a committed Gothic architect. His *Gothic Ornaments* was published in 1848, and during the time Eden studied with him he was writing *Details of Gothic Architecture*, published in 1852. He and Eden visited churches and abbeys together, taking careful measurements and making drawings of ornamental and architectural details. The first evidence of their work is at Wenlock Abbey in Shropshire in 1850, where Eden made an elevated coloured drawing of the arcades in the Chapter House (possibly his first true architectural drawing). In 1851, he and Colling visited Somerset, where they sketched in Huish and Weston Zoyland churches, and Eden witnessed 'old Farmer Higgs sitting in his pew.'[5] Always attracted to the picturesque, he could not resist making a drawing of a Greek seaman in Bridgewater Dock. The following year the two men spent time together, for there is a measured drawing by Eden, dated 16 January, of the bench ends at Ufford Church, Suffolk.[6] In February of the same year

1 Rosemary Hill, *God's Architect: Pugin and the Building of Romantic Britain* (Penguin Books, 2007), p. 229.

2 *Ibid.*, p. 454.

3 *Ibid.*, p. 464.

4 Charles Barry was knighted by Queen Victoria on 3 February 1852 when she opened Parliament, at the time of the opening of the new chamber. Pugin received no such acclaim.

5 Eden Nesfield's Sketch Books, Royal Institute of British Architects, Drawings and Archives Collections, British Architectural Library.

6 *Ibid.*

they visited Norwich Cathedral, and Bradfield and Cottingham Churches in Norfolk. These excursions around the countryside provided an opportunity to take accurate architectural measurements of medieval detail and painting, and to sketch picturesque scenery, which Eden often also did with his father. In 1851 he accompanied his father on one of William's professional visits to Yorkshire, where, 'after a visit with Dad to Castle Howard where he was seeing Lord Carlisle', they called on his father's step-sister Marianne, who had married Charles Darley of Burtonfield, Stamford Bridge. Here they took the opportunity to paint and draw at Kirkham Priory, Bolton Abbey, Whaley Bridge and Wawn Church, where, on 6 March, Eden made a measured drawing of the west window in the nave. Eden's work had elements associated with a painter as much as an architect, and although he became a great draughtsman he was able to draw freehand with a sureness of touch that has been described as remarkable and of 'the most beautiful and delicate kind.'[1] Eden was also in Shropshire during 1851 (possibly with Harding) and visited Buildwas Abbey, the churches at Acton Burnell and Leominster and Hill's Mansion in Shrewsbury.

During Eden's time with Burn he met Richard Norman Shaw, perhaps the most important event of this period: the pair were to become inseparable for many years and ultimately set up in practice together. Shaw was the youngest of six children, the son of an Edinburgh lace merchant whose father died intestate in 1833, leaving his wife heavily in debt. It must have been a struggle for Shaw's mother to bring up her four surviving children. However, she came from upright Scottish stock, and was a survivor. In 1846 she moved to London, where her eldest son Robert had found work with a firm of shipping agents, and Richard was articled to Burn for two years. Richard was a kind-hearted and self-effacing man, but doggedly ambitious and hard-working, having had to struggle to attain his goals, unlike Eden who had never needed to struggle for anything! These two, therefore, were complete opposites. Eden was four years Shaw's junior, full of enthusiasm, confident in his own abilities and impetuous, and he swept Shaw along with him. His new friendship and his busy, interesting life at York Terrace must have opened up an entirely different world to the young Scot.

Although in 1852 Eden was still measuring and drawing churches with Colling, he and Shaw were spending more and more time together. In fact, they spent almost two years in the winters of 1852-1853, on Saturday afternoons and sometimes on a Sunday, drawing and measuring in the Houses of Parliament. They were able to gain access to what was still primarily a building site because William knew Charles Barry and got his permission for the two to draw and measure Pugin's decorative work. They copied stained glass, tiles, metalwork in iron and brass, linen fold panels, bosses, keyholes, bell and door handles, carved woodwork and cresting, sometimes with coloured washes in red, blue and gold. On 6 March that year, Eden was in Westminster Abbey and the British Museum, where he drew part of Scipio's tomb and a gate leading to St Bartholomew's

1 R. Phene Spiers, *William Eden Nesfield's Drawings: Journal of the Royal Institute of British Architects*, 2 (1895), p. 60, Drawings and Archives Collections, British Architectural Library.

in Smithfield. On 9 June he was in Lincoln's Inn drawing brick-angle corbels, and in a passage where he drew a boss in a groin. On 2 April he was at Hampton Court, and in May and on 2 June he visited Pugin's masterpiece, St Augustine's Church in Ramsgate. Both Eden and Shaw were there on the day of Pugin's funeral on 21 September, and again in July 1853.

Unlike Eden, who considered it to be vulgar and unnecessary to advertise his work in order to further his career, Shaw needed the kudos exhibiting his work would bring him. In December 1852 he was awarded the silver medal from the Royal Academy for a finished drawing of the cloisters in Westminster Abbey, and the following year the gold medal for a classical design for a Military College in honour of the Duke of Wellington.

In 1853 Eden, always impatient, broke his Articles of Indenture with Burn for the more congenial atmosphere of Salvin's office at 30 Argyll Street, close to Oxford Circus. In the meantime, although Shaw was still doggedly pursuing his articles with Burn, the two remained close friends, and after 1853 their shared excursions became a regular feature of their summers. In that year they spent two weeks on a walking tour which took them to some of the most beautiful counties in the British Isles: Worcestershire, Gloucestershire, Wiltshire and Hampshire. A leap of imagination is needed to envisage life in England in those days, free of motorways, cars, street lights, overhead wires, pylons and supermarkets. Although there was, by this time, a comprehensive train service that covered the major towns, coaching inns still existed, and the main means of transport was on foot, horseback or coach. Eden and Shaw travelled mostly on foot along untarmacked roads and country lanes, drawing and measuring as they went, seeking out churches and abbeys with medieval detail, Gothic ornamentation and heraldic design. In June they were in Worcester, where Eden prepared a plan of some groining in Worcester Cathedral which he felt gave a 'very fine effect.'[1] On 4 July a window on the east side of College Hall in Worcester that caught his eye, whilst on the fifth he drew an oriel window on the south side of the choir. By the eighth they had moved on to Tewkesbury, where Eden drew a doorway in the Sacristy in Tewkesbury Abbey, and on the ninth the Piscina in the Triforium in Gloucester Cathedral [sic]. Finally, on the tenth, he drew the gateway to Llanthony Secunda Priory near Gloucester. A measured drawing by Eden of Bishop Bridport's tomb in Salisbury Cathedral, although unfinished, has been described as 'remarkable for the accuracy and beauty of its lines.'[2] On 16 July he was in Winchester Cathedral, measuring one of the bays of stalls and doorway in the Lady Chapel. He drew the stairway to the dining hall and a view of the Tower from the south west. In December he went to Gloucester Cathedral, drawing the east end of Abbot Parker's tomb and St Peter's Church, Sandwich, Kent. In March 1854, conscious that Shaw was working towards obtaining a travelling scholarship from the Royal Academy, Eden did a sketch

1 Eden Nesfield's Sketch Books, *op.cit.*
2 *Ibid.*

for a college with a plan and elevation, which he described as 'designed to hold 550 Scholars in St George's Cathedral in ye fields, Southampton'. This was probably probationary work for the Royal Academy. However, he never had to complete this or send it in. Whilst travelling in Wales he visited Conwy, Flint, Prudhoe and Caernarvon Castles, and at both Conwy and Caernarvon there are demonstrations of how intrigued he was with seemingly insignificant detail; in this visit with the jointing of ashlar and rubble masonry.

Shaw was hard at work in 1854 and was given the Royal Academy Travelling Scholarship for a late Gothic palace design. Therefore, after completing his final year with Burn, he went off on his travels to France, Italy and finally Germany. In the summer of 1854 Eden joined him, and they went to Normandy together to draw and measure the cathedrals and churches of that region. They visited St Martin's Church, Honfleur and the Palais de Justice in Rouen. The latter, late-Gothic building, with its steeply pitched roofs and tall dormer windows, was begun in 1493. At Evreux Cathedral, Eden drew the clerestory from the roof of the aisle. They then moved to Gisors Cathedral and Beauvais, a High Gothic structure of 1247, which, although never completed, contains beautiful coloured glass. Amiens Cathedral, built between 1220 and 1288, was a must-see for the two aspiring Goths, as 'its portal sculptures and great carved choir screen are medieval masterpieces.'[1] Eden and Shaw parted company at the end of July and Eden returned home.

Eden spent the next two years learning lithography and engraving, writing on one piece of work 'ye first time of trying Sept. 1856.' In April 1855 he was in Canterbury Cathedral, drawing a detail of Archbishop Meopham's tomb on the south side of the choir. Nothing that was unusual or quaint escaped Eden's eye, for example, on the 16 August, in the south-east angle of cloisters in Worcester Cathedral, the following inscription caught his eye: 'Sacred to the Memory of Joseph Buggins His Virtues and More Especially His Very Forgiving Temper &c &c &c'. The inscription apparently appealed to his sense of humour. Whilst he was there he drew the roof of the Refectory, which, he said, 'fairly takes one's breath away.' By the 22 August he had moved on to Herefordshire, and drew the fireplace in the Lower State Room at Ludlow Castle. At Stokesay Castle he drew the view of part of the courtyard windows in the Great Hall, and the oak roof over the college cloister in Hereford Cathedral. In the same year he travelled to Paris with the Salvins for the Exposition Universelle des Beaux Arts. At this time, Salvin was designing a revival fourteenth-century castle for Lord Tollemache in Cheshire, and the model was exhibited in the architectural gallery. According to Salvin's daughter it had 'a stand by itself and it looks very grand.'[2]

In 1855, whilst in Salvin's office, Eden submitted a design for Grantham Lodge for the 7th Duke of Rutland at Belvoir Castle in Leicestershire, a design which he adapted from French town gates, possibly the ones at Port du Croux, Nevers. He was also given

1 Doreen Yarwood, *The Architecture of Europe* (Chancellor Press, 1974), p. 205.

2 Eliza Anne Salvin, *Reminiscences.*

the opportunity to work for one of his father's most important and long standing clients, Lord Crewe, on his estate in Cheshire. In 1856, Eden designed a Puginian-style canopied tomb to commemorate Lord Crewe's ancestor, the 3rd Baron Crewe, in the nearby church in the village of Barthomley, where the Crewe family worshipped at that time. This was designed to form one side of the Crewe Chapel and consisted of heraldic family shields. Between two cusped arches was a soffit rich with colour and decorative effect.

Eden was also been given the opportunity to spend some time at Keele Hall in Staffordshire, where between 1854 and 1860 Salvin designed a new mansion for Ralph Sneyd, as the old manor house had become derelict. Eden reflected, when he came to write Salvin's Obituary in *The Builder* in 1881, that Keele was 'one of the best planned houses of its time and drew attention to the way it was adapted to the slope on which it stood.'[1]

In July 1856 Shaw joined Eden in Salvin's office and started to learn lithography and engraving in order to transfer the drawings he had produced whilst on his Continental tour onto stone. Day & Son ultimately published these drawings under the title *Architectural Sketches from the Continent* in the summer of 1858.

In 1857, whilst undertaking extensions to the domestic range for the 4th Earl of Warwick at Warwick Castle, Salvin had a stroke that left him partially paralysed, and he took longer than he hoped to recover. His daughter wrote: 'My father was much more hopeful during the first part of his illness, his slow recovery disappointed him; he felt the powerlessness of his left hand and side in a greater degree and to rouse his spirits and to give him greater strength it was settled we should take a house in Dover.'[2] The Salvin family remained in Dover until March 1858 until Salvin recovered, when they moved to 11 Hanover Square in Regent's Park, where they were once again living near the Nesfields.[3] During Salvin's illness, with the help of his principal clerk William Harroway, his three main assistants, Anthony Salvin Jr, Shaw and Eden, took over the reins. However, Anthony Jr suffered from chronic ill-health and had no talent for architecture, and it fell to Eden, in particular, to take the principal role. Both Eden and Shaw, however, were anxious to develop their own ideas and styles, and although 'Salvin was an agreeable friend, a competent architect who could rebuild Old England for his clients . . . it was the class of client, their circumstances and their lack of any desire for the full-blown Gothic Revival or Victorian classicism as it manifested itself in the mid-nineteenth century, that was to inhibit and finally destroy any originality

1 Jill Allibone, *Anthony Salvin Pioneer of Gothic Revival Architecture* (The Lutterworth Press, Cambridge, 1987), p. 50.

2 Eliza Anne Salvin, *Reminiscences*.

3 'On the 19 December 1854 there was a gathering of relations at Uncle William Nesfield's in York Terrace, Regent's Park. Such a meeting had not taken place for years & was destined never to be again. There was gathered round the dinner table seventeen near relations – amongst them was Fanny Nesfield, Aunt Bessie, Mrs. Fred. Cookson & her daughter Bessie, Uncle William & Aunt Emma Nesfield, their sons and ourselves'. *Ibid.*

Commemorative Tomb at St Bertoline's Church, Barthomley, Cheshire, designed by Eden Nesfield.

that Salvin might have developed in his later work.'[1] Consequently, in 1857, when Eden was twenty-one years old, and upon receiving £300 from his godfather Sir John Eden, he was able to emulate Shaw and travel extensively on the Continent, indulging his love of medieval architecture, and leaving a firm which did not nurture his interests. His journey was to take him through Europe and on to Constantinople. It also meant that he did not have to complete the drawing for the Royal Academy Travelling Prize for which he had been reluctantly preparing designs. He was the first to leave the practice, and although Shaw stayed on until early 1858, he too had itchy feet. Perhaps he felt he was not receiving the recognition and responsibility given to Eden, who had been in a privileged position. He too left to become the principal assistant in the office of George Edmund Street in Montague Place. It was in Street's office that Shaw became acquainted with Philip Webb, who would shortly leave the practice to help William Morris and Edward Burne-Jones set up a new firm that would concentrate on the decorative arts. They ultimately became Morris, Marshall, Faulkner & Company in 1861, and were to be pivotal in the Arts and Crafts Movement which was to influence both Shaw and Eden's designs in the future.

1 Eliza Anne Salvin, *Reminiscences.*

12.

Breaking Free

The period of Eden's travels on the Continent was to be one of the most fulfilling and innovative of his life. He could indulge his love of ornamentation in the great medieval buildings on the Continent to his heart's content. His tour began with an extended visit to the atelier of Eugène-Emmanuel Viollet-le-Duc, the architect aspiring young Goths most wanted to emulate. Viollet-le-Duc had rebuilt and reconstructed a number of Gothic masterpieces, including the Cathedral at Notre Dame, La Sainte Chapelle, and the Abbey Church of St Denis in Paris, as well as extensive restoration work in the walled town of Carcassonne. His work had been admired by Salvin, who saw a copy of Viollet-le-Duc's design for the Tour du Tresor at Carcassonne at the Exposition Universelle in Paris in 1855; as, presumably, so too had Eden. Consequently, when Salvin was asked to rebuild the Curfew Tower at Windsor Castle by Her Majesty's Commissioners of Works between 1862 and 1863, he emulated Viollet-le-Duc's Carcassonne designs by choosing a part-gabled, part-conical roof. From Viollet-le-Duc's Atelier Eden travelled to St Lo, Amiens Soissons, Leon, Chartres and Rouen. In Bayeux he drew an armoire, which he reproduced in his forthcoming book and to which Viollet-le-Duc may have drawn his attention.

By September 1857, travelling with his friend, the architect John Hebb, Eden moved to Blois, Augers, Bourges, and Dijon. By October they were at Lake Geneva, and they then travelled on into Italy where they visited Siena, Padua and Pisa. By December they had reached Rome, where Eden had his portrait painted by Edouard Brandon in the style of Holbein. From Rome they travelled to Naples. In January the following year Eden was again in Italy, and in March he was joined by James Smollet Donaldson, the son of Professor Thomas Levington Donaldson. They wandered through Greece and did a number of drawings of the Parthenon and Propylaea, the old cathedral, and a general view of the Acropolis. After visiting Constantinople they returned to England via Rome, Florence, Siena, Padua and Orvieto.

By the end of 1858, with his extended tour over, Eden established himself in a small practice at 15 Bedford Row in London, by this time in the enviable position of not having to worry too much about acquiring commissions. For this he could, to a large extent, thank his father, who did not hesitate to recommend him to his network of influential landowning clients. Although some of these commissions were small, they marked the beginning of Eden's very successful career and gave him what he really wanted: work on estates where his father was well-established, and where he could indulge his love of ornamental decorative detail by embellishing intimate little buildings in his own style. These were the situations in which he was at his happiest and most comfortable.

In 1859, he agreed with Day & Son to produce a book based on the drawings he had produced on his travels, but in order to augment his existing drawings he needed to undertake a further series of shorter journeys to France, which he did in the summers of 1859-61. He travelled with the artist Albert Joseph Moore (1841-1893). Moore co-operated with Eden on a number of important commissions and, although unfortunately not as well-known today as he should be, he was a versatile and accomplished artist Born in York, he was the youngest of fourteen children and the son of William Moore (1790-1851), a portrait and landscape painter. After his father's death, Moore moved with his mother to London and, in 1857, aged fifteen, he exhibited at the Royal Academy. The following year entered the Royal Academy Schools. In 1862-63, possibly due to Eden's influence, he spent four or five months in Rome. He turned his hand to designing tiles, fabrics, wallpaper and stained glass for Morris, Marshall, Faulkner & Company, but his first love was classical sculpture which he painted all his life. Even by artistic standards Moore was a somewhat strange and eccentric figure, who, according to his pupil W.G. Robertson,

> lived in a curious building at the corner of Holland Street, its accommodation consisting of two large studios, a sitting-room with nothing in it to sit upon, a bedroom and, I suppose, a kitchen. His constant companion was Fritz, a dachshund of depressed appearance. . . . Cats pervaded the whole house; vaguely, unofficially, holding no recognized position, they swarmed in the studios and passages. . . . Albert Moore regarded them mournfully but placidly as inevitable. . . . There were also the spiders and their cobwebs, the dust, the leaks in the pipes, and other like phenomena.[1]

During the autumn of 1861 Eden's travelling companion was his brother, Arthur Markham, who recorded their journey in his diary on 23 October that year: 'Leaving York Terrace at 6 o'clock in the evening. Met Willy at Bedford Row – stopped on the way for him to swallow a mouthful of ham sandwich.'[2] They crossed to France via Newhaven-

1 Victorian High Renaissance Exhibition Catalogue, Minneapolis, Brooklyn and Manchester 1978-9, p. 130.

2 Arthur Markham Nesfield's Diary, Nesfield Archives.

An illustration from *Specimens of Medieval Architecture.*

Dieppe, where they stayed at the Hotel de l'Europe and explored what Markham described as a fine watering place. From there they took the train to Rouen, where Markham considered the 'iron spire on top of Rouen Cathedral an abomination that was erected by a French architect years ago and will be probably pulled down.' After breakfast on the 26 he and Eden went to the Cathedral, where he 'assisted Willy to measure a window as he is making very careful drawings of it for his book.' On the 27 they took the train to the Port de l'Arche where they 'went into a café where Willy stopped some years ago and ordered dinner for half past 5, and then went to l'Abbeye de Bonport which was then owned by an English gentleman a Mr Martin who obtained it through his wife.' They sketched there, and Markham assisted Eden to measure a window at the end of the refectory, which Markham said was used at present as a hay loft. They returned by rail to Dieppe and had a very rough passage back to England – everybody was sick![1]

Eden's book, *Specimens of Medieval Architecture of the Twelfth and Thirteenth Centuries in France and Italy*, was published in 1862. It contained 100 lithographed plates of Gothic architecture, the majority being thirteenth-century churches, 89 in France, and the remainder in Italy, 5 of which had been set in stone by Eden. Albert Moore designed a frieze-like composition for the lower section of the front cover with five draped figures: a female representing Architecture, and four males representing Egypt, Greece, Rome and the Middle Ages. Eden's drawing techniques suggest that 'many lines were ruled or set out with compasses. Traced over freehand. Probably using a magnifying glass with the results being far from mechanical. He never exaggerated age or ruin or proportion. He used shading in a consistent manner rather than for pictorial effect.'[2]

In 1859, Eden and Shaw had submitted a proposal for what was probably their only joint commission. This was for the Manchester Assize Court. Although their design was much acclaimed, exhibited with other designs in Manchester and displayed at the Architectural Exhibition in London the following year, the commission was ultimately awarded to Alfred Waterhouse. Three years later, in 1862, Eden and Moore collaborated at the International Exhibition, for which Eden designed a fountain with panels in Greek and Gothic form by Moore. Once Eden returned from his Continental tour, his

1 On Sunday 30 September 1860 Eden wrote in his Sketch Book: 'Pulled to Kew and back with Markham. No steerer, tide against us both ways nearly swamped at Vauxhall.' Drawings and Archives Collection, British Architectural Library.

2 Roger Turner, *William Eden Nesfield (1835-1888), Some Houses* (*Canterbury School of Architecture Review*, no. 1, 1990).

Pages from *Specimens of Medieval Architecture.*

Detail from *Specimens of Medieval Architecture*

work over the next few years was largely on estates where his father was well known, and in some cases these commissions were minor; as, for example, at Swillington Hall near Leeds, where he designed a pavilion and gates for Sir John Lowther; at Clumber in Nottinghamshire where he designed a boat-house, pavilion, terrace and terrace seats for the Duke of Newcastle; various commissions at Woolverstone Hall in Suffolk for John Berners; two Gothic-style lodges at Kirtlington Park, Oxfordshire for Sir John Dashwood; a laundry, summerhouse and lodge for Mdm. Van de Weyer of New Lodge, Windsor; a conservatory and ferneries at Linton Park, Kent for Viscountess Holmesdale; some heating grilles and a gate at Tregothnan in Cornwall; and walls, terraces, steps and a fountain at the Royal Horticultural Society's garden in the Museum Complex at Kensington Gore, London.

Sometimes, however, these commissions led to bigger ones. For example, outside the gates of the Croxteth estate in West Derby village, Eden had designed a stone Cross for J. Pemberton Heywood-Lonsdale, a Liverpool Banker. It was twelfth-century Gothic in concept, with coupled shafts holding up a seated Christ under a canopy, reminiscent of a drawing he had done in 1861 at Reims Cathedral. Later, Heywood Lonsdale commissioned him to design his country house in Shropshire.

Eden also built cottages in the village, and at Croxteth Hall itself, for the 4th Earl Sefton, and also designed a laundry and ornamental dairy decorated with mosaic tiles depicting the *Twelve Months of the Year*, and a fountain which was placed in the centre of the courtyard. The fountain supported figures sculpted by Albert Moore, which represented the four seasons. So impressed was the Crown Princess of Prussia (later Empress Frederick) with the dairy that she commissioned a replica for her estate, Fair, in Potsdam in 1863. Eden later produced plans to reface the north front at Croxteth, remodel the interior, and build a new wing, which was intended to match the west front, a brick addition of 1702. Unfortunately, the plan was never executed, but this style was not forgotten by Eden; later in his career he was to design buildings that became part of a movement known as the Queen Anne Revival.[1] Another commission, again on an estate where his father was well-known, was in 1861 at Shipley Hall, near Heanor, Derbyshire, for A.N. Mundy. It was at Shipley that Eden's disaffection with strictly orthodox Gothic first manifested itself. Here he designed an ornamental dairy and farm, and Albert Moore decorated the ceilings. He included a turret, dove-cot and central tower, with pitched roofs, half-hipped in the same brick, diaper-patterned polychromy he would have seen at Crewe Hall. It was all very reminiscent of Salvin's Elizabethan/Jacobean Revival style.

Gothic Cross in West Derby Village.

In 1862, Eden received what was to evolve into a major and prestigious commission at Coombe Abbey, Warwickshire, for the 2nd Earl of Craven. He was initially asked to provide a scheme for a range of service buildings which included a servants' quarters, offices for the estate steward, a billiard room, laundry, and a kitchen, which was open to the roof. Albert Moore spent many months in 1863 remodelling the interiors of both the dairy and kitchen, where he produced images of classically-robed figures carrying food and drink, dressed in pale draperies against a background of pale yellow brown, and which he painted directly on the plaster of the walls in oils. Eden designed various culinary objects, including Burgesian roasting jacks. The Georgian stable block was extended to provide a new coach-house and hay loft, with decorative tiles on the side of the building. Eden's love of ornamentation comes over strongly at Coombe; for on the gable end just below a window in the stable block, the Craven coat of arms was placed in red clay, with the date 1863. The stable block included a clock tower made entirely of wood and clothed in decorative lead sheeting, with a dovecot. There was a Latin inscription, *Vivite Fugio* (enjoy life because time flies).

The following year, Eden was given the chance to design his first complete house. This was Sproughton Hall, a small manor house in the village of Sproughton near Bury St Edmunds in East Anglia, where Nesfield family connections were strong.

1 The Plan, dated 1863, is in Croxteth Hall. William Nesfield worked at Croxteth for Charles William Sefton, 3rd Earl, there was a *parterre* at the front of the Hall that was probably his work, and in 1851 he received £166 from the estate for work completed there. I am grateful to Andrea Ellis for her help. In the Bodleian Library, Oxford there are drawings by Eden for suggestions for estate cottages.

Sproughton Manor, Suffolk.

The commission came from Lt Col. and Mrs Henry Phillips, the story being that Mrs Phillipps wanted a house that would resemble the French chateaux that they had seen during their honeymoon, although they were not able to fulfil their dream until years later when Mr Phillipps was fifty-seven and the couple had six children. Eden, fresh from his travels in France, was the ideal architect for this project, and the small manor house received the Nesfield touch; the widespread use of decorative features. The initials HP 1863 appeared on the cast-iron rain hoppers and in the circular plaster moulding in the dome of the main hall. There is a coat of arms set into the brickwork at the front of the house with the motto *Voto Pete Finem* (I will be faithful to the end). At the rear of the building there is a twin set of initials on shields HP and JBP (Lucy Burch Phillipps), whilst semi-circular shaped bricks adorn the upstairs windows, reminiscent of the Croxteth estate cottages in West Derby village.

The last tour of any length that Eden and Shaw took together was to Sussex between 24-28 September 1862. During this visit it became apparent that, although they still believed in the Gothic virtues of avoiding counterfeit materials and honesty of design, their great urge to be inventive with decoration opened their eyes to the delights of Old English vernacular architecture. A great many villages still contained a wealth of picturesque cottages with tile hanging and tall chimneys, and for the two men the Old English style came to represent a much truer English past than the Gothic, which originated on the Continent. They were not the only architects who became enamoured with this style of architecture: 'In the 1860s a number of the younger and abler Gothic Revival architects, who had started life as enthusiasts of the Gothic style, found themselves having doubts about the sense of reviving Gothic for nineteenth-century people to live in. In one way or another they kicked over the traces!'[1] Although they still continued to visit churches, the pair were becoming increasingly aware of the vernacular style to be found in the old cottages in the south of England, particularly in the deeply rural Weald of Kent, from which they were to evolve their own variation on what was to become the Vernacular or Old English Revival. Eden would have known that area well; he and Harding had sketched there and both his father and Salvin had had a number of commissions in the area. For example, William was consulted regarding the arrangements for the garden at Penshurst Place for Lord de L'Isle, and he had also designed a formal garden at nearby South Park for Lord Hardinge, which Salvin rebuilt in 1848. There were also other professional connections in this part of the world. Decimus Burton also worked at Penshurst Place and George Devey, who had been a pupil of Harding's, and whose office was near to Argyll Street where Salvin had his practice, designed a number of cottages in the Vernacular style in Penshurst village. This method of construction must have been a revelation to Eden and Shaw, with its coving, leaded lights, decorative brickwork, stained glass, very large brick chimneys, heraldic devices, mottoes, casement windows, half-timbering, tile hanging, hipped gables, inglenooks, great halls and stone mullioned windows, and it was to become the preferred style for both men. Its possibilities were confirmed for Eden when he visited Tunbridge Wells and Speldhurst the following year and he realised that his love of ornamentation could be given full rein not only through the Wealden and Sussex vernacular, but also with the pargetting to be found in East Anglia. These he combined with Japanese ornamentation for artefacts including Nankin blue and white porcelain, prints, sun and petal designs and sunflowers, which were all in fashion in the 1860s and collected avidly by a group of Bohemian artists, craftsmen and writers. Although Arthur Lasenby Liberty was not to open his store in Regent's Street devoted to the decorative arts until 1875, it was these early collectors who led the way for the full flowering of what came to be known as the Aesthetic Movement. In the 1850s, Dante Gabriel Rossetti was amongst the first to use the Japanese-inspired small whorled discs, with which he embellished his picture frames. Ultimately, both Eden and Shaw incorporated them into their architecture, and Eden referred to them as 'pies'.[2]

1 Mark Girouard, *The Victorian Country House*, pp. 66-67.
2 For the Japanese influence see author, 'Japanese Ornamentation', *The Builder*, May 2, June 13, 1863.

During the tour the two visited the church at Pulborough and Amberley Castle farmhouse, Arundel Castle, and the church at Tortington in Sussex, where Eden saw 'two sows lying back to back, head and tail, for mutual support against the combined efforts of their respective litters of about 13 suckling pigs each. Good dodge.'[1] The two had started their journey on the 25 September at 8.30 a.m., when they left Littlehampton to look at the church at Rustington. Eden's comment on this first day was: 'Rustington Church, very good. Augmering an awful sell totally restored by Tuelon in his best manner. Went to Clapham thro the most beautiful lanes and found a queer little plaster church of no interest & rather picturesque farm went on to Broadwater long walk this is a most abominable church. Went on to Sompting curious old church & well restored by Carpenter got to Shoreham very tired at 8.30 – went to a beastly bad inn.'[2] On the 27 September they visited New Shoreham Church: 'had a beastly bad breakfast at the station inn the den we turned into last night & went down to the church. The choir is not good work. The church is in a shocking state. Walked to Old Shoreham 12th c. small church good. Went on to Bramber nothing to see in either the castle or church. At Steyning nothing but a bad Norman church – Found very good quarters.'[3] On 28 September, which was a Sunday, they visited the Brotherhood Hall, Steyning. They walked to Bramber at 9 a.m., but as it rained they returned to London. They had been away for five days. Although the pair were still very keen church-seekers, this journey was the catalyst for a change of direction in their work.

---

1 Eden Nesfield's Sketch Books, Drawings and Archives Collections, British Architectural Library.
2 *Ibid.*
3 *Ibid.*

13.

Witley Court and Stoke Edith

During the 1850s William was as hard at work as his son, and one of his most important commissions, which was to continue on into the 1860s, was at Witley Court in Worcestershire. It included the creation of a vast baroque fountain, known as the Perseus and Andromeda fountain, which was designed as the centrepiece for the most prestigious garden at Witley and to act as a theatrical backdrop to the house. It still dominates its space. William described the Witley commission as his 'monster work', not only because the project went on well into the 1860s, but because it was an extremely lucrative commission for him and an impressive and costly undertaking for his client. The estate had been purchased in 1837 from the 4th Baron Foley by the trustees of William Humble Ward, 11th Baron (1818-1885), who was later to become the 1st Earl Dudley. As a result of the Industrial Revolution, Lord Ward was reputed to be one of the richest men in Britain, his wealth deriving from coal, iron, limestone and fire clay mines, iron smelting works, chemical factories and railway construction. Consequently, when he came into his inheritance, he was able to transform the mansion at Witley into a seventeenth-century, Italianate-style villa, employing the architect Samuel Whitfield Daukes (1811-1880) to undertake the task.

Daukes added a large conservatory, but retained the existing Ionic stone porticos designed by John Nash (1752-1835), c. 1805, for the 3rd Baron Foley. These porticos were eight columns wide and said to be the largest in any country house in Britain. Further additions included two stone lions to guard the portico steps and support garlanded decorations flanked by two stone vases, which were decorated with flowers and swags. A flight of steps with a curved balcony led down from Nash's portico, with a central avenue leading down to two symmetrically placed circular flowerbeds (a number of rejected designs for these beds were submitted before one was considered suitable). These beds were surrounded by bastions of rhododendrons and azaleas, but the main feature of the scheme was the massive fountain.

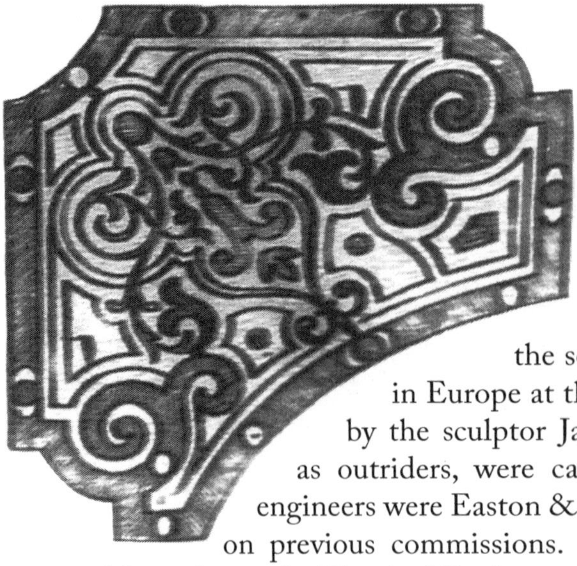

To the north of the fountain were two flanking pavilions designed by Daukes. The whole scheme was surrounded by low, pierced balustrades, giving the impression, as William always aimed to give, that the formal garden was a picture set within a frame.

The Perseus and Andromeda fountain William designed as the centrepiece for the south garden was reputed to be the largest in Europe at the time, and was carved in Portland stone by the sculptor James Forsyth. Two sea nymphs, featured as outriders, were carved by Charles Raymond Smith. The engineers were Easton & Company, who had worked with William on previous commissions. Eighteen thousand litres of water were pumped from the nearby Hundred Pool to a reservoir a kilometre away and thirty metres above the level of the mansion to feed the fountain. It was driven by a forty horsepower steam engine, coupled to two Cornish boilers. This water supplied the fountain and the main jet, which issued from the open mouths of sea monsters, the latter reaching a

Designs for unexecuted flowerbeds in the South Gardens at Witley Court.

An Overall Plan for the South Garden at Witley Court, c. 1870.

height of thirty-six metres. There were also numerous subsidiary jets and sprays. The dolphins had reeds fitted inside their open mouths, which could be adjusted to make varying pitches of sound as the water jets issued from them. Beneath the fountain were three chambers, reached by a passageway which started outside the balustraded grounds. Mythological figures for fountains were inspired by the statues and fountains in late fifteenth-century Italy, which often took Greek and Roman legends as their subjects. William's classical education would have taught him the significance of these legends, and that figures representing Greek and Roman mythology had been discovered on ancient Roman sites that were being excavated at the time, such as the villa of the Emperor Hadrian at Tivoli. Figures relating to the sea were, not surprisingly, thought to be highly appropriate for fountains. 'The myth behind the Perseus and Andromeda fountain is well known. Perseus, having obtained the head of Medusa with the help of his winged sandals and his helmet of invisibility, flies to the rescue of Andromeda, who has been tied to a rock by Poseidon, angry at the suggestion that she is more beautiful than the sea nymphs. A sea monster threatens to devour Andromeda, but before it can do so Perseus carries her off – in this case on the back of the winged horse Pegasus.'[1]

To the east of the mansion, overlooking the ballroom, William provided a subsidiary garden, which included a *parterre-de-broderie* surrounded by clipped evergreens and ornamental vases filled with flowers. The fountain in this garden denoted Flora, the Goddess of Spring, standing on a pedestal holding a cornucopia, from which a jet of water issued from a variety of sources. Other examples of statues holding cornucopias can be found at Chatsworth in Derbyshire, and at Petworth in West Sussex by Cibber dating from about 1690. William also included smaller jets and shells around the 164-inch circumference of the basin.

These gardens continued to act as impressive backdrops to many house parties at Witley well into the Edwardian period, when the 2nd Earl of Dudley took up residence. The gardens have been restored by English Heritage and the *parterre-de-broderie* in the east garden, although still lacking Flora, is an authentic reconstruction of Nesfield's original *parterre*.[2]

In August 1850 Queen Victoria visited Castle Howard on her way to Balmoral and was disappointed to find no flowers or gravel walks. Although by this date William had already been commissioned by Lord Carlisle to design a formal garden there, it was felt prudent to delay the work until after her visit. By September 1850, however, work had commenced on the pleasure grounds to the south of the mansion, which consisted of a large *parterre-de-broderie* and a huge fountain known as the Atlas Fountain. It depicts Atlas carrying a Globe on his shoulders, surrounded by a group including Triton and outriders blowing conches. The engineers were once again Easton & Company, and the fountain figures were cast in Portland stone by the sculptor John Thomas, who is reputed to have been Prince Albert's favourite sculptor, and who was responsible for the decorative sculpture on the entrance piers of Buckingham Palace. The globe, six feet in diameter was made in London, using £10 of copper. By December 1850 William had submitted a scale drawing for the fountain figures, and in February of the following year Lord Carlisle had seen all the detailed plans and given his final approval. Ten pieces, weighing a total of twenty-four tonnes. were sent from London by rail to Castle Howard railway station, and the tazzas, pedestal, shells and basin were executed by local masons working from models that Thomas sent from London. Thomas' total bill, which included the provision of models, supervision and the cost of transport, was £1,183 10s. 5d., whilst expenditure for the pleasure grounds from 22 July 1850 to 23 December 1852 reached £3,579 9s. 2d. The work was completed to schedule by October 1852.

---

1 Jeremy Musson, Shirley Evans, *et.al.*, *The Gardens of Witley Court*, English Heritage, 1997, p. 33.

2 See Shirley Evans, *Nesfield's Monster Work: The Gardens of Witley Court* (Peter Huxtable Designs, 1994).

The Perseus and Andromeda fountain before the restoration.

The Perseus and Andromeda fountain after the restoration.

The restored South Garden at Witley Court.

The East Garden at Witley Court during (top) and after (bottom) the restoration.

The Cascade in the Lake at Castle Howard.

William's association with Castle Howard was a long one and one which apparently had given him great satisfaction. The south *parterre* at Castle Howard survived until changing fashions swept it away in the 1890s in favour of an easier arrangement of lawns and yew hedges, whilst the south lake's formal banks were softened and naturalized.

In December 1853 William received two letters from Lady Emily Foley, his client at Stoke Edith, Herefordshire, and his reply gives one of the most revealing insights we have into his landscape gardening philosophy and his sensitivity to any criticism of his work. Lady Emily's letters referred to a *parterre* design William had submitted, which she was not satisfied with; therefore, she asked him: 'would or could you condescend to arrange something that would look well resembling in a slight degree one or other of these two sketches?'[1] These were designs that had been drawn up by Lord Graham. William's reply on 2 January 1854 leaves no doubt that her comment had upset him, for he was quickly on the defensive. He said he had been studying Art and Nature for thirty-six years and it was only, 'thro unremitting practice that the mind becomes more sensitive to the least trifling deviation from the latter.' He explained that: 'an error in Art may be compared to the offence which the touching of a false note would cause to the ear of a cultivated musician.' He used his criticisms of Lord Graham's design to set out all the attributes he considered necessary to make a picturesque garden. For example, although he considered colour important, it

1 Lady Emily Foley to William Nesfield, letters dated 21 and 22 December, 1853, Herefordshire Record Office, Hereford, Foley Papers.

was *form* in pictorial art that 'most justly precedes colour and if this were not so, we might then be content with the most hideous objects if they were only beautifully coloured.' He quoted from one celebrated artistic Author who maintained that '*Proportion* is to form what time is to music or measure to Poetry.' The crowding together of features, such as a group of flowerbeds, 'is . . . as objectionable as overloading a small room with furniture which is not only adverse to *Repose* but is the very means to make little appear less.' He also maintained that there was another quality in art: 'viz. *Expression* . . . as every object, artificial as well as natural has more or less of this, we surely ought to give each its due, if worthy of notice, or why rid a fine Tree of inferior and obtrusive accompaniments as in the case of the Cedar of Lebanon and Holly etc.' He also explained that it was necessary to avoid compounding small parts with large so that neither are sufficiently distant from one another; if this is not achieved, '*Simplicity* fails'. Breadth in a *parterre* was another important factor, especially where it acts 'as a frame to a picture with the aid of a general surrounding walk.' William likened the shapes in his *parterre* designs to music when he explained that: 'Some few lines are intentionally single (i.e. 3 inches square) acting with others on a graduated scale as the octaves in musical chords they constitute the charm of good composition inasmuch they not only produce *Variety* but give energy to all the broader lines which are as base notes.' The most important principle, however, in his opinion, was *Consistency*: 'w'thout which the most valuable materials must inevitably be non-effective.' His design was eventually put in place, but not until he had produced at least three other plans for *parterres-de-broderie* for Lady Foley's consideration.

His final *parterre-de-broderie* design for Stoke Edith contained large liminal scrolls on the four corners, with a floret running up the centre, and culminating in a volute. The architectural feature he provided to give height to the scheme was an armillary sphere. He used topiarized evergreens for the border around the *parterre*, which acted as a frame. The arabesque shapes were outlined in box and laid on coloured gravels. Two lines of box infilled with gravel were used to outline the plant-like shapes, and statues were strategically placed on each side of the *parterre*, together with tazzas for flowers.

The unification of house, terrace and the formal garden was an important architectural principle, and by 1853 William was explaining this concept to Lady Foley. He pointed out the significance of the stone lions which were to be installed on top of two piers attached to the balustrades, the intention of which was to link the terrace with the garden. His opinions appear to have been acceptable to Lady Foley, for by 1859 he was giving her advice regarding interior decoration! A duchess of Lady Foley's acquaintance had advised that red blinds should be used on the windows at Stoke Edith, to which William replied: 'red blinds upon a red house, I confess disagreement with the Duchess – considering that the large pictures have already a very objectionable contrast to the *nondescript* painted panels below, it appears to me that red wd obviously disturb the colouring of the said pictures whereas a quiet grey, with a *very tender* pinky border & diaper would be less violent.'[1]

1 The above quotations refer to correspondence from William Nesfield to Lady Foley, 2 January 1854, *Ibid.*

Detail of the Perseus and Andromeda Fountain at Witley Court.

Witley Court and the Perseus and Andromeda Fountain

Parterre-de-Broderie at Stoke Edith in Herefordshire, reproduced in *Country Life*, 6 June 1903.

In the early 1860s William was back in Cheshire, at Rode Hall, with his client Roger Wilbraham. Rode Hall has been the seat of the Wilbraham family since 1669, when it was bought from Randle Rode by his cousin, Roger Wilbraham of Nantwich, for the latter's younger son. Roger was descended from Sir Richard de Wilbraham, Sheriff of Cheshire in 1259, and the house continued to descend through the male line until 1900, when Katherine, an only child who had married a George Baker, assumed Wilbraham as their principal surname. The estate today is owned by Sir Richard and Lady Baker Wilbraham. At Rode, William designed rose gardens and the formal drive leading to the west front of the house, and provided a plan for the formal treatment of the ground to the south west and north east fronts of the house. His plans are still held in the archives at Rode Hall.

14.

30 Argyll Street

When Salvin relinquished his lease on 30 Argyll Street, Eden and Shaw decided to take it on. By February 1863, Eden had crossed out 15 Bedford Road on his headed notepaper and substituted his new address. His office at the new practice has been described as: 'a sight in those days, containing a valuable collection of blue-and-white Nankin china and Persian plates, Japanese curios, brass sconces and other metal work, nick-nacks of various descriptions, and a well-stocked library in a case designed by himself. It was the studio of an artist, rather than the business room of a professional man; any samples of building materials being conspicuous by their absence.'[1] Eden attracted a large circle of friends, all interested in the principle of 'Art for Art's Sake', all charismatic and dominant personalities. Amongst their number was the painter and poet Dante Gabriel Rossetti, who eventually died of drink and drugs, and who was the main driving force behind the pre-Raphaelite Brotherhood of painters. This group included John Everett Millais and William Holman Hunt, and it aimed to change British art, disdaining anything that had been produced after Raphael. In 1856 Rossetti formed a friendship with William Morris and Edward Burne-Jones, and together they decorated the Oxford Student Union Library with scenes from the Arthurian legends. Eden certainly admired Morris' work, as he did the work of all talented, versatile craftsmen. In reply to an enquiry regarding Morris' abilities as a craftsman, Eden said: 'I fear I did not quite answer your letter Re Morris, Topsy, is his name, on account of his curls, & cos he growed as he got bigger. Well let's see – he has done everything most splendidly – cant do otherways. . . . In short he is a clipper but privately and confidentially if your esteemed friend thinks he will get a window, at the time he stipulates, he will be in grievous error. . . . But both the delay, & price, are well worth going in for, as there is no-one who can do anything approaching his work.'[2] Another friend of Eden's was James McNeill

1 J.M. Brydon, *Architectural Review*, May 1897, pp. 236-237.

2 *A Deuce of An Uproar: William Eden Nesfield's Letters to the Rector of Radwinter Church, Essex*, Friends of Radwinter Church, 1988, p. 282.

Whistler, whom Eden probably met through Albert Moore. Whistler was introduced to classical sculpture by Moore and particularly admired Moore's *The Marble Seat*, which was exhibited at the Royal Academy in 1865, showing figures in classical dress which Whistler had copied in 1864 in his *Captice in Purple and Gold* and *The Golden Screen*. In turn, Whistler opened Moore's eyes to Japanese motifs and woodcuts. However, Whistler became worried that their work was too similar and Eden was asked to arbitrate in their dispute. Diplomatically, Eden pronounced that the influence was reciprocal: Moore was influenced by Whistler's colour harmonies and Whistler was influenced by Moore's classically draped figures, but he felt their scenes depicting women by the seashore were sufficiently varied that they did not affect one another's work excessively. Eden was also acquainted with the poet Algernon Charles Swinburne, the illustrator Randolph Caldecott and the architect William Burges. Eden and Burges had much in common, both being described as: 'rich, mercurial, jovial young egotists, fascinated by decoration, ornament and heraldry. Both enjoyed the masculine company of their peers . . . '[1] Burges was a member of the FABS with Eden and a Freemason at the same Lodge .[2] A fondness for dogs and parrots was something else they had in common. When the office parrot died, either Burges or Eden drew a design for a gabled sarcophagus with a tulip vase in front, candles at its corners, P.P.P.P. along its frieze, feathered friends 'Jane' and 'Tommy' looking on, and an inscription which read:

> Poor Polly
> Died on Feby 19
> 1863 She was a
> Gentle Bird.

Over the next few years, Eden continued to sketch and measure, sometimes alone and sometimes with Shaw. On Sunday 9 July, 1865, Eden made an excursion with the FABS and a group of architects into Kent. He wrote in his Sketch Book: 'Knowle with ye FABS doing the staircase. Went down with FABS to Sevenoaks & stayed at the Crown from Saty till Monday July 8-10.'[3] His career continued to flourish at Argyll Street, and by 1863 his commission at Combe Abbey had been extended to include alterations and additions to the main house. He remodelled the south front and gave it a chateau-like appearance, influenced no doubt by the great moated chateaux he had seen in France. He also designed a new east wing using red sandstone as a complete contrast to the buff colour of the rest of the building. To do this he needed to demolish the old east cloisters of the Cistercian abbey – a decision he later regretted. A long moat was dug along the

1 Andrew Saint, Richard Norman Shaw (the Mellon Centre for Studies in British Art Limited by Yale University Press, New Haven and London, 1983), p. 18.

2 This was the Westminster and Keystone Lodge No. 10, a fashionable lodge that mainly consisted of Oxford Undergraduates. They feasted annually in Greenwich or at the Star and Garter. The Foreign Architectural Book Society, or FABS was formed in 1859 with fifteen members.

3 William Eden Nesfield's Notebooks, Drawings and Archives Collections, British Architectural Library.

entire length of the south front and extended beyond the building at the eastern end. This terminated in a waterfall and four cataracts through which flowed water, gravity-fed from a top pool through a system of glazed conduits. It curved round the terraced western front and at a point immediately in front of the west range of buildings, formed a straight canal that met with the Great Lake, separated only by an ornamental Balustrade. With the surplus soil from the moat canal, terraces were created on the west front and retained by stone walls. These terraces formed bases for large ornamental gardens and straight gravel pathways and drives, which were laid out by his father.

During the same year, J. Pemberton Heywood-Lonsdale, for whom Eden had designed the Gothic Cross in the village of West Derby, commissioned him to design a new house, Cloverley Hall, on his estate at Calverhall in Shropshire.[1] It had all the hallmarks, as one would expect at this time, when Eden was experimenting with the English Vernacular, of a typical English manor house, but with a French flavour. Sixteenth-century Tudor, built of brick, local stone and English oak and cleverly designed on a slope (could Eden be remembering his time at Keele Hall?), it had sculpted gables and a frieze by James Forsyth depicting *The Seasons*, using Albert Moore's designs. The bricks were reminiscent of the Tudor period, two-and-three-quarter inches wide for the lodge house, and two-and-one-quarter inches deep for the main house, made from local clay quarried on the site. It was designed on three levels with an Entrance Hall and Great Hall fifty-five feet long and twenty-eight feet wide, its bay window lit from the south and east. The high stone fireplace had a band of panels depicting nine of *Aesop's Fables*, carved by James Forsyth from Albert Moore's drawings. Stairs led to the dining-room, library, drawing room and a staircase hall. The lower ground floor, the male domain, contained business and billiard rooms and had a view of the garden at the rear. The fireplaces at Cloverley were splendid; for example, the chimneypiece in the dining room was of oak, with three panels in alto-relievo also by James Forsyth from designs by Albert Moore, with the motto 'East and West Home's Best'. The walls were English oak panelled with a seventeen-inch ceiling of oak, eight light bay windows and heraldic stained glass located at the corner of the main block following sixteenth century precedents. The entrance to the stable court was below a massive clock tower under a Flemish style gabled roof. The tower had a penthouse for the stable keeper with carved stonework panels representing zodiac signs by Albert Moore. Eden sought the advice of his friend and client, the Revd Frederick Bullock of Radwinter in Essex, regarding a motto to adorn the clock on the stable block. Eventually, on reflection, Eden told Bullock that: 'on second thoughts I "concluded" (nasty Yankee word) that for a domestic clock something less pious & ecclesiastical wd be better.'[2] Eden's motto read:

1 Arthur Markham Nesfield also worked at Cloverley. On 20 August 1866; 20 September and 29 'he staked out dried ground which will have to be rained over, and returned on 30 and 31 On 25 May 1867 he went over the Avenue staked out fresh conifer trees took measurements for dressing the ground by the approach. 5 July again staked out ground'. Arthur Markham Nesfield's Notebook of Travelling Expenses.

2 *Deuce of An Uproar*, letter dated 11 October 1867, p. 266.

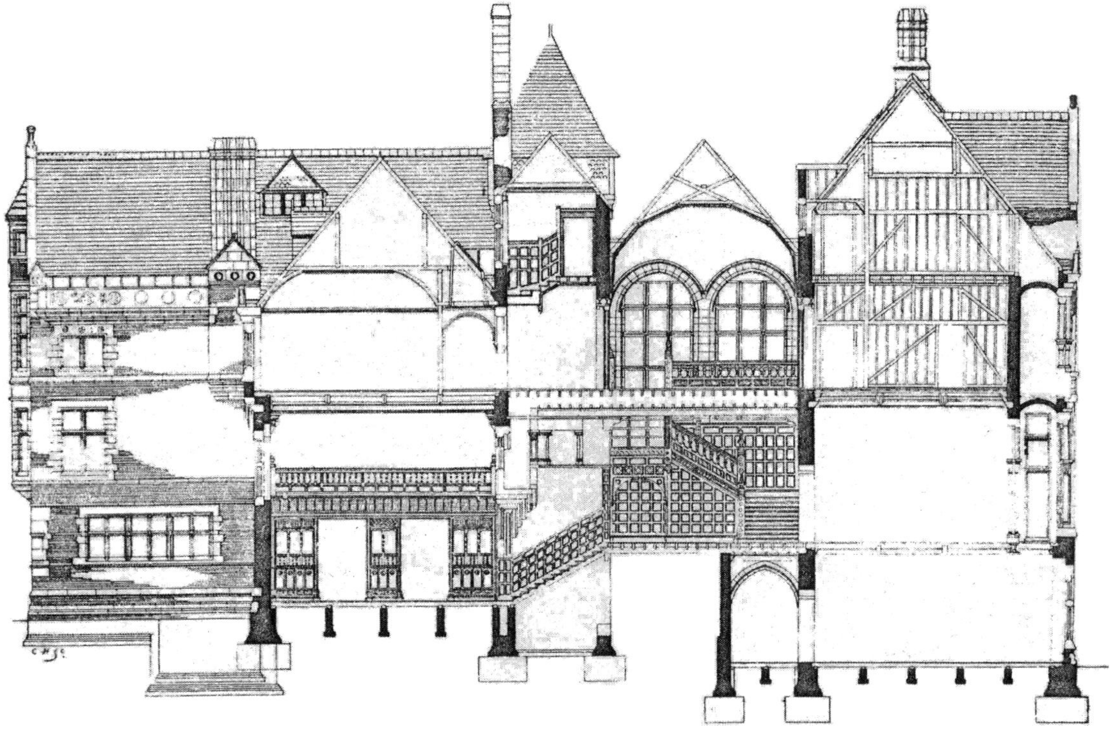

Cross-section through Hall and staircase, Cloverley Hall, 1896.

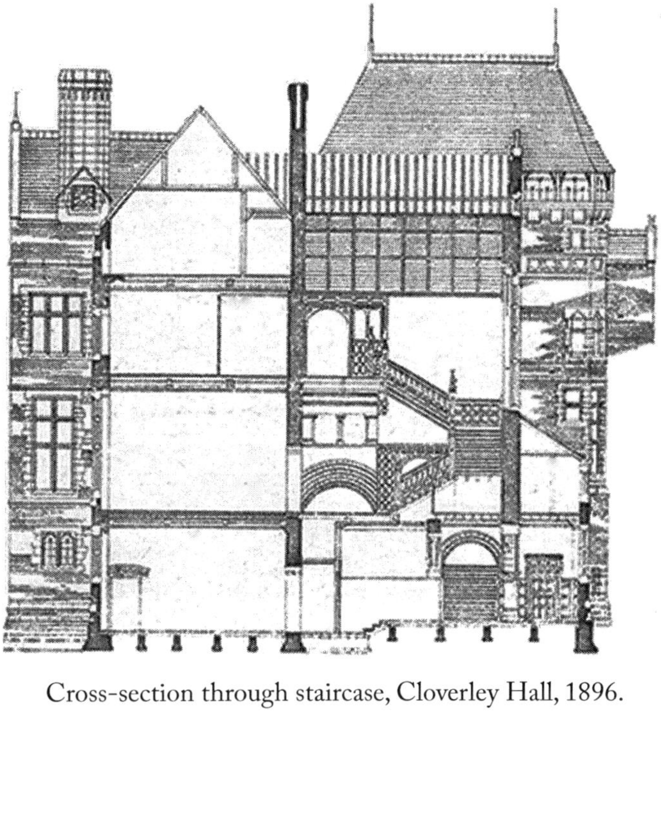

Cross-section through staircase, Cloverley Hall, 1896.

Lo though we
Sleep or wake
or roam or ride
Aye fleeth the time;
It will no man abide.[1]

These clock towers were some of Eden's most successful innovations and demonstrated his unrivalled ornamental flair. A similar example exists at Hampton Manor in Warwickshire. Here Eden also designed a curved larder with a rectangular gable, diaper brickwork with carved texts interspersed with sunflowers and pies, and a number of lodge houses. It was a commission that was to influence both Shaw at Leyswood in Kent in 1868 and William Burges at Knightshayes Court in Devon in 1869.[2]

Cloverley Hall today.

1 *A Deuce of An Uproar*, Letter dated 11 October 1867, p. 166. This is a quotation from *The Clerk's Tale* from Geoffrey Chaucer's *Canterbury Tales*.
2 The house has now been partly demolished.

Left: Clock Tower, Cloverley Hall. Right: The Lodge House, Kinmel, North Wales.

Lodge House, Cloverley Estate.

Clock Tower (top left), Hampton-in-Arden, Warwickshire.
Church (top right) and cottages (below) Hampton-in-Arden, Warwickshire.

Eden also worked in estate grounds, building lodge houses and carrying out alterations and additions at Cora Church in Calverhall village between 1872 and 1878, where he designed a new nave with roof pie discs, two aisles, a tower, an alabaster reredos, and a semi-circular lectern. The stained glass for the south window in the chancel was supplied by William Morris' firm. In 1878 Eden received a further commission from his client at Calverhall to undertake some alterations at his London home, 23 Grosvenor Square.

There is no doubt that it was Eden's father who secured Eden's commission to design a series of estate cottages for Lord Crewe on the Crewe estate, as William had continued to offer advice to Lord Crewe well into the 1860s. Eden designed them in the Old English Revival manner and they included Yew Tree Cottage, a Smithy, and a pair of cottages to the east of the main drive known as Stowford Cottages, to which William referred to in his correspondence with Lord Crewe:

> 3 York Terrace,
> Regent's Park N.W.
>
> My Lord,
>
> I was out of Town when your Lordship's letter arrived, which accounts for the delay in reply – I have consulted with my Son regarding the Cottages which are to be near Weston Lodge, & although I certainly did agree with Mr Martin that single cottages might be preferable to double ones, yet my Son's opinion (to which I attach much importance because of his very superior taste as an Artist) now is, that as there is to be provision for 4 families – One double & 2 single cottages (as affording most variety of effect) would be preferable to introducing them all single – Thus as his reasoning in the matter is so convincing I now entirely coincide with him & therefore hope you will sanction this, as our great desire is to take the utmost pains in improving the domain of Crewe Hall.
>
> Yours faithfully, W.A. Nesfield.[1]

In 1866 Eden and Shaw decided to put the years of their friendship and co-operation on a more solid footing, and in 1866 they went into partnership. One would have assumed that, knowing Eden as well as he did, Shaw would have hesitated before taking such a decisive step; it proved to be a mistake. A partnership for Shaw would have meant they would have gone forward on an equal footing, but it evidently took such a move for him to realize that Eden was not, and never could be, a team player. His outward bonhomie, inventive flair and genuine kindliness masked his inability to relinquish his desire to dominate. This tendency, which could have been dismissed as youthful high spirits when he was young, was the cause of irritation later in life. Shaw was a more mature individual, and by then was intending to marry and take up a more settled existence – not a concept that Eden would have understood. Although, as far as is known, the two men never had

1 Cheshire Record Office, Chester, DCR/15/2.

a serious quarrel, and indeed continued to share offices until the lease ran out in 1876, they grew apart. Shaw's marriage to a very conventional lady probably hastened the decision to revert to organizing their own affairs. These years, however, were extremely busy and productive for Eden. Between 1866 and 1867, for example, he designed a lodge house at the Royal Botanic Gardens, Kew. It had been decided that a grand carriage entrance should be made opposite the Temperate House, that would be suitable for receiving Royalty, but another factor in this decision was that the London and South Western Railway was to have a terminus at Kew, which would inevitably attract more people to the gardens. The lodge Eden designed was opposite to these gates, and it was his first attempt at designing in the manner which came to be known as Queen Anne Revival style.[1] There were mixed feelings about this style at the time, one description being that it was an: 'architectural cocktail, with a little genuine Queen Anne in it, a little Dutch, a little Flemish, a touch of Robert Adam and a dash of François'. However, what Eden produced at Kew was a little gem, and the entrance front as a whole has been described as 'a masterpiece.'[2] He was a pioneer of this style, for Shaw did not design New Zealand Chambers until 1871, and, small though this building is, it is one of Eden's most interesting projects. It has an exaggerated roof overhung at the eaves to provide an excessively long cornice, and a massive central rubbed brick chimney decorated with the Royal arms, which were carved in red rubbed brick on a panel set in the west and east sides of the moulded ribs of the stack. It has very prominent pedimented dormers and brick pilasters and large sash windows of different sizes and shapes of glass panes, all reminiscent of the 1630s. Eden's inspiration for this building is said to have been the nearby Dutch House, and Thackeray's house of 1861, in the early eighteenth century style, at No. 2, Palace Green.

One of Eden's most important and largest commissions during the two years he and Shaw were in formal partnership was at Kinmel Park near Abergele in North Wales, where William had laid out a large formal garden. Their client was Hugh Robert Hughes (852-1911), and his acquisition of the estate can be described as a rags to riches story. Kinmel came to the Hughes family when Edward Hughes, a curate from Anglesey, married his rector's daughter, May Lewis, in 1765. May had inherited Parys Mountain near Amlwch, which, it was subsequently discovered, contained a rich vein of copper. In 1774 the Parys Mining Company was formed and Edward and May became very wealthy, purchasing the Kinmel Estate in 1786. Hugh Robert Hughes inherited the estate from his uncle William Lewis Hughes, 1st Baron Dinorben (1815-1852). In 1865, possibly due to Eden's work on estates elsewhere, he was asked to undertake the design of some estate buildings at Kinmel. In 1866 he designed the Home Farm, Plas Kinmel, which had a dovecot and dairy, and in 1868 the Golden Lodge, which was a copy of his Temperate Lodge at Kew with stained glass windows, ornamental sunflowers and other

1 For details of the Queen Anne Revival style see Mark Girouard, *The Listener,* 22 April 1977, pp. 504-506.

2 Clive Aslet, 'Bodrhyddan', *Country Life*, 27 July, 1978, p. 229.

Stowford Cottages at Crewe Hall Estate, Cheshire.

flowers. He also designed new wrought-iron gates for the forecourt of the mansion. The Smithy was built in 1867 and featured pargetting, a form of decoration Eden could have seen used by the Chester architect, John Douglas, in Great Budworth, Cheshire, when Eden was designing some cottages for his father's clients the Warburton family of nearby Arley Hall. However, it was also a common decoration in Saffron Walden, a happy hunting ground for Eden. In 1867 he added an ornamental well, eight cottages, a chapel, a further row of cottages in 1867, and, in 1875 another estate building which contained the Gas Works.

Eden went on between 1871 and 1874 to partly rebuild and enlarge the manor house at Kinmel in the Queen Anne Revival style. On 25 May 1865 Eden recorded in his diary that, accompanied by 'Mr Hughes, Mrs Hughes & children [we went] to Hampton Court, Mr Hughes drove the dray, Very pleasant day.' The purpose of their visit was to see Christopher Wren's Quadrangle and the rubbed brickwork it featured. Eden prepared a bird's-eye view of the proposed alterations to show Mr Hughes, but his first design proved to be too costly, so it had to be reduced and done over again. Despite the reduction in size, this was to be Eden's largest country house. He made use of rubbed brickwork featuring carved heraldic designs and musical instruments above the original ballroom. Interestingly, the plan for Leicester Town Hall, which was submitted by Eden's assistant Francis Hames in 1873, is strikingly reminiscent of Kinmel. How much was Hames' work and how much Eden's is not known, but the design influenced the construction of a number of other buildings, including the Town Halls at Oxford, Wakefield and Sheffield.

In 1868, when Eden and Shaw decided to end their short-lived partnership, but continued to share offices, Eden was entering into one of his most productive professional periods. It was at this time that he was given many of the long-standing commissions which he relished. For example, during the latter years of the partnership, he had received a commission from the Rt Hon. Sir Frederick Peel, the son of the Prime Minister, Robert Peel. Peel had bought land in Hampton-in-Arden in Warwickshire in 1840, and refounded the manor there. In 1868 Eden was asked to design a number of estate cottages on the High Street, opposite the entrance to the manor drive. They have all the hallmarks of his hand, with tile hanging, 'pies', pargetting, armorial masonry, tall chimneys and ornamental plasterwork. One of his most interesting buildings was the lodge at the end of the manor drive, little altered since it was built, incorporating sunflower and pie decoration and tall chimneys. In the early 1870s the alterations and additions to the manor house included an octagonal Gothic clock tower with an exuberant high roof, dormers on four sides, and a top lantern with carved panels featuring the Signs of the Zodiac, executed by Albert Moore. Eden also undertook restoration work on the church of SS Mary & Bartholomew in the village. He measured the church in June 1868, and on 5 May 1869 submitted his initial report to Frederick Peel. The church was built c.1130 and the chancel, which Eden restored, stands on the original Norman structure. There are still traces of its origin in the jambs and lintels in the north outer wall, fifteenth-century stained glass, fourteenth to fifteenth century floor tiles, and the remains of thirteenth-century stone coffin lids with incised crosses. At that time it retained its trefoiled fleur-de-lys box pews, which Eden unfortunately removed.[1] He also wanted to replace the spire, which had been destroyed in a violent thunder and lightning storm at night on St Andrew's day in 1643, but this change was not implemented. One of the most interesting features to Eden at Hampton Church was a damaged Heart Tomb, one of the few remaining, with Early English hood-moulding. It probably contained the heart of some noble (a Crusader?). It was restored by Eden in 1878 before being replaced in the church. Walking through this village today, in spite of the traffic on what is now a busy main road, it is still possible to appreciate how idyllic it must have been in the late 1860s.

1 This Report, together with plans and photographs of the church during construction, is held in the Warwickshire County Record Office, Warwick DRB63/50.

Lodge house for the manor, Hampton-in-Arden, Warwickshire.

The Hampton-in-Arden commission was followed by one in Radwinter in Essex from the rector, the Revd Frederick Bullock. This project began before the end of Eden's partnership, as a communication of 24 February 1868, headed 'Nesfield and Shaw Architects', testifies. It was to be a lengthy commission for Eden, and the letters written by him to Frederick Bullock throw a great deal of light, not only on the work being carried out at Radwinter, but on the personal connection between the two men. Bullock had been curate to Eden's paternal uncle, Charles Nesfield, and was a few years younger than Eden. Arthur Markham Nesfield was his particular friend, and Markham's diary describes a continental journey he and 'Fred.' took together.[1] Eden's work at Radwinter

1 On 11 June 1861 he set off with Frederick Bullock, travelling to Boulogne, then to Paris and from thence they proceeded along the Rhine into Germany and then Berne – where they admired the clock with its procession of bears. From there they went to Lugano, Markham noting particularly the Swiss cemeteries where every grave was numbered and generally had no headstone, each formed into a separate *parterre* with the edges neatly lined with box, and three poles about half an inch diameter and six to seven feet high and painted black and white onto which were trained

was to enlarge, embellish and alter the fourteenth-century church of St Mary the Virgin in Radwinter village, at a proposed cost of £1,500. This project was initiated by the Bullock family in memory of their father, who had been the previous incumbent at Radwinter.

In February 1869, the church was closed in order for the alterations to begin. Eden warned the Revd Bullock to be prepared for 'A Deuce of an Uproar'. He remodelled the east end of the church, enlarged the nave and aisles, designed a new chancel, richly embellished and inscribed with texts an organ case, and provided stained glass in three windows in the Vestry depicting Gabriel, Raphael and Michael.[1] Externally, he added tiled inserts in flint walling and his signature pies on the hoppers. Eden was called in again by the Revd Bullock in the mid-1870s when, on Friday 1 May 1874, a fire virtually destroyed the centre of Radwinter village. The small cottages built of thatch and wood soon caught alight, and many of the villagers were made homeless. By 1875 Eden had built a new shop, a row of four cottages on the south of the village, a pair of semi-detached cottages and a tailor's shop. Almshouses, a Reading Room and a Dispensary were built to his designs, but were not finished until after his death.

During the time Eden was at Radwinter he undertook commissions in the nearby town of Saffron Walden, where, between 1873 and 1875, he designed Gibson's Bank (now Barclays) internally and externally. It still dominates the Market Square. Built in brick and stone, the main block is symmetrical, whilst the one on the right hand side has a large Gothic doorway with a pointed arch. The structure is three storeys high with a lead-lined parapet and an attic storey. It has tall brick chimney stacks, large mullion windows, stone facings and a carved stonework panel on which Randolph Caldecott carved a flight of storks in low relief. Inside are plastered ceilings, a tiled fireplace, coloured window glass and panelling depicting the Saffron Crocus. Originally, there was also a carved fountain in front of the Bank. Eden refaced in plaster the front of the Rose and Crown Hotel across the square with colourful pargetting depicting Roses and Crowns, which has since been demolished.

---

standard roses. They then moved on to Lake Geneva, where Markham observed that the lake was 'certainly a beautiful colour although there are quite as many streaks of bright sparkling green as rich dark blue, and here and there the base note of reddish purple the clearness is marvellous.' On 21 June they were in Bonneville and stopped at a hotel overlooking Mont Blanc, before going on a walking tour which took them through the Simplon Pass to Lake Maggiore, where they took a gondola to Isola Bella. This Markham found merely curious on account of the mechanical contrivances used in winter 'by means of which tropical plants flourish under the very nose of the Alps. To artistic taste and design it has no pretensions in truth it is money for the most part mis-spent.' From Stresa the two men went by boat to Arona, took the railway to Milan thence to Lugano and Interlaken where a foot infection, due to too much walking, forced Markham home; but first he went with Frederick as far as Hindenburg. From this city they made for home via Antwerp and the Ostend ferry arriving back on Saturday 3 August – Frederick leaving the same day for Saffron Walden: Taken from Arthur Markham Nesfield's Notebook of Travelling Expenses.

1 Signed 'Eden Nesfield, 1870'.

Kinmel Hall and William Nesfield's formal Garden, watercolour by Cyril Blakeman, 1944-45.

Right: the Lion Tazza in the Avenue Gardens, Regent's Park.

Left: the Cable Frieze in the Avenue Gardens, Regent's Park.

Below: the Flower Garden in the Avenue Gardens, Regent's Park, pastel.

15.

Two Public Commissions

Not surprisingly, when William's designs for the Buckingham Palace gardens were rejected, he was very disappointed; especially as he had refused at least one commission in order to concentrate on these plans (at Bowood House in Wiltshire, for the 3rd Marquess of Lansdowne). However, Prince Albert did not forget him, and he was to receive commissions to improve a number of London parks. For example, in 1861 William was consulted regarding a series of complex geometric borders along the Hyde Park boundary: 'These were filled with low "carpet" bedding (so called because the patterns reflected those found in carpets); these bright colourful borders spread along the Bayswater Road boundary and to the Serpentine'.[1] Also through the auspices of the Prince he acquired two further commissions during the 1860s, the first at the Royal Horticultural Gardens at Kensington Gore, London.

The Gardens were the centrepiece of the Museum Complex dedicated to the 'Arts and Sciences', Prince Albert's special project, and opened by him on 5 June 1861. The event that had enabled this scheme to come to fruition was the 'Great Exhibition of the Works of Industry of All Nations' (The Great Exhibition), which was opened by Queen Victoria on 18 May 1851 in Hyde Park. It was the first International Exhibition to be held in the United Kingdom, and was that rare event, a complete success. Over six million people from all walks of life attended, and it had generated a surplus income of £186,000 when it closed on 15 October 1851. Its legacy was to be the Museum Complex, or 'Albertopolis' as it was known to its detractors. It was said of the Prince that 'it is to his energy and judgement that the world owes both the original design and its harmonious and rapid execution.'[2] Prince Albert was an industrious and far-sighted man, interested in both the arts and sciences, and, during the years he was married to Queen Victoria, he worked hard to try to help reconcile

1 Hyde Park Historical Survey, Land Use Consultants, London, 1981.

2 Hermoine Hobhouse, *A Quartier Latin of a Dignified and Popular Sort* (Templegate Publishing Limited), V & A Album 2, 1983, p. 367.

the conflicting ideologies of modernization and tradition that were of particular concern to the upper classes. In a speech he made at the Mansion House in 1850, he observed that no-one who 'paid attention to the particular features of our present era, will doubt for a moment that we are living in a period of most wonderful transition, which tends rapidly to accomplish that great end, to which, indeed, all history points – the realization of the unity of mankind.'[1] It has been suggested that the Prince's inspiration for the Museum Complex could have come from the 'complex of university and museums at Munich laid out by von Klenze; in its breadth of scale and comprehensive nature it was much grander than any other contemporary scheme for an educational foundation in England.'[2]

Before the doors of The Great Exhibition closed, the Prince was already planning the Museum Complex, and in 1853 a site was purchased for it. The revenue from The Great Exhibition was doubled by the government, and in August of that year the Prince set out his intentions for the site in a memorandum and plan. Approximately eighty-six acres of land were bought for the purpose, extending south from Hyde Park to the village of Brompton, west of central London. The area was to be centred on the Brompton Road, and a three-hundred-yard approach along the Cromwell Road would lead to a group of museums, with the South Kensington Museum (renamed the Victoria and Albert Museum in 1899) as its principal building. It was also hoped that the National Gallery would relocate to the site now occupied by the Albert Hall, but the directors refused to move from their home in Trafalgar Square. A committee was set up to organize the museums plan. Henry Cole (1808-1882), who had been an invaluable, hard-working stalwart of The Great Exhibition planning committee, was to prove his worth in the creation of the new complex. He had the necessary energy and drive to match the Prince's own, and was to be instrumental in the creation of the South Kensington Museum in particular. In 1852 the Department of Science and Art was established, headed by Henry Cole, Lyon Playfair (who became head of the Science Department) and Richard Redgrave (who was the Inspector of Art). Under their auspices the South Kensington Museum collection was built up.[3]

In 1858, Her Majesty's Commissioners for the Exhibition were appointed, and the Horticultural Society requested twenty acres of land for flower shows in the capital. The Society had been formed in 1804, mainly for the benefit of the aristocracy and landed gentry, by a small group of men, which included John Wedgwood and Sir Joseph Banks. Their request was wise, for the Prince's interest revived their flagging financial fortunes. Their total liabilities at the time were £10,752; but by 1860 this had dropped to £4,295. From the beginning of that year, 801 new fellows had been enrolled. In 1858 Prince Albert became President of the Horticultural Society, and a new Charter transformed them into the Royal Horticultural Society.[4] On 8 July 1859 it was agreed

1 *Ibid.*
2 *Ibid.*
3 *Ibid.*, p. 373.
4 H.R. Fletcher, *The Story of the Royal Horticultural Society 1804–1969* (Oxford University Press, 1969), p. 191.

that an area of land in the Museum Complex should be allotted to them. This granted the Society a lease of ground for thirty-one years at a cost of £50,000. In turn they would be responsible for laying out the grounds at an equal cost. It was proposed that the gardens should be at the heart of the complex, surrounded by museums representing trade, patented inventions, art and industry, together with colleges of Art and Science. A twenty-two-and-a-half acre site was earmarked for the garden adjacent to the current location of the Albert Hall. William was chosen by Prince Albert and Henry Cole to undertake the detailed horticultural layout of the new garden, and on 1 May 1860 he appeared before the Committee in the Museum of Science and Art with his detailed designs for the gardens.[1] Francis Fowke and Sydney Smirke were engaged as architects, Godfrey Sykes and Joseph Durham as sculptors, and George Eyles, previously foreman at The Great Exhibition site, was engaged as foreman and eventual superintendent. Prince Albert took a great interest in the gardens and made regular visits to the site as the work progressed: 'Nothing in any part relating to art was done without his personal inspection and approval, and in at least one instance, being dissatisfied with what had been done, he ordered it be altered at his own cost'.[2] The Prince's interest in Italianate design was well-known: he had chosen the style for his own gardens at Osborne on the Isle of Wight, which he and Queen Victoria had acquired in May 1845. The gardens there had been laid out by Ludwig Gruner of Dresden, the Prince's art adviser, under the Prince's close supervision. Osborne has been described as a villa looking back to the Italian Renaissance, and it certainly contained Italianate elements including terraces, balustrading, statuary, fountains, and two large Medici Lions which had been recast from ones seen by the Prince in Florence. Nevertheless, the gardens at Osborne were a strictly Victorian interpretation in the tradition of Thomas Hope's Deepdene, which Loudon, in his *Encyclopaedia of Cottage, Farm and Villa Architecture* of 1833, had hailed as: 'the finest example in England of an Italian villa united with the grounds by architectural appendages.'[3] The Prince made it clear that he hoped the gardens at Kensington Gore would be in an Italian or Palladian style when the architectural structure was put in place. Not surprisingly, the architects endeavoured to comply with his request. This must have been a problem on a relatively small, flat site in London: key features of the Italian Renaissance garden were steeply descending terraces, the use of mechanical devices, grottoes and cascading water features. Nevertheless, the effect was partially achieved with the construction of a cast-iron conservatory designed by Frances Fowke, which had a

1 The Survey of London XXXVIII, *The Museum Area of South Kensington and Westminster*, published for the Greater London Council, 1975, pp. 93 and 127: 'The Prince and Cole were content to settle for W.A. Nesfield, Barry's favourite Italianate gardener, to do the detailed horticultural layout . . . The Prince and Cole both thought the formalist landscape gardener W.A. Nesfield suitable, and the Society engaged him. The Prince had been appointed Colonel-in-Chief to the Rifle Brigade in September 1852, on the death of the Duke of Wellington. This was Nesfield's old Regiment, a factor which could have added to the rapport between the two men.'

2 H.R. Fletcher, *The Story of the Royal Horticultural Society 1804-1969*, p. 191.

3 Roy Strong, *Royal Gardens* (BCA and Conran Octopus Limited, 1992), p. 211.

tessellated mosaic floor of Minton tiles based on Pompeian, early Italian and Renaissance models, and which included a copy of the altar slab from Santa Maria in Trastevere in Rome. A series of arcades were built, representing fifteenth century Milanese brickwork: a Byzantine-style Lateran model and an arcade based on details from the Villa Albani.[1] This meant that the architectural structure within which William was required to lay out his designs was already in place when he was called in. The restraints imposed on him as part of a team, working within the remit of a Committee was not something he was accustomed to, as his private clients usually gave him a free hand to develop his schemes, whilst overseeing the appointment of a head gardener to ensure that his designs were kept in pristine order. However, Kensington was an important commission and one to which the public would have access. Therefore, although he did raise certain objections, especially to the installation of canals, which were not even Italianate in style, but Dutch, he was overruled. When the garden was later criticized after Prince Albert's death by some members of the public for its lack of flowers and shelter, the Kensington Garden Committee consulted William about alterations. He was quick to point out that they had originally rejected some of his suggestions.[2]

In a series of articles in the *Gardeners' Chronicle and Agricultural Gazette*, the first of which appeared on 26 April 1862, William wrote about the embroidered compartments he had designed for the gardens at Kensington, whilst George Eyles described the method used for laying out and maintaining these beds. He emphasised the danger of 'baldness', which resulted in monotony, and which should be avoided in the flower garden. Kensington Gore gardens were no exception: 'cutting beds upon Grass, either rectangular, circular, or tortuous which although effective during the flowering season, are yet wretchedly bald and unmeaning in our long winters'. This resulted in 'green as opposed to green (i.e. Grass and permanent shrubs).'[3] Therefore, although he conceded dwarf evergreens such as aubuca, holly, and Portugal laurels applied to the scene in winter were better than nothing, his solution was to use them sparingly in combination with gravel, spar and slate. He also designed four beds entirely of gravel and box, presumably as a gesture towards the Italianate style, where flowers were rarely used in *parterres*. He also included a maze, which suggested the gardens of Elizabethan England rather than Italy.

The initial response to the gardens was a favourable one, the garden writer Donald Beaton, announcing that: 'I should hail the flowing lines of Mr Nesfield, at Kensington Gore, as the best auxiliaries to what I have myself been aiming at in my doings and sayings for the last twenty years . . . I never yet saw flower gardening carried on in such high order.'[4] The opening of the gardens was to be the occasion of Prince Albert's last public appearance in London before his untimely death in December of that year. His demise was a tragic loss not only to the nation, but to the South Kensington project, for

1 Brent Elliott, *Victorian Gardens* (B.T. Batsford Limited, 1986), p. 141.
2 *Ibid.*, p. 143.
3 *Gardeners Chronicle and Agricultural Gazette*, Saturday 26 April 1862.
4 *Journal of Horticulture*, I, 1861, pp. 373-5.

once his influence, firm hand, attention to detail, enthusiasm and vigour were removed, factions soon began to develop within the Committee. By the mid-1860s an adverse reaction was under way: there were disputes over the rent and in 1882, the year after William's death, the garden came under the direct management of the Commissioners, although the Royal Horticultural Society did not vacate the site until 1889. The garden was eventually swept away to make way for the Science Museum and Imperial Institute.

In 1861, the year that the Royal Horticultural Society's garden was opened, William received what must have been one of the most enjoyable commissions of his career, at Regent's Park near the Nesfields' family home in York Terrace. By this time he had been joined in his business by his second son, Arthur Markham (1841-1874), who was making a name for himself as a talented garden designer. Eden too was to play his part in this project. It is a work that has endured, having undergone a very comprehensive restoration programme.[1]

The development of urban parks for the public was a Victorian phenomenon, and was seen as a social necessity. After the end of the Napoleonic Wars there had been a vast growth in population, coupled with rapid and unplanned urban development. Therefore, by the time Queen Victoria came to the throne in 1837, the overcrowding, poverty and squalor associated with the poorer parts of the country were becoming more obvious. These conditions resulted in growing unrest and unruly behaviour, for although in London there had been a tradition for generations of public access to open spaces, especially in the Royal Parks for walking and, in the case of Hyde Park, for riding, these spaces were not available to the poor, living in the over-crowded areas of east London. In 1833 the Select Committee for Public Walks confirmed that there had been a substantial loss of recreation areas available to the general public in major towns, and set in motion an operation to provide them for the benefit of the poor, not only in London but across the country. This was not an altogether altruistic measure, for it was hoped the recommendation would help to diffuse social tensions by providing physical, moral and educational benefits. There was also the possible added incentive that recreation areas could provide financial investment for entrepreneurs. The availability of fresh air to improve the health of the poor city dweller would also, it was hoped, stop the spread of disease, which was no respecter of persons and could spread from the slums to the more affluent areas of cities and towns. Manchester was one of the first places to organize a plan of action. In 1844 a large public meeting took place in the town hall where it was agreed that the acquisition of parks for exercise and active sports, 'would contribute greatly to the health, rational enjoyment, kindly intercourse, and good morals for all classes of our industrious population.'[2]

Originally, parks were associated with open spaces for walking and recreation; but

1 In the 1990s the Avenue Gardens were sympathetically restored by the Royal Parks Department, together with the landscape architects Land Use Consultants, London.

2 Hazel Conway, *People's Parks: The Design and Development of Victorian Parks in Britain* (Cambridge University Press, 1991), p. 50.

when William became involved he promoted the addition of complex geometric beds incorporating colourful floral displays, an important new departure. This horticultural notion did not become universally popular in municipal parks until the last quarter of the nineteenth century. In the 1850s in Hyde Park, 30,000 bedding plants were laid out along the eastern avenue by William and Markham Nesfield.[1] The Nesfields, therefore, can be credited as being the first to copy the floral displays which had hitherto been the prerogative of large private gardens in public parks. The presence of floral displays in the centre of the city meant that poorer members of society could also enjoy displays of spring and summer bedding. However, there were vested interests who were opposed to the notion of flower gardens in public parks. For example, Joseph Paxton contested the idea in Parliament, possibly because he thought it would deter people from travelling to Sydenham, where the Crystal Palace had been re-erected, and where elaborate gardens were used as focal points. Sydenham was not a municipal park, and an entrance fee was required.

Until the eighteenth century the area which became known as Regent's Park had been part of the Marylebone Estate, the property of the Crown, to which it again reverted in 1803 'after being leased to the Duke of Portland who also owned the land to the south and north of the park.'[2] By 1809 it was felt necessary that a main thoroughfare should be laid out to link the estate with the city, and 500 acres of undeveloped land was earmarked for a new housing estate. A competition was organized to design the new thoroughfare, but none of the entries were acceptable to the Committee. Ultimately, the commission was offered to John Nash (1752-1835), a lake was excavated, the ground re-modelled and planning of the site got underway. As part of the scheme a small palace or 'guignette' was proposed for the Prince Regent (the future George IV). Although this was never built, an avenue intended to lead to the palace, intersected by a Broad Walk, was constructed. Originally, Regent's Park had been planned as a 'fashionable residential estate set in extensive private parkland and occupied by wealthy merchants and professional people.'[3]

Regent's Park was partially opened to the public in 1835, and in 1851 the parkland of Regent's Park and Primrose Hill was transferred by means of the Crown Land Act from the management of the Commissioners of Woods, Forests and Land Revenues, Works and Buildings to the newly formed Ministry of Works.[4] In January 1861, William's professional advice was sought in regard to the removal of existing trees from the southerly end of the lower section of the Broad Walk. He recommended that as some of the horse chestnuts, which were stunted to such an extent that they could not be saved, should be removed. In December of that year he put forward a plan for 'dressed ground in a geometric arrangement',[5] and was asked to undertake this work. In January 1863

1 *Gardeners Chronicle*, 1868, p. 941. Also Land Use Consultants, London.

2 Ann Saunders, *Regent's Park: A Study of the Development of the Area from 1086 to the Present Day* (David & Charles, Newton Abbot, 1969), p. 61.

3 J. Summerson, *The Royal Parks Survey*, Directorate of Ancient Monuments and Historic Buildings, Department of the Environment, 1981, pp. 56-60.

4 Crown Estate Commission, Crown Land Act, 1851.

5 Public Record Office Work 16-168 & Work 16/33/9 1-4.

his plans were approved by the Office of Works. His design consisted of strictly formal planting within a strong structure of straight vistas and axes, with stonework in the shape of tazzas and urns. The area was conceived as a promenade along which many people were to pass daily. Long, relatively narrow beds, with many brightly coloured flowers, were set out and into these beds he introduced coloured gravels, box and topiarized evergreens. The design was a departure from the sophisticated *parterres* he provided for his private clients, and many of them can be classed as simple flowerbeds. The pattern rhythms were linear, intended to lend variety and interest to the public as they walked up and down the central avenue. Whilst the beds were strictly formal, they were not designed to reflect one another symmetrically across the avenue. When the design was put in place it must have had a strong appeal for the large numbers of people who passed along it daily, especially those who came from the poorer areas of London.

> The project was said to have been: a characteristic development for the period being a public garden, intricate in layout and planting design. . . . The Chestnut Avenue of the Broad Walk was thinned and retained and on either side were gravelled walks, box or stone edged flowerbeds, high vases combining to create an Italian-style garden. Turfed areas were surrounded by low railings and neatly clipped hedges and Lombardy poplars lined the straight walk. It was an intricate design of a complexity which satisfied the Victorian taste.[1]

An important component within the garden was a large cable frieze consisting of six circles containing one type of bedding, each circle surrounded by a ribbon of Verbena Purple King and edged with *Cerastium*.[2] These friezes or embroidered compartments were popular in the 1850s, and were devices which William used to great effect in a number of his gardens (for example at Stoke Edith in Herefordshire and Tregothnan in Cornwall). The origin of these friezes can be traced to Italy, where the pattern was used in stone for church floors. An example of a reproduction can be seen in the Cosmati Pavement at Westminster Abbey in London.

The gardens were laid out within four existing rows of trees. A row of wych elms formed the outer edge, and on the inner was a row of horse chestnuts. They were set on a square grid with an inner avenue of poplars in the north and south compartments of both the west and east sides. The gardens consisted of gravelled paths bounded by turf panels, in which were planted formal beds and individual specimen shrubs, for the display of summer bedding and spring bulbs. They were edged with ornamental iron railings supplied by Hill & Smith, and the plants were provided by James Veitch of Chelsea. Twenty-four curved flowerbeds, eight large tazzas (five feet in diameter with pedestals), eight upright vases with pedestals (to stand about seven feet high, both to contain flowers), four ornamental kerbs to surround circular beds and a large lion tazza to act as the centrepiece to the gardens were bought from the artificial stone works of Austin and Seeley & Company of 371-375 Euston Road, London.

1 The Regent's Park and Primrose Hill Royal Parks Survey, July 1981, p. 31.
2 William Nesfield's plan is in the Public Record Office Works 16/33/8/13.

By June 1863, the western side of the garden was complete. The eastern side was finished in August, and the whole scheme completed by the winter of 1863-1864. Eden had designed a small lodge house in the Old English style as a terminus to the garden in 1864, and was seen, attired in a blue smock like those worn by French artisans, busily incorporating green bottle tops into the windows of the lodge.[1] It was said of this little building: 'with its handsome gables and verandas nestling among the trees, it will form an elegant finish to the vista in the western garden looking southwards'. [2] Unfortunately, the Lodge was destroyed in a bombing raid during World War II.

Two years after the completion of the Avenue Gardens, Markham Nesfield designed an additional garden to the east of the Avenue Gardens. It was known as the Coliseum Garden, but was described by Markham on his plan as a 'Picturesque Shrubbery'. Here Markham planted over 150 plants, both evergreen and deciduous, and incorporated a water garden. Markham, like Eden, travelled extensively on the continent, examining and recording gardens and nurseries. Whilst he was travelling in France and Holland he would have become aware of the architect and gardener Jean-Pierre Barillet-Deschamps' (1824-1875) work in introducing exotic specimens into his designs. In 1860 Barillet was made chief gardener to the city of Paris and designed the Bois de Vincennes in the Champ Elyssées and Park Monceau, and provided plans for the Bois de Boulogne and the Paris Exhibition of 1867.

The caption on Markham's Sketch Plan for the Picturesque Shrubbery reads:

No.1 Concentrated display of all the new foliage plants as they are brought out by Mr Barillet:

No.2 Evergreen and Deciduous plantings of Arbutus, Rhododendron, Laurestinus, Ilex, Mahonia and Aucuba yellow and green, etc. Snowdrop Tree, Sophera, Cotoneaster, Thorn, Acacia, Laburnum, Apple, Pear and Plum Trees, etc. etc.

No.3 Water Garden – sides wattled with osier work and on its north side and near termination of mound. To be filled with waterlillies, the Bull Rush, Egyptian Rush, etc. and all common weeds, with ferns, forget-me-not and wood ivy and periwinkle. margining the banks (N.B. All water plants to be grown in it)

No.4 Large Mound to give an undulation of the surface and relieve its monotony.

Markham was gradually taking over from his father and by the late 1860s was indispensable to him, especially as William's surveyor, James Howe, left to set up his own business in Ireland. Therefore, although William was responsible for drawing up the original plans and plantings for the Avenue Gardens, it was Markham, whom he described as his 'clever and deserving son', who produced the planting plans after the first year. These survive for 1864, 1866, 1867 and 1869.[3]

1 Andrew Saint, *Richard Norman Shaw* (Yale University Press, 1983), p. 45.
2 *Gardeners Chronicle and Agricultural Gazette*, 17 September 1864, p. 890.
3 Arthur Markham Nesfield's plans and plantings are in the Nesfield Archives.

16.

The End of an Era

Prestigious commissions at Regent's Park, Witley Court and Crewe Hall helped maintain William's reputation into the late 1860s and early 1870s. Continuing interest in his designs is demonstrated by an article relating to Woolverstone Hall in Suffolk, which appeared in the *Gardeners Chronicle and Agricultural Gazette* as late as February 1869. At the time the writer recorded that he had never seen: 'a happier combination of Box embroidery, flowering plants, gravel and Grass than in the garden at Woolverstone. It is perfect of its kind.' Woolverstone had been built around 1776 for the Berners family, who still owned the estate when William was called in. The scheme consisted of a large *parterre-de-broderie* which was almost circular in shape, with liminal scrolls on each side of a central ray. The dominant feature of the design was a statue set in a water basin, and colourful bedding plants in blocks of one colour were also used. The whole scheme was axially aligned to the mansion and approached by steps which led down to a gravelled terrace walk, the whole bounded by beds of evergreen shrubs, rhododendrons and azaleas.

Unfortunately in 1874, at the age of thirty-three, Markham was killed whilst travelling towards St John's Wood in London. His horse bolted and he died almost instantly.[1] It was a devastating blow for his family. In 1866 he had married Fanny Catherine (Kate) Powell of Milton Heath, Dorking and they had five children: Avila and Lilian, who both died young, Bertram, Margaret and Dorothy.[2] After Markham's death William made

1 See Arthur Markham Nesfield's Obituary in *The Garden*, 20 June 1874, p. 538.
'We deeply regret to announce the death of Mr A. Markham Nesfield, son of Mr Nesfield, the distinguished painter and landscape gardener, and well-known to many of our readers. He was riding from his house, in Dorset Square, in the direction of the Regent's Park, and when near the Hanover Gate his horse ran away, carrying him in the direction of St John's Wood; on entering the St John's Wood Road he was thrown and killed almost instantaneously, the horse kicking him in the head. He had for the past ten years or so carried on the practice of landscape gardening, succeeding to his father's business, and was in the front rank of his profession. He was only in his thirty-third year.'

2 Markham heard of Avila's birth whilst he was undertaking a commission on the Tehidy Estate in south-west Cornwall. See his diary, Nesfield Archives.

Parterre Design for Woolverstone Hall, Suffolk.

Planting Plan: 1. Coleus Verschaffeltii; 2. Bijou Pelargonium; 3. Purple King Verbena; 4. Indian Yellow Pelargonium; 5. Andre Verbena, circle of Aurea Floribunda Calceolaria; 6. Lady Middleton Pelargonium; 7. Orange Nosegay Pelargonium; 8. Flower of the Day Pelargonium; 9. Stella Pelargonium; 11. Amaranthus melancholleus; 12. Mrs Pollock Pelargonium; 13. Purple King Verbena; 14. Centauro eau viridissima; 15. Christine Pelargonium; 16. Ariosto Verbena edged with Golden Chain Pelargonium; 18. Calceolaria aurea verschaffeltii; 22. Golden Chain Pelargonium; 23. Lobelia speciosa.

a will leaving everything to Eden. Kate and the children went to live at 8 Rose Hill, Dorking, so that she could be close to her own family. William kept in close touch with them and loved them all, especially Bertram, his grandson. A few months before he died he wrote to her:

> Dearest K. Your report on the two dear lambs (read this morn) proves what a kind old girl you are, for endeavouring to cheer me. Altho' Daisy (Dorothy) seems better I cannot but fear she must be a delicate plant, requiring more than ordinary attention in a sanitary sense, and altho' first rate medical advice is desirable my faith rests

> more on proper diet and cheerful recreation than physic but you are so awake for the welfare of your pets, I fervently hope you will find some promising discipline to promote more constitutional strength. Altho' our weather, of late, has been mild it does not equal what you describe in Dorking, in as much as we have thick fog every morning, sometimes all day, but my misery does not decrease, I seldom venture out. . . . As to dear Bertie [Bertram], I hope you will contrive to bring him here, if only for a few days especially, as Harry can pilot him to see sights etc. Should he require winter clothing, he must go to Hyam's and the needful shall not be wanting. . . . Harry unites with me in best love. I remain Ever affectionately yours.[1]

Although Eden had moved into another office at 19 Margaret Street, Cavendish Square in 1876 he remained in the family home until his father's death. In 1872 he was asked to submit plans for additions and alterations to a 1690s Welsh mansion, Bodrhyddan Hall, near Abergele in North Wales, owned by Captain Conwy Grenville Hercules Rowley-Conwy, who would have known of the Nesfields work on the nearby Kinmel estate. Eden's work at Bodrhyddan Hall demonstrates his mastery of the art of the Queen Anne Revival style. In addition to the work on the manor house, an intricate scroll-pattern *parterre* with a central fountain, surrounded by clipped evergreens, was laid out in the garden. Unfortunately all the plans were lost in a fire at Bodrhyddan, but it must have been William's hand that can be seen in the designs for the *parterre-de-broderie.* Fortunately, this combination of mansion and garden remains virtually unchanged today, the only remaining complete collaboration between the two men.

When William died on 3 March 1881, Eden was with him. In a letter to Frederick Bullock of Radwinter, he said: 'Had the privilege of 24 hours with the dear old Dad's last moments – his hand in mine his end was very peaceful.'[2]

William must have had his fair share of financial worries, especially when his four sons were being educated at Eton College, and he probably felt some disappointment that his two younger sons did not pursue the careers he had planned for them.[3] Nevertheless,

1 William Henry ('Harry') Nesfield was the black sheep of the family who had persuaded his brother, David, to join him in an unsuccessful sheep farming venture in Australia and New Zealand. By January 1881 Henry was travelling once again, his father wrote to Osbert Salvin (Anthony's son) on 16 January: 'Harry departed a week ago for Egypt and must now be about the Bay of Biscay. Although I cannot but despair (at my age) of ever greeting him again in this world of trouble, yet am consoled by being told that his secular welfare will be much enhanced by the experience. So I must grin and tolerate his unpalatable absence with equanimity.' I am grateful to Sybil Rampden for this information.

2 *A Deuce of an Uproar*, p. 287, William Eden Nesfield's letter to the Reverend Frederick Bullock, 17 August 1881.

3 David Nesfield was an accomplished pianist but he became estranged from his family. He relinquished his training to read for the Bar, and on 29 May 1865 he arrived in Australia, where he had a spell in what he called 'theatricals'; a fiasco according to his later account. He then decided to carry on with his training to become a Barrister. He wrote to his elder brother, Markham and told him that he was working for a Barrister who gave him 25/- per week for drafting, plus three rooms, wood and lighting. He also took pupils for piano lessons. He intended to settle down to work towards being admitted to the

in many ways he had led a charmed life. He had spent many years travelling in some of the most beautiful areas in the British Isles, whilst contributing to the landscape on the estates of his wealthy clients, and throughout his long career had been well regarded by most of his clients.

Two statements, one written at the beginning of his career, and one near the end, confirm this. The first was written on 4 November 1841 by Katherine Clarendon of The Grove, Rickmansworth in Hertfordshire, who said: 'When he [Nesfield] does come I mean to ask Tom to meet him for it would be a great thing to have a person of that gentleman's exquisite taste at one's elbow & I have no doubt he will be good natured & run down per Rail and Back again.'[1] In 1869 Alexander Forsyth, the head gardener at Alton Towers in Staffordshire, wrote in an article in the *Gardeners Chronicle*:

> After fruitless attempts had been made by Lord and Lady Shrewsbury to agree about cutting down overgrown trees, &c., at Alton Towers, it was arranged that W.A. Nesfield, Esq., the eminent landscape gardener, should be called in, and that his decision (to use a law phrase) should be final and binding on both parties. This gentleman was particularly fitted for such a task, being a landscape painter, as he could strike off at a heat the thing as it then was.[2]

William was a product of his class, upbringing, his education and his place within the family hierarchy. He was what would now be considered as a man of his time: a true Victorian, hardworking, somewhat pompous, unshakeable in his belief that his philosophy was the right one, self-confident and self-reliant. After his father's death Eden moved to Delahay Street, and then to 6 Waverley Place, St John's Wood (which had been the home of James Duffield Harding), and although he continued to undertake a select number of architectural commissions, mainly for people he knew well, the deep commitment he had felt in the early years to his craft was no longer there. Once his brother and father had died, it became apparent how important the special relationship between client and the family firm had been to him. A good example of their interplay

---

Bar in 1872, but the rules for admission of Colonial Barristers differed greatly from those of the English Bar. He asked for £100 to be sent to him so that he could commence his studies. Unfortunately, before it arrived, his younger brother Henry persuaded him to throw in his lot with him and farm sheep in New Zealand. In order to do this Markham was asked to sell David's reversion and pay the proceeds into the Union Bank of Australia; this was money his father had provided for his sons during his lifetime and amounted to £1,200. The venture was a failure and David eventually emigrated to America.

Henry was initially sent to Germany to acquire a knowledge of the language so he could enter the Civil Service. However, this did not work out and he spent a short of period time in a ship-broking firm in Leadenhall Street. He said he was not cut out for a life devoted to business – his ideas of this being as vague as his father's! So he travelled to Australia and New Zealand. (Nesfield Archives.)

Henry Nesfield wrote: *A Chequered Career: 15 Years in New Zealand and Australia* (1881), Bodleian Libraries, Oxford.

1 Correspondence of Katherine Clarendon and Mrs George Villiers, 1839-55, 7 June 1841, 4 Nov. 1841. Manuscript English c. 2141, fols. 112-115, Bodleian Libraries, University of Oxford.

2 *Gardeners Chronicle*, 1869, p. 416.

View towards Brodick Castle, watercolour by William Nesfield.

Brodick Bay, Isle of Arran, watercolour by William Nesfield.

Bodrhyddan Hall and *Parterre*, North Wales.

Bodrhyddan Hall *Parterre*, North Wales.

of connections can be seen at Broadlands in Romsey, Hampshire. Eden's client was the Rt Hon. William Francis Cowper-Temple (later 1st Baron Mount Temple). He was the first Commissioner of Works and Buildings, and William, Eden and Markham had all received commissions through his recommendation. It was through Cowper Temple's patronage that William and Markham obtained the commission for the planting schemes they carried out in the London Parks. The commission Eden received to design the Lodge House at Regent's Park was also at Cowper Temple's behest All three worked on his Broadlands estate, where Eden designed two lodge houses: Southampton Lodge in 1866, which has half-timbering, leaded windows, moulded plasterwork and an iron sunflower on the main gable; and another lodge in 1868. He also designed a group of cottages known as Lee Cottages in 1870, and an Orangery. In 1872 he built a Boys' Grammar School and Headmaster's house in Romsey. In 1878 he designed a very picturesque villa on the cliffs at Babbacombe as a holiday home for Lady Mount-Temple. When the house was built, Babbacombe was a small fishing village and watering place for the rich. In its day it must have been idyllic. The villa is a mixture of Tudor and Gothic, two storeys high with large gabled dormers. It is built according to an L-shaped plan, with characteristic tall brick chimneys and an arched entrance way. To the left of the entrance the ground floor is of stone with mullioned windows and leaded lights. The first floor is slate-hung on two storeys, with an oriel window rising into the roof. A side opening within the archway gives a breath-taking framed view of the sea and a path runs from the courtyard to the sea. The plans show that an inglenook was intended for one of the rooms, but this was either never executed or has since been removed. Today the villa is a hotel and very little of his internal work remains except for some Minton tiles in the porch and oak panelling. In many ways Eden was his own worst enemy, for his working methods meant that a revival of interest in all things Victorian in the mid twentieth-century led to Shaw's contribution to architectural design coming to the attention of historians rather than Eden's. Eden's all-or-nothing approach to his work, his distaste for publicity, and reluctance to allow his work to be published contributed to it being overlooked. Also, his relatively early retirement and death meant that he did not produce as much as Shaw. Yet when they first went into partnership together Shaw is reputed to have said to Eden: 'You do the designing, I'll do the donkey work',[1] demonstrating the regard he had for Eden's skill as an innovator and designer. Shaw, however, was also aware that Eden's mercurial personality did not enable him to cope with the everyday, mundane commitments that were necessary to run a busy office.[2] In 1877 Eden wrote to Mrs Walker, the wife of his client at Lea Wood in Derbyshire: 'Personal work is very difficult and I think

1 I am grateful to Robert Markham Nesfield for this information.

2 Eden was over-indulged by both his parents. A letter from Emma to her mother, dated Bath 26 December 1839, indicates that he was a fat, greedy baby whose digestive powers were weakened because he ate too much and too quickly and her mother's reply, dated Bath, which she considered to be more beneficial than medicine, was to try the Bath waters, which had produced great changes in Emma's own digestive powers many times. Nesfield Archives.

becomes more so in one's sere and yellow. It used to be so nice.'[1] He was, however, undoubtedly highly regarded in his day, and the following assessments give a fair indication of how he was perceived by his contemporaries. The poet Simeon Solomon claimed he was: 'one of our very best architects, a man of great knowledge, invention, and consummate amiability, he is a fat, jolly hearty fellow, genuinely good natured, very fond of smoking, and I deeply grieve to say of women.'[2] The other comment, written by the stonemason and carver James Forsyth, who worked with both of the Nesfields over the years on a number of commissions, claimed that: 'Of all the members of the architectural profession who have flourished during the last 50 years, few have left a greater mark or created more influence on modern English domestic work than the late William Eden Nesfield, not so much by the number of his works, as by originality of conception, refinement and delicacy of detail, and his power of obtaining extremely artistic results.'[3]

One of Eden's last letters was to Frederick Bullock, and is worth quoting in full as it explains his state of mind in 1885 and how deep his disillusionment with his profession was by this time. It is sad that work that had meant so much was so little regarded by him at the end. The letter was written a year before his marriage to Mary Annetta Blackwell, the daughter of John Sebastian Gwilt. She was, a divorcee whom, it is reputed, he married in order to make an honest woman of her! They went to live at 45 Buckingham Road in Brighton.

> First let me thank you, old friend, for the very kind expression you are pleased my hand writing called forth. I know, or conscience tells me, there is a gentle rebuke conveyed which I richly deserve. Thanks for cheque, I had forgotten about it, but on reference to my office books find it is correct & enclose receipt. I had many heart burnings about that shifty little beast Whiffin. It was really up hill work to get any righteousness out of him, although he frequently asserted that the Lord was his might & his protection. The fact is that next to Attorneys Builders are the most cunning of scamps. I did all in my power to get those cottages well built. I gave Whiffin two large jobs really as his own (or nearly so) valuation. Lord Mount Temple's & Hampton in Arden for Sir F. Peel some 10 or £12000. The trouble and anxiety at both was considerable. The pious little beggar failed but I have strong reasons for thinking at an opportune moment as he did not liquidate until all accs were settled as far as I was concerned, & Ld. M.T. made him a present of £150 – just like him, but then he is a rich man with no incumbrances beyond his watch key. Bell is really no better, the worry I had to get Lea Wood properly built was heart breaking & then we had litigation. To sum up the pitiful condition of things as

1 Andrew Saint, *Richard Norman Shaw* (Yale University Press, 1976) p.51.

2 Simeon Solomon to Algernon Swinburne, from the Saracen's Head, Beddgelert, c. 1869, British Museum.

3 James Forsyth, *Architectural Association Notes*, August 1901. As a compliment to the Nesfields James Forsyth named his son James Nesfield Forsyth.

> practiced by shirking & crafty builders in this latter end of our century, I must say that from the day a contract is signed to the closing of accs all a contractor aims at, is scanty work and large extras, & to get 10 per cent more on his bargain. Clerks of works are in 99 cases open to backsheesh in some form or other – & even if honest, a sappy joist is turned topsy turvey & shoved into a floor when his back is turned or some old mortar mixed into the new soup – weary work Sir. I look back on my professional career with wonder that so noble an occupation is mixed up with such a blaguardly crew, & that Hanwell had not opened its doors to me 10 years since. I have been invalid for the last 2 years & away – left Delahay St 18 or 20 months since. My friend Mileham Essex Street Strand has looked after work which has been imperative. I am all right now and principally occupy myself with painting which I am passionately fond of.[1]

On 25 March 1888, Eden died in Brighton of cirrhosis of the liver, at only fifty-three years old. It is probably fair to say that the high life had at last caught up with him.[2]

Art and painting were the defining influences upon the works of both Nesfields. William can perhaps best be described as an artist who became a landscape designer, not a landscape designer who happened to be an artist. In the past he has been dismissed as a 'mere builder of *parterres*' who copied from the work of others. This is a simplification and a complete misunderstanding of the ethos that lay at the core of his work. Apart from possessing the obvious skills needed to lay out *parterres-de-broderie*, he was an artist who did not consider it anomalous to juxtapose the strictly formal and the naturalistic. To his artistic eye, both natural landscapes and artificial gardens were seen as beautiful pictures. His work was guided by a strong sense of the appropriate. In his opinion, man-made gardens should be formal and not attempt to hide their artifice. Outlying landscape, however, should be as naturalistic as a painter of rural scenery could conceive.

> Eden's need to express his individuality was what drove him on, and when he could no longer apply it to his architecture (the excitement he had felt in his early years in experimenting with a variety of architectural styles turned to disillusionment, especially with the workmen he had trusted to carry out his schemes), he retreated to his first love, painting. Eden's underlying melancholic nature came to the fore after his father's death in 1881. This had been submerged during his younger years by outward high spirits, bonhomie and his delight in discovering and making his own a variety of architectural styles. The house at 3 York Terrace was sold, the family had dispersed and Eden, for the first time in his life, no longer had the support and encouragement he had always received from his father and on which he had relied throughout his life. He gave up his practice, although he was only 45, ill health probably adding to his decision.

1 *A Deuce of An Uproar*, letter dated 10 June 1885 from 6 Waverley Place, St John's Wood.
2 Obituary in *The Builder*, J.M. Brydon, 1888.

For both Nesfields, the definition of the Picturesque was that understood by Uvedale Price. William in particular admired the way he merely 'tweaked' the landscape on his estate at Foxley in Herefordshire in order to open up interesting views, whilst retaining ancient woodland, rocks, water and old rutted lanes. William had a romanticized view of old England, fostered by memories of his early years in the village of Brancepeth, which he considered to be completely opposed to the vast open spaces of Lancelot Brown with their wide carriage drives, clumps and belts of trees. His objection to the ha-ha was that it was pretending to be something that it was not. Fences, on the other hand, could be seen. Boundaries were necessary for a variety of reasons but William would argue that fences were doing the opposite of the ha-ha – they avoided artifice. He believed in calling a spade a spade.

The ideals of the Nesfields were the forerunners of those expressed in the Arts and Crafts Movement, pioneered by William Morris (1834-1896). He attempted to return to the traditional crafts of the past in his art and design. These ideals were expressed by painters such as Helen Allingham (1848-1926), who depicted idealized cottage gardens, quaint old buildings and clean and beautiful children in her watercolours. Whilst there have been many artistic revolutions since the Nesfields produced their own particular brand of architectural and landscape gardening styles, an appreciation of beauty and nature does not change. The satisfaction to be gained in the work of skilled craftspeople, an appreciation of beautiful objects, and the notion of nostalgia and romance based on escapism, is as important today as it has ever been.

List of William Andrews Nesfield's Commissions

Editor's Note

By 1866 it becomes apparent from Arthur Markham Nesfield's Diary of Expenditure that in many respects he had taken over the business from his father.

William Andrews Nesfield's commissions are arranged geographically; by county, in alphabetical order. C.M. Refers to William Nesfield having marked the estate on his County Map.

Avon

Claverton Manor, near Bath
Client: Mrs Vivian.
Dates: unknown.
Summary of Work: Plan for a lodge house.
Source: Nesfield Archives. C.M.

Berkshire

Basildon Park, near Reading
Client: James Morrison, M.P.
Dates: 1840 onwards.
Existing Reports: In March 1840, first report for parkland together with recommendations and criticisms.
Source: Nesfield Archives. C.M.

New Lodge, Windsor Park
Client: His Ex. Van de Weyer (son of Belgian Minister married to Georgina, daughter of 2nd Earl of Craven).
Source: Nesfield Archives. C.M.
From 1866 this commission was an important one for Arthur Markham Nesfield.

Sandleford Priory, Newbury
Client: William Charteris.
Source: Nesfield Archives C.M.

South Hill Park
Client: Rt Hon. W.G. Hayton.
Source: Nesfield Archives. C.M.

Tittenhurst Park, near Sunningdale
Client: Mr T. Holloway, M.P.
Source: Nesfield Archives. C.M.

Wellington College
Clients: Queen Victoria, Prince Albert and Lord Edward Smith-Stanley, 14th Earl of Derby.
Dates: October 1856.
Summary of Work: Submitted a plan for the grounds at the College, and there is correspondence between Nesfield, the architect John Shaw and John Chance relating to this commission. Unfortunately, due to lack of funds, it was not implemented.
Sources: The plan and correspondence are in the Royal Archives, Windsor Castle RA PPTO/PPWEL/CSP Box 1. I am grateful to John Phibbs for drawing my attention to these archives.

Breconshire

Treberfydd, Brecon Beacons
Client: Mr Raikes.
Dates: 1852.
Summary of Work: Laid out Garden incorporating the Raikes monogram in the *parterre*.
Existing Plans: Formal garden layout including *parterre*.
Source: Treberfydd Archives.

Buckinghamshire

Addington Manor, near Winslow
Client: Mr J. G. Hubbard (later Baron Addington).
Source: Nesfield Archives C.M.

Clifden
Client: Duke and Duchess of Sutherland.
Summary of Work: Advised on the placing of trees in the landscape, it is not known whether he carried out any work before he was dismissed.
Source: Nesfield Archives C.M.

Latimer Place, Chesham
Client: Lord Charles Cavendish.
Source: Nesfield Archives.

Mentmore Towers, Leighton Buzzard
Client: Baron Mayer Amschel de Rothschild.
Summary of Work: Formal Garden.
Existing Reports: Recommendation for the best site for new mansion, engineering work for the supply of water to the house by Messrs. Easton & Co.
Source: Nesfield Archives; *Gardeners Chronicle*, 17 June 1869, p. 389: 'Nesfield's Italian garden, as good an example of this style as can be found in this country, will soon be finished'.

Taplow Court, near Maidenhead
Client: Mr C.P. Grenfell.
Date: 1858.
Source: A letter of 23 February 1852 from William Nesfield to Mr Grenfell reads: 'I am hampered with quantities of engagements & it is unfortunate that I did not receive earlier notice of your wishes . . . I am to depart for Worcester on Monday & shall have much travelling afterwards with few & short intervals in town till 1st week in May . . . I will send my surveyor – Mr Howe – down during the week, and he will plot the work to be done on paper. . . . I will try and consult with you one day during Easter.' Mr Howe went down to Taplow Court with his theodolite on 14 March 1852. Nesfield Archives. C.M.

Cambridgeshire

Hemingford Grey, near Hemingford Abbots
Client: Dandy Sadler.
Existing Plans: Plan for a *parterre*.
Source: Nesfield Archives

Cheshire

Arley Hall, Great Budworth
Clients: Rowland and Mary Egerton-Warburton.
Dates: 1842 onwards.
Summary of Work: Luggage Approach to the west door of the house. An elaborate *parterre-de-broderie* constructed in the east garden to compliment the family chapel designed by Anthony Salvin and built between 1842 and 1845.
Existing Plans: Detailed plan of proposed *parterre* dated November 1846: Plan labelled '2nd Plan Luggage Approach'.
Source: Arley Hall Archives, where there is also correspondence between William Nesfield and Rowland Egerton-Warburton, together with an additional copy of the plan in the Nesfield Archives C.M.

Betley Court, Betley, near Crewe
Client: Mr Thomas Fletcher-Twemlow.
Dates: 1858.
Existing Plans: Plan dated 1st October 1858 for new entrance at front of house. Staffordshire Record Office, Stafford, D.3098. Not executed.
Source: County Record Office, Stafford D.3098; Professor N. Brown.

Capesthorne Hall, near Macclesfield
Client: Arthur Henry Davenport.
Dates: Not known, but Anthony Salvin virtually rebuilt the Hall after a fire in 1861.
Source: Nesfield Archives C.M.

Carlett Park, Eastham, Wirral
Client: Mr J. Torr.
Dates: 1859.
Source: Nesfield Archives C.M. Abstract of accounts dated September 1859. House demolished.

Combermere Abbey, near Wrenbury
Client: Viscount Combermere.
Summary of Work: Nesfield Archives. The gates and lodge on the south-eastern border of the Park at Combermere are similar to those at Dorfold Hall, but according to the English Heritage Historic Buildings and Ancient Monuments (19 May 1986), Stone Lodge on the south-eastern border of the Park was built to the designs of the Irish firm of Morrison in the 1830s. However, there is a small pencil sketch of trees in the park by William Nesfield and Viscount Combermere carried out alterations during his tenure during the middle years of the nineteenth century (1865). No further information regarding whether William Nesfield carried out any work at Combermere is at present available.

Crewe Hall, Crewe
Client: Lord Crewe.
Dates: 1842 onwards.
Summary of Work: Large formal pleasure ground to the north of the house and a broad walk leading from the eastern *parterres* to the eastern pleasure ground. Boundary walls, gates and entrance courtyard, new access road and avenue to the southern entrance of the house, improvements to the kitchen garden. Extensive work on estate including the cutting and re-siting of trees and the thinning of plantations, the enlargement of the western end of the Park, the planting of shrubs, the screening of the railway embankments to the North Staffordshire Railway line and possibly a tunnel to allow cattle to pass below the terrace to and from Crewe Hall Farm without disturbing the gardens.
Existing Plans: Plan for a small village green at Crewe Green in the vicinity of the Church and Plan of 'North *Parterre*' 1863 and drawing for balustrading and pedestal. Small pencil drawing by William Nesfield of a view down the drive from the tower. Planting Scheme.
Sources: Nesfield Archives; Royal Institute of British Architects; County Records Office, Chester, DCR/15/2 where there is correspondence between William Nesfield and Lord Crewe and initial Report dated February 1842; Land Use Consultants, London.

Dorfold Hall, Nantwich
Client: Wilbraham Spencer Tollemache.
Dates: 1849 and 1861 onwards.
Summary of Work: On William Nesfield's recommendation trees were removed and the avenue straightened to the front of the house and the pond drained and re-aligned. Advised on the building of gates, a lodge, coachhouse and clock tower. Paved the forecourt, installed a carriage sweep in he middle of which was a grass circle with a statue of Mastiff and Pups. At the rear of the property he designed a small *parterre* with liminal scrolls.
Existing Reports: Report on the present state of the accompaniments to Dorfold Hall with propositions for improvement.
Sources: Nesfield Archives; Planting plans are in the Dorfold Archives Mr R. C. Roundell; *Country Life*, 1908, vol. 24, pp. 594-606.

Eaton Hall, Congleton
Little information except it is listed on C.M.

Eaton Hall, Chester
Client: Hugh Lupus Grosvenor 2nd Marquess (1825-1899) created 1st Duke of Westminster 1874.
Dates: Late 1840s onwards.
Summary of Work: Extended garden over part of the area covered by the formal garden of the new eighteenth-century plantations were formed and shaped to enhance the middle distance from the main rooms of the Hall, which took in a framed view of Beeston Castle seven miles away. East of the house were laid out two large, impressive reflecting *parterres-de-broderie* in sunken panels with scrolls and rays outlined in box. In each compartment he incorporated large monogrammed Ws to commemorate Robert Grosvenor (1767-1845), created 1st Marquess of Westminster 1831.
Sources: Nesfield Archives where there is a watercolour entitled *No.9 Working Drawing for the Construction of Embroidery on the main Parterre Eaton Hall* and sketch looking towards Beeston Castle; Eaton Hall Archives; Eaton Hall Gardens OS Map 1911; East Garden *Parterre*, E. Aveno Brooke *Gardens of England* c. 1857.

High Legh, near Knutsford
Client: George Cornwall-Legh.
Existing Reports: Report containing recommendations and criticisms.
Source: Nesfield Archives.

Hooton Hall, Childer Thornton
Client: Mr R. C. Naylor.
Dates: 1854.
Summary of Work: Laid out gardens.
Existing Plans: Plan of a *parterre*.
Source: Nesfield Archives C.M.
House demolished c.1935.

Marbury Hall, Comberbach
Client: James Hugh Smith-Barry.
Dates: Not known but Smith-Barry inherited in 1856 when Anthony Salvin greatly enlarged the house. House demolished in 1969, grounds now a public park.
Source: Nesfield Archives C.M.

Peckforton Castle, near Tarporley
Client: 1st Baron Tollemache.
Dates: Not known, but castle designed by Anthony Salvin between 1844-50.
Source: Nesfield Archives C.M.

Rode Hall, Rode Heath, near Congleton
Client: Mr R. Wilbraham.
Dates: 1861 onwards.
Existing Plans: Plan for a terrace, rose gardens and formal drive leading to the west front of the House and No.1 Skeleton Plan of proposed geometrical treatment of dressed ground on south west and north east fronts of House, etc. March 1861.
Sources: Rode Hall Archives, Nesfield Archives C.M., *Country Life*, May 2 1985.
Arthur Markham Nesfield also worked here.

Tabley House, Tabley Inferior, near Knutsford
Client: 1st Baron de Tabley
Dates: 1843.
Existing Plans: Ground Plan for *parterres* and disposition of dressed ground in connection with the house and alterations to approaches. 1st November 1843.
Sources: Nesfield Archives C.M.
Additional information from the Tabley Hall Collections Trust: The date of 1843 on William Nesfield's plan coincides with the time the 2nd Baron de Tabley made extensive changes to the house, with the original front entrance to the house turned into the Garden Room and a new front door on the north side. Nesfield's plan is aligned north-south and when held in portrait mode it accurately reflects the shape of the building, the bulge being a Palladian-style portico over the old front door.

Toft Hall, Toft
Client: Ralph Gerard Leycester.
Source: Nesfield Archives C.M.

Wythenshawe Hall, Wythenshawe, near Manchester
Client: Mr T. W. Tatton.
Date: 1850s.
Source: Nesfield Archives C.M.

Cornwall

Tregothnan, near Truro
Client: Lord Falmouth.
Summary of Work: Formal garden sited on main rooms of House.
Existing Plans: There are a number of plans in the Estate Office at Tregothnan relating to work undertaken by William and Eden Nesfield; A design for a proposed pedestal for a vase together with a *parterre* in the Nesfield Archives. The *parterre* has recently been reinstated in simplified form.
Source: Nesfield Archives and Tregothnan Estate Office.

Tregrehan House, Par
Client: Edward Carlyon.
Dates: 1845 onwards.
Summary of Work: *Parterre* containing statues, a fountain and formal flower beds. Carriage sweep to the front of the House incorporating the sculpture of a Lion, a play on the family name.
Existing Plans: There are two identical plans for the *parterre*, one at Tregrehan and one in the Nesfield Archives.

Trewithen, near Probus
Client: Christopher Henry Thomas Hawkins.
Dates: 1845.
Summary of Work: Not executed.
Existing Plans: Plan for an Approach and site for a lodge dated 10 May 1845.
Source: Nesfield Archives.

County Durham

Barrock Park, Low Hesket
Client: William James (Powell).
Source: Nesfield Archives. C.M.

Cumberland

Castlerigg Manor, Keswick

Patterdale Hall, near Ambleside
Clients: John Marshall of Castleriggs, M.P. for Leeds, second son of Walter Marshall of Patterdale Hall.
Existing Plans: At Patterdale plan for the lower garden July 1849.
Source: Nesfield Archives. C.M.

Greystoke Castle, near Penrith
Client: Mr H. Howard.
Source: Nesfield Archives. C.M.
Arthur Markham Nesfield also worked here.

Whitehall, Allhallows, Wigton Post Town
Client: Mr G. Moore.
Source: Nesfield Archives C.M.

Derbyshire

Beauchief Abbey, near Broomfield
Client: Mr Burnell.
Source: Nesfield Archives C.M.

Longford Hall, Ashbourne
Client: Thomas William Coke, 2nd Earl of Leicester.
Source: Nesfield Archives C.M.

Osmaston Manor, Osmaston, Ashbourne
Client: Henry T. Wright.
Source: Nesfield Archives C.M.
House demolished 1956.

Shipley Hall, near Ilkeston
Client: Mr Alfred Edward Miller-Mundy.
Summary of Work: Nesfield Archives C.M. Abstract of Professional Accounts September 1859. William Eden Nesfeld designed a farm house, lodge, labourers' cottages and new porch to hall c.1862.

Stancliffe Hall, near Bakewell
Client: Mr Whitworth.
Source: Nesfield Archives C.M.

Sudbury Hall, Ashbourne
Client: Lord Vernon.
Dates: 1852.
Existing Plans: Plan for a *parterre* dated Sept. 1852.
Source: Sudbury Hall Archives.

Wingerworth Hall, Wingerworth
Client: Sir Henry T. Hunloke.
Existing Reports: General observations relative to the defects and improvements at Wingerworth Hall.
Source: Nesfield Archives.
Arthur Markham Nesfield also worked here.
House demolished 1927

Devon

St Marychurch, Torbay
Client: Isambard Kingdom Brunel.
Date: 1848.
Existing Plans: Plan for the layout of a small property and recommendations and criticisms.
Source: Nesfield Archives.

Watcombe Park, Torquay
Client: Isambard Kingdom Brunel.
Date: 1847.
Existing Reports: Report dated 12 February 1985, William Nesfield: 'helped plan the Italian and other gardens round the house-site and the woodlands that sweep dramatically along the hillsides. Many kinds of recently introduced trees were obtained from Veitch and these are now very large.'
Source: Conservation of Historic Parks and Gardens, University of York, and letters and sketch books referring to the estate are held in the University of Bristol Library.

Dorset

Canford Manor, Canford Magna
Client: Sir John Guest.
Existing Plans: Recommendations and criticisms regarding Approaches to the property.
Sources: Nesfield Archives C.M.

Motcombe House, Stalbridge
Client: Marquess of Westminster.
Source: Nesfield Archives C.M.
There is a drawing of the Market Cross, Stalbridge by William Nesfield 31 August 1854.

Pennsylvania Castle, near Penn
Client: William Penn.
Source: Nesfield Archives C.M.

Essex

Birch Hall
Client: Charles G. Round.
Source: Nesfield Archives C.M.
House demolished 1954.

Felix Hall, Kelvedon, Colchester
Client: Mr J.G. Western.
Source: Nesfield Archives C.M.
House demolished 1941.

Forest Hall, Stansted Mountfitchet
Client: J.M. Bramstone-Stone.
Source: Nesfield Archives C.M.

Wivenhoe Park, Colchester
Client: Mr Gordon Rebow.
Source: Land Use Consultants, London have done a survey on the park, and have ascertained that William Nesfield's contribution was a considerable one as he seems to have laid out a large area of the park in addition to advice on the entrances and gate piers.
Nesfield Archives C.M.

Gloucestershire

Adlestrop, near Stow-on-the-Wold
Clients: Lord and Lady Leigh.
Dates: commenced March 1848.
Existing Plans: Profile of Ground entitled 'No.1 Skeleton Plan to shew the Construction of Ground at Adlestrop March 1848 W.A. Nesfield.'
Source: Nesfield Archives C.M. and Shakespeare Birthplace Trust, Stratford-upon-Avon.

Escourt Grange, near Tewkesbury
Client: Lord Blantyre.
Existing Reports: Report on the Lake.
Source: Nesfield Archives.

Highgrove House, Tetbury
Client: Sir Edward Strachey.
Source: Nesfield Archives C.M. Sir Edward Strachey of Somerset, where William Nesfield also worked.

Pull Court, near Tewkesbury
Client: Dowdeswell Family
Source: Nesfield Archives: drawing labelled 'Present garden very bad'.
Arthur Markham Nesfield also worked here.

Sudeley Castle, Sudeley
Client: Mr P. Dent
Source: Nesfield Archives. C.M.
'The Dents then turned their attention to the garden, begun in September 1859. This was a landmark in historic garden design for it was one of the first major revivals of topiary in a formal layout and was designed to compliment the architecture of the house. W.A. Nesfield was paid £57 18s in 1858 for giving his advice but the final layout was devised by the Dents themselves.' *Country Life*, 19 April 1990, p. 156.

Thornbury Castle, Thornbury
Client: Henry Howard.
Source: Nesfield Archives. C.M.

Tortworth Court
Client: Henry Reynolds-Moreton 2nd Earl of Ducie
S: Nesfield Archives. C.M.

Hampshire

Bramshott Grange, near Hazlemere
Client: Sir William Erle
Source: Nesfield Archives. C.M.

Broadlands, Romsey
Client: Rt Hon. William Francis Cowper-Temple (Lord Mount Temple)
Date: 1860s.
Source: Nesfield Archives
Arthur Markham Nesfield was working at Broadlands in 1869 and William Eden Nesfield designed an Entrance Lodge and Cottages. He also altered a marine villa for Lady Mount Temple at Babbacombe in Devon in the Old English style in 1878. Victoria and Albert Museum, March 1869, DD11 D 1340-41. November 1871 1346-47; R.I.B.A. Drawings Collection; University of Southampton (Broadlands). Papers WFC/N11.

Dogmersfield Park, near Odiham
Client: Sir H. Mildmay.
Source: Nesfield Archives. C.M.

Froyle Place, near Alton
Client: Sir Charles Miller
Source: Nesfield Archives. C.M.

Heckfield Place, Heckfield
Client: Baron Eversley.
Source: Nesfield Archives. C.M.

Idsworth Park, near Bishop Waltham
Client: Sir Jervoise Clarke-Jervoise.
Existing Reports: Report on the comparative merits of seven proposed mansion sites on Idsworth Estate dated December 1846 with recommendations and criticisms.
Source: Nesfield Archives.

Minley Manor, near Basingstoke
Client: Raikes Currie
Source: Nesfield Archives

Herefordshire

Belmont House, Clehonger
Client: Mr Wegg-Prosser.
Source: Nesfield Archives C.M.
William Nesfield's involvement is mentioned in the Diary of Richard Snead-Cox of Broxwood Court. Arthur Markham Nesfield also worked here.

Broxwood Court, Leominster
Client: Mr Richard Snead-Cox.
Existing Plans: Formal Garden.
Source: Nesfield Archives. C.M.
At Broxwood Court there is a plan of the gardens, and in the journal of Richard Snead-Cox he records having met William Nesfield in London and at Broxwood. I am grateful to Mrs A. Allen for this information.

Downton Castle, Downton-on-the-Rock
Client: Mr A.R. Broughton-Knight.
Source: Nesfield Archives C.M.

Garnstone, near Weobley
Client: Captain Peploe.
Existing Plans: Plan of Gardens.
Existing Reports: Recommendations and criticisms October 1845.
Source: Nesfield Archives C.M.
House Demolished.

Newport House, Almeley
Client: Mr James Gibson-Watt.
Dates: 1860s.
Source: Nesfield Archives C.M. There is a large tazza still in place at Newport House: I am grateful to David Whitehead for telling me about this commission.

Rotherwas, near Hereford
Client: Mr C.T. Bodenham.
Source: Nesfield Archives. C.M.
House demolished 1913.

Saltmarsh, Bromyard
Client: Mr C. Higginson.
Source: Nesfield Archives. C.M.

Shobdon Court, Shobdon
Client: Lord Bateman.
Source: Nesfield Archives C.M.
This was to be one of Arthur Markham Nesfield's most important commissions. House demolished.

Stoke Edith, near Ledbury
Client: Lady Emily Foley.
Dates: 1853 onwards.
Summary of Work: Large formal garden to the west with a *parterre-de-broderie* Existing Plans: County Record Office, Hereford hold a large collection of correspondence, plans and plantings (Foley Collection E12).
Source: Nesfield Archives C.M.

Hertfordshire

Beechwood, Near Markyate
Client: Sir J.S. Sebright.
Source: Nesfield Archives C.M. Plans which probably were not executed.
Arthur Markham Nesfield also worked here.

The Grove, Rickmansworth
Client: Lord Clarendon.
Dates: 1841-43.
Existing Plans: Plan for additions and substitutions of trees and shrubs and a heathery on the long walk 1842.
Source: Nesfield Archives.

Moor Park, Rickmansworth
Client: 1st Marquess of Westminster.
Dates: 1843.
Existing Plans: Plan of garden and terraces to the rear of the house dated 1848.
Existing Reports: Recommendations and criticisms.
Source: Nesfield Archives.

Huntingdonshire

Cunningham Castle
Client: Mr T. Heathcote.
Dates: 1847.
Existing Plans: Revised plan for a *parterre* September 1847 and in June 1848 a plan for a *parterre* with two compartments.
Source: Nesfield Archives C.M.
House demolished 1955.

Kent

Acrise Place, Canterbury
Client: Mr Papillion.
Source: Nesfield Archives C.M.

Ashurst Park, near Tunbridge Wells
Client: Mr George Field.
Source: Nesfield Archives C.M.

Barham Court, Maidstone
Client: Lord Gainsborough.
Dates: 1844.
Summary of Work: Report to the Solicitors of Lord Gainsborough on the Artistical Injury done to his estate by the proposed Maidstone Branch Railway, 11 March 1844.
Source: Nesfield Archives.

Bickley Park, Bromley
Client: Mr Dent.
Source: Nesfield Archives C.M. Listed on William Nesfield's Professional Accounts September 1859.

Bourne Park, Bishopsbourne, near Canterbury
Client: Matthew Bell.
Dates: 1848.
Summary of Work: Alterations and improvements to the landscape. *Parterre* on the south side of the house. Dammed up stream for a lake and designed a classical bridge with pierced parapets.
Existing Reports: Recommendations and criticisms.
Source: Nesfield Archives and Lady Juliet Tadgell.

Broom Hill, Christchurch, near Bromley
Existing Reports: Report on the present state of Broom Hill with general propositions for improvements.
Source: Nesfield Archives. C.M.

Chislehurst, near Bromley
Client: Mrs Labouchere.
Source: Nesfield Archives. C.M.

Doddington Hall
Summary of Work: On 7 January 1857 William Nesfield submitted a Before and After watercolour from the Boudoir.
In February 1873 Markham Nesfield produced his *No.1 Plan of Details for the Proposed general arrangements of garden, forecourt &c. around the house*, together with a plan.
Source: Nesfield Archives and the late Mrs Alexandra Oldfield.

Frognal, Chislehurst, near Bromley
Client: Lord Sydney.
Source: Nesfield Archives. C.M.

Hadlow Castle, Hadlow
Client: Mr Barlow (or Robert Rogers).
Source: Nesfield Archives. C.M.

Halcot, near Bromley
Client: Mr F. Dashwood.
Source: Nesfield Archives. C.M.

Huggins College, near Gravesend
Client; Mr John Huggins.
Source: Nesfield Archives. C.M.

Linton Park, near Maidstone
Client: Lord Holmesdale.
Source: Nesfield Archives. C.M.

Oxon Hoath, West Peckham
Client: Sir William Geary Bart.
Dates: 1847 onwards.
Summary of Work: Formal pleasure ground with two flanking *parterres* and Rosarium to the side of the house.
Source: Nesfield Archives C.M. Plan held at Oxon Hoath.
Arthur Markham Nesfield also worked here.

Penshurst Place, Penshurst
Client: Lord de L'Isle.
Existing Plans: Plan entitled 'Penshurst the alterations show Mr Nesfield's arrangements' held by the Royal Institute of British Architects, Victoria and Albert Museum.
Source: Nesfield Archives C.M.

Preston Hall, Aylesford
Client: Mr E.L. Betts.
Summary of Work: Large formal terraced garden.
Existing Reports: Recommendations and criticisms.
Source: Nesfield Archives. C.M.

Sandling Park, Hythe
Client: Mr W. Deedes.
Existing Plans: Ground plan of *parterres* etc. preparatory to the formation of terraces; 1844 plan of additions and shrubbery; 5 August 1845 revised plan of *parterre*.
Source: Nesfield Archives. C.M.

Scotney Castle, near Lamberhurst
Client: Mr Edward Hussey.
Source: Nesfield Archives C.M.
Suggestions not executed.

Somerhill, near Tonbridge
Client: Mr James Alexander.
Source: Nesfield Archives C.M. together with plan of ground work and *parterres*.

Surrenden Dering, near Ashford
Client: Sir E. Dering.
Source: Nesfield Archives C.M.

South Park, Penshurst
Client: 1st Baron Harding of Petherton.
Summary of Work: Pleasure ground with *parterre*.
Source: Nesfield Archives. C.M.

Torry Hill, near Lenham
Client: Lord Kingsdown.
Dates: 1843 onwards.
Existing Plans: Plan of arboretum and ground plan of *parterres* October 1843.
Source: Nesfield Archives C.M.
Parterre designs and plantings by Arthur Markham Nesfield, dated April 1869 at Torry Hill.

Lancashire

Croxteth Hall, Liverpool
Client: Charles Molyneux, 3rd Earl of Sefton.
Dates: 1851 onwards.
Source: Nesfield Archives C.M.
Notes by Robert McQuillian lodged at Preston Record Office in November 1977 record that 'Mr Watt received Eleven Pounds for plans and to complete and set out Croxteth Gardens – ridiculously low compared with One Hundred and Fifty-Five Pounds paid to W.A. Nesfield 80 years later.' It is thought by the archivist at Croxteth Hall that this information could have been from letters by R. Lodger, steward concerning the estate (May 1844/June 1854, DDM 4.6.67, pp. 97-266). A formal garden is known to have existed.
William Eden Nesfield worked for the 4th Earl on estate buildings and designed a new wing (not executed).

Duxbury Hall, near Chorley
Client: Mr W.C. Carr-Standish.
Source: Nesfield Archives. C.M.
House demolished 1957.

Knowsley Park, Knowsley
Client: Earl of Derby.
Existing Reports: Report on the propositions for the improvement of Liptrops Ground.
Source: Nesfield Archives C.M.

Worden Park, Leyland
Client: James Nowell ffarington.
Dates: 1840s.
Summary of Work: Formal garden with *parterres* and small fountain and a maze of hornbeam hedges with a mound in the centre surmounted by a single hornbeam tree with a fool's or false entrance between stone pillars.
Source: Leyland Historical Society, Mrs E. Shorrock.
Anthony Salvin rebuilt what was then Shaw Hall between 1840-45.

Worsley Hall, Manchester
Client: Lord Ellesmere.
Dates: 1840s.
Existing Plans: Plan for Panels of Embroidery for the Bastion; Ground Plan for planting a Mound 13th November 1845.
Existing Reports: Recommendations and criticisms.
Source: Nesfield Archives.

Wrightington Hall, near Parbold
Client: Charles Scarisbrick (in 1860 Mrs Clifton inherited the estate).
Source: Nesfield Archives C.M.
Arthur Markham Nesfield also worked here.

Leicestershire

Gopsall Hall
Client: Lord Ripon.
Dates: 1845 onwards.
Existing Plans: Plan of south *parterre* incorporating the letter 'R'.
Source: Nesfield Archhives.
House demolished.

Lincolnshire

Aswarby Park, Sleaford
Client: Sir Thomas Whichcote.
Dates: 1845 onwards.
Existing Plans: Plan for a *parterre* January 1846.
Source: Nesfield Archives C.M.
House demolished.

Elkington Hall, Elkington
Client: Revd William Smythe.
Dates: 1844 –
Existing Plans: Plan of *parterres* and a ground plan for a carriage sweep and stable approach together with planting scheme.
Existing Reports: Recommendations and criticisms.
Source: Nesfield Archives. House demolished.

Nocton Hall, Nocton
Client: Lord Ripon.
Dates: 1846.
Existing Plans: Plan of south *parterre* incorporating the letter 'R' November 1846.
Source: Nesfield Archives.

Rauceby Hall, Sleaford
Client: Mr A. Peacock Wilson.
Dates: 1845.
Existing Plans: Ground Plan of Details for Terraces etc.
Source: Nesfield Archives.
House demolished.

Stoke Rochford Hall, Stoke Rochford
Client: Christopher Turnor.
Dates: 1846.
Existing Plans: Revised plan of details for the terraces, etc with the initials 'C.T.' labelled 'No.5'.
Source: Nesfield Archives.

Middlesex

Alexandra Park, London
Client: Office of Woods and Forests.
Source: Nesfield Archives C.M.

Buckingham Palace, London
Client: Commissioners to Her Majesty Queen Victoria and Prince Albert.
Dates: 1849.
Existing Plans: Watercolour plans for a grand Baroque Gardens to the east of the Palace.
Letter from William Nesfield to the Earl of Carlisle in which he states 'In obedience to your Lordship's instructions communicated to me at Grosvenor Place of the 23rd ultimo I now beg to submit the following Estimate of expenses for the formation and construction of the decorative Gardens in front of Buckingham Palace according to the designs I prepared under the direction of His Royal Highness Prince Albert and accompanied by my report of 31st Dec. 1849.'
Source: Victoria and Albert Museum, Royal Institute of British Architects and Nesfield Archives where there are details of the cost of the work.
Scheme not implemented. It is tempting to speculate that the designs for the Buckingham Palace fountains were adapted by William Nesfield for his great fountain at Castle Howard in Yorkshire. There is also a watercolour by him of Britannia surrounded by sea horses, which he suggested as an alternative to the Perseus and Andromeda at Witley Court in Worcestershire, the original of which was intended for Buckingham Palace.

14 Fortis Green, Muswell Hill, London
Client: William and Emma Nesfield.
Dates: c. 1836.
Summary of Work: An avenue of sycamores bounded on each side by a laurel hedge, pleasure ground, kitchen garden, shrubberies, terrace bordered by flower beds geometrically shaped containing low flowers surrounded by miniature roses and jasmines with a single standard rose in the centre.
Source: Nesfield Archives, where there is a watercolour of the house; *Gardeners Magazine,* February 1840. House demolished.

Greenwich Park
Client: Commissioners of H.M.Woods and Forests.
Existing Reports: Summary of Work: Report on tunnel proposed by South Eastern Railway through the Park and Recommendations and criticisms 30 April 1846.
Source: Nesfield Archives.

Hillingdon Court, Uxbridge
Client: Mr Charles Mills.
Dates: 1856.
Existing Plans: Plan for a *parterre.*
Source: Nesfield Archives.

Kensington Palace Gardens, London
Client: Office of Woods and Works.
Existing Plans: Plan for a *parterre*.
Source: Nesfield Archives.

Regent's Park, London
Client: Office of Woods and Works.
Dates: 1860s.
Summary of Work: Avenue Gardens in the Broad Walk.
Source: Nesfield Archives where there are plans and plantings by William and Arthur Markham Nesfield; Land Use Consultants London Feasibility Study November 1992 and Restoration Proposals for the Avenue Gardens for the Royal Parks. Planting Schemes for the Picturesque Shrubbery Public Record Office Work 32/234.
There are a series of articles in the *Gardeners Chronicle* and *The Garden*, 21 June 1873 relating to the gardens.

Royal Horticultural Society's Garden, South Kensington
Client: Royal Horticultural Society.
Summary of Work: Designed the Gardens.
Source: Royal Archives, Windsor; Royal Horticultural Society, Lindley Library; Royal Parks and Gardens of London 1877. N. Cole, pp. 11-14; GLC Survey of London 1975, v. 38; Museum of South Kensington and Westminster 124-132.
Planting Plans reproduced in the Gardeners Chronicle and Agricultural Gazette Saturday 26 April 1862.

Syon House, London
Client: Duke of Northumberland.
Existing Reports: Observations on various details at Syon – Plan No.1.
Source: Nesfield Archives C.M.

South Eltham Gardens, Woolwich
Existing Plans: Plan for a *parterre*.
Source: Nesfield Archives.

Trent Park, Barnet
Client: R.C.L. Bevan.
Source: Nesfield Archives C.M.

Norfolk

Bylaugh Hall, Dereham
Client: Sir Henry John Lombe.
Dates: Not known but the house was completed in 1852.
Existing Plans: General plan of the proposed railings and walls enclosing the entrance court, terrace gardens and kitchen garden with the principal lines of the paths, roads etc. Plan and elevation of the terrace wall enclosing west *parterre*. Plan and elevation of the south *parterre*. General Ground plans of the park, forecourt and mansion and approaches. Planting Scheme.
Existing Reports: Observations on the choice of a mansion site.
Source: Public Record Office, Chancery Lane, London. MPA 66(3) (ex C 103/3).

Haveringland Hall, Reepham
Client: Edward Fellowes.
Existing Plans: Plan for a garden layout.
Source: Norfolk Record Office MS 8593, 10 B1, 20 B3 and Public Record Office, Chancery Lane, London.

Holkham Hall, Holkham
Client: 2nd Earl of Leicester.
Dates: 1849 onwards.
Summary of Work: A series of terraces around the house on the west front. The *parterre* to feature the Earl's initials in box. On the south side, a pair of sunken panels with flower beds in a Louis XIV pattern on coloured gravels. A fountain designed by William Nesfield and sculpted by Raymond Smith, who also sculpted the fountains at Keele Hall, Eaton Hall and Stoke Edith, the engineers were Easton & Co.
Source: Nesfield Archives where there is a plan for a *parterre* and vase.
This scheme is the only one of William Nesfield's private commissions that remains intact today.

Honingham Hall
Client: Revd Henry Vicar.
Existing Plans: Ground plan of *parterre* and rosarium and courts.
Source: Nesfield Archives.
House demolished 1866.

Kimberley Hall, Kimberley
Client: John, 2nd Baron Wodehouse.
Dates: 1847 onwards.
Summary of Work: Garden terrace on the south west, including retaining wall and general layout.
Source: Nesfield Archives and according to the *Gardeners Chronicle* of Saturday, 20 September 1884, p. 359: 'The garden in front of the mansion is one of Nesfield's largest and best'.

Lynford Hall, Thetford
Client: Stephen Lyne-Stephens.
Dates: 1858 onwards.
Existing Plans: Geometric elevation for proposed tazza for fountain basin of east *parterre*.
Source: Nesfield Archives and Norfolk Record Office.

North Runcton Hall, King's Lynn
Client: Mr Daniel Gurney.
Dates: Late 1830s – Salvin was building the house from 1834.
Summary of Work: Plans and Reports: Plan 1 Ground Plan of *parterre*; Explanation of Plan 1; Explanation of Plan 2; Plan for Trellis Work; Proposed improvements at North Runcton: Approach; A Section of proposed slopes and Plan of Improved Pond.
Source: I am grateful to the late Dr Jill Allibone for this information. House Demolished.

Northamptonshire

Althorp House, Daventry
Client: Lord Spencer.
Summary of Work: British Library and the Royal Botanic Gardens Kew, who hold a letter which indicates that William Nesfield met the Earl in London in 1853, it is not known whether a commission ensued.

Drayton House, Kettering
Client: Mrs Stopford-Sackville.
Existing Plans: Ground plan No.8 of details for east *parterre* incorporating initial 'S'; Source: Nesfield Archives; Northamptonshire Record Office; Cambridge University Photograph Collection.

Easton Neston, near Towcester
Client: Sir William Fermor Hesketh.
Dates: 1850 onwards.
Existing Plans: Plan for *parterre* and geometrical improvements December 1850.
Existing Reports: Remarks on detailed plan for a *parterre* and other geometric improvements in connection with the house at Easton Neston December 1850.
Source: Nesfield Archives.

Overstone Hall
Client: Lord Overstone.
Source: Nesfield Archives, Nottinghamshire Record Office.

Northumberland

Alnwick Castle
Client: 4th Duke of Northumberland.
Dates: 1847 and 1860.
Summary of Work: Panoramic watercolour view from the castle ramparts 1860. William Nesfield also submitted a plan for a formal garden away from the environs of the castle. Although a *parterre* was executed resembling this plan, it is not known whether it was laid out by him.
Source: Nesfield Archives and Alnwick Castle Archives.
The above garden has now been re-designed.

North Wales

Bettisfield Park, near Hanmer
Client: Sir J. Hanmer.
Source: Nesfield Archives C.M.

Bodrhyddan Hall, near Abergele
Client: Captain Conwy Grenville Hercules Rowley-Conwy.
Dates: 1872.
Summary of Work: Formal garden with *parterre*. It is not possible to verify whether this was the work of William Nesfield as a fire in the house destroyed any evidence. William Eden Nesfield redesigned the exterior in a Queen Anne Revival style and undertook a number of alterations to the interior, including an inglenook fireplace decorated with Spanish leather.
Source: Lord Langford.

Kinmel Park, near Abergele
Client: Hugh Robert Hughes.
Summary of Work: Large Formal Garden and sketch of proposed approach through St George Village.
Source: Nesfield Archives; Kinmel Hall Archives; Victoria and Albert Museum Royal Institute of British Architects; *Architectural Review* 1896; University College of North Wales.
William Eden Nesfield built Kinmel Hall and estate buildings. Arthur Markham Nesfield also worked here.

Pendyffryn, near Llandudno
Client: Mr S.O. Derbyshire.
Source: Nesfield Archives. C.M.

Nottinghamshire

Babworth Hall, Retford
Client: Hon. Bridgeman Simpson.
Source: Nesfield Archives. C.M.

Clumber Park, Worksop
Client: Duke of Newcastle
Existing Reports: Explanation for improvements at Clumber; Clumber 2 List of scattered plants in a Rosarium; Clumber 3 'Recommendations relating to a Waterfall'; Plan dated May 1851 for a Gun Battery.
Source: Nesfield Archives; University of Nottingham Manuscripts Department NeC 13, 829, NeC 7302, NeC 7, 302/1; Nottingham County Council Record Office.
William Eden Nesfield was engaged in architectural work at Clumber where he designed the Lincoln Terrace and Boat House in the 1860s.

Kelham Hall, Kelham
Client: John H. Manners-Sutton.
Dates: c. 1860.
Existing Plans: Ground plan with *parterres*, plan of proposed steps on bastion of south garden, scale ¼ inches = 1 foot, signed W.A. Nesfield July 23/60.
Existing Reports: Recommendations and criticisms.
Source: Nesfield Archives C.M. and Newark & Sherwood District Council.

Ollerton Hall, Ossington
Client: Mr F. Dennison.
Source: Nesfield Archives. C.M.

Rufford Abbey, Ollerton
Client: 8th Earl of Scarbrough.
Source: Nesfield Archives. C.M.

Wellow House, Wellow
Client: 8th Earl of Scarborough.
Existing Plans: Plan of Improvements.
Source: Nesfield Archives.

Oxfordshire

Hamels Park, Boar's Hill, Oxford
Client: Catherine Mellish.
Existing Reports: Report on present state of Hamels Park and Recommendations and criticisms.
Source: Nesfield Archives.

Kirtlington Park, near Oxford
Client: Sir George Dashwood.
Source: Nesfield Archives C.M.

Shirburn Castle, Thame
Client: Earl of Macclesfield.
Source: Nesfield Archives C.M.

Tusmore House, Bicester
Client: Earl of Effingham.
Source: Nesfield Archives. C.M.
House demolished 1860.

Wroxton Abbey, Banbury
Clients: Lord and Lady North.
Existing Plans: Plan for a formal *parterre* garden incorporating the initial 'N'; ground plan of details for *parterre*, entrance court, etc. March 1846.
Source: Nesfield Archives, Bodleian Library Oxford MSS North 17(R)2.
This scheme was probably not executed as the letter containing the above plan of 6 March 1846 from Eton College, Windsor from William Nesfield to Lord North states: 'I sincerely hope that because I dissented from Lady North's proposition regarding the *side of the* hill southward it will not be supposed I did so out of any spirit of contradiction or because the original idea did not emanate from myself – on the contrary, I assure you that had not experience at once suggested the utter impossibility of doing anything *professionally* creditable, or eventually satisfactory to Her Ladyship, it would have given me the greatest pleasure to have realised her wishes.'

Scotland

Balcaskie, near Pittenweem, Fife
Client: Sir Ralph Anstruther.
Existing Plans: Design for a flower garden incorporating the letter 'A' and plan.
Source: Balcaskie Archives and Nesfield Archives where there is correspondence between William Nesfield and Sir Ralph Anstruther 3 June 1848; also for information from Dr S. Piebenga.

Blackadder House, near Chirnside, Borders
Client: Mr G. Houston Boswell.
Existing Plans: Plan of the south front and proposed opening in the belts and additions to the clumps. House demolished c.1925 but there was a large *parterre* with fountain.
Source: Nesfield Archives.

Brodick Castle, Isle of Arran
Client: Duke of Hamilton.
Dates: 1847 onwards.
Summary of Work: Approach which now serves as the entrance to the castle grounds.
Existing Plans: Plan of a *parterre* depicting entwined letters.
Source: Nesfield Archives where there is a watercolour by William Nesfield of a distant view of Brodick Castle; National Trust for Scotland and Lady Jean Forde.

Dunira, near Comrie, Tayside
Client: Sir David Dundas.
Dates: 1853.
Source: Nesfield Archives where there is a sketch of Dundas looking from the entrance door. Plan for balustrade in connection with north-west and north-east angles of main building dated 1854 sent from 6 Stratton Street London.

Erskine House, Erskine, Strathclyde
Client: Lord Blantyre.
Existing Plans: Design for a carriage sweep, *parterres* and a plan of the landscape. Terracing and formal garden still survives.
Existing Reports: Recommendations and criticisms.
Source: Nesfield Archives.

Inveraray Castle, Inveraray, Strathclyde
Client: 8th Duke of Argyll.
Dates: 1849 onwards.
Summary of Work: Garden layout and approaches – new approach along riverside swept away dark laurels – formal garden of flower beds on south side.
Source: Nesfield Archives where there are recommendations and criticisms. Royal Commission on the Ancient and Historical Monuments of Scotland where there is a drawing of the castle approach.

Poltalloch
Existing Plans: Plan for a *parterre.*
Source: Nesfield Archives.
Sketch for a gardener's cottage by William Eden Nesfield, 20 February 1862.

Tulliallan Castle, Firth of Forth
Client: Margaret, Baroness Keith (created Baroness of Nairne 1837).
Source: Nesfield Archives where there is a report on the present state of Tulliallan Castle with recommendations and criticisms. There are *parterres* to the south west of the house.

Shropshire

Aldenham Park, Morville
Client: Sir J. Acton.
Dates: 1843 onwards.
Existing Plans: Ground plan of proposed *parterre* and entrance court and the opening up of belts and additions to the clumps October 1843.
There is a watercolour by William Nesfield labelled 'Alderham Park Shropshire from Summer House 1843.'
Source: Nesfield Archives. C.M.

Boreatton Park, near Baschurch
Client: Mr Rowland Hunt.
Source: Nesfield Archives. C.M.

Buntingsdale Hall, near Market Drayton
Client: Mr W. Taylor.
Source: Nesfield Archives. C.M.

Burwarton House, near Ditton Priors
Client: Lord Boyne.
Existing Plans: Ground plan of *parterre* and terrace.
Source: Nesfield Archives. C.M.
Estate still owned by the Boyne's who came originally from Brancepeth Castle. Anthony Salvin designed the house for the Hon. Gustavus Frederick Hamilton (later 7th Viscount Boyne) between 1835 and 1838. He also made some additions for the 8th Viscount.

Netley Hall, near Dorrington
Client: Mr Hope Edwards.
Source: Nesfield Archives C.M.

Willey Park, near Bridgnorth
Client: Lord Forester.
Date: 1850.
Existing Plans: Two plans for the garden, ground plan of proposed architectural arrangements to ground contiguous to the house.
Source: Lord Forester, County Records Office, Shrewsbury, Nesfield Archives C.M.
It is thought no work was carried out.

Staffordshire

Alton Towers, Alton
Client: 16th Earl of Shrewsbury.
Dates: 1844 onwards.
Summary of Work: Two *parterres* framed with Irish yews, in one a Rose, a Shamrock and a Thistle in filled with coloured gravels and a small fountain standing on carved lions paws flanked with three tazzas, in the other a large monogrammed letter 'S'. In the area referred to the Quarry William Nesfield designed what is known as Lady Mary's terrace. Arthur Markham Nesfield also worked at Alton Towers.
Existing Plans: 'Proposed parterre &c for the Conservatory Court Jan. '46.'
Existing Reports: Report on the gardens dated October 1844 and a small pencil drawing of the main garden at Alton Towers.
Source: Nesfield Archives.

Aqualate Hall, Newport
Client: Sir Thomas Fletcher Fenton Boughey.
Dates: 1854 onwards.
Existing Plans: Plans for the alterations to the landscape.
Source: Nesfield Archives where there is a 'Before and After' drawing, dated 20 September 1854, from the centre dining room window. Family and estate papers of the Boughey family are held in the Staffordshire Record Office, Stafford.

Ingestre Hall, Ingestre
Client: Earl of Shrewsbury.
Existing Plans: Plan for the parkland and a plan of the estate.
Source: Nesfield Archives.

Keele Hall, Newcastle-under-Lyme
Client: Ralph Sneyd.
Dates: 1842 onwards.
Summary of Work: Alterations to a Bowling Green in order to make it into an Italian Garden also advised about changes around the hall, formal garden.
Existing Plans: Plan for a Pomarium November 1845 scale 3/8th inches which included Apple and Pear Standards, Cherries, Plums, Dwarf Medlars, Apple half standards, Filberts, Cobnuts and Hazels.
Source: Nesfield Archives; University of Keele 89 S2768, 90 S (RS/HWV) 120 Spring 1844, Ralph Sneyd to H.W. Vincent 91 S2768, 29 June 1843, W.A. Nesfield to Ralph Sneyd 92 S 80/9 (Box 38).

Sandon Hall, Sandon
Client: 2nd Earl of Harrowby.
Dates: 1854 onwards.
Existing Plans: Plan for Terrace.
Source: Nesfield Archives.

Shugborough Hall, near Stafford
Client: Earl of Lichfield.
Dates: 1855.
Source: Staffordshire Record Office, Stafford where there is a letter dated 24 September 1855, two bills and a receipt from William Nesfield for professional services, an approximate estimate for the forming of a garden at Shugborough (D615/E(H)54).

Stone Park, Stone
Client: Lord Grenville.
Dates: 1845 onwards.
Existing Plans: Plan for ground work 1846.
Source: Nesfield Archives.

Teddesley Hall, Near Penkridge
Client: Lord Hatherton.
Existing Plans: Plan for a terraced garden at the front of the hall.
Source: Nesfield Archives.
House demolished 1954.

Tixall Hall, Tixall, near Stafford
Client: Thomas Clifford.
Existing Plans: Plan of the estate.
Source: Nesfield Archives.
House demolished 1928/9

Trentham Park, Trentham
Clients: Duke and Duchess of Sutherland.
Dates: 1844 onwards.
Existing Plans: Plan of a mound for an obelisk, poultry yard, fish stews and approaches to same. A new drive west of the hall and a section of a line from the western entrance towards the gravel pit gates.
Existing Reports: Recommendations and criticisms.
Sources: Stafford Record Office [D593/H.13/45], 46, 48 and [D593/H/13/47] and the Nesfield Archives.
A diary entry of Ralph Sneyd's of Keele Hall, Staffordshire reads: 'Passed the whole day in staking out an approach from the Whitworth side with Messrs. Nesfield, Barry and Lock. My advice was accepted.' University of Keele Archives S.3707, 15 April 1844.

Suffolk

Bradfield Hall, Bradfield Combust
Client: Arthur Young.
Summary of Work: Not known, but there were close social connections between the Nesfields of Bury St Edmunds and Arthur Young, and there was an ornamental lake on the east side of the house and formal gardens encircled by standard laurustinus and bounded by a yew hedge that are familiar features of William Nesfield's work. Also, William Eden Nesfield was responsible for designing the house.
Source: Nesfield Archives. C.M.

Brantham Court, Wangford
Client: Mr W. Gurdon
Existing Plans: Plan for a *parterre.*
Source: Nesfield Archives.

The Chantry, Ipswich
Client: Sir Fitzroy Kelly
Source: Nesfield Archives. C.M.

Flixton Hall, Flixton
Client: Sir Robert Shafto Adair Bart.
Dates: 1842 onwards.
Existing Plans: Skeleton plan of proposed disposition of dressed ground.
Parterre for the Priest's House.
Source: Nesfield Archives. C.M. Suffolk Record Office (HA.12).

Glevering Hall, Easton
Client: Andrew Chaloner Arcedeckne.
Source: Nesfield Archives C.M.
House demolished.

Henham Hall, Wangford
Clients: Earl and Countess of Stradbroke.
Dates: 1859.
Existing Plans: Skeleton plan for proposed forecourt dated March 1859. Design for a pavilion taken from the circular one at the Borguese Palace in Rome (but not a copy as the client wanted a design unlike other places) accompanied by 10 tazzas with flowers. Proposed gates for forecourt. Probably not executed.
Source: Nesfield Archives C.M. and County Record Office, Ipswich, Suffolk (HA 11/(C46/22), HA 11(C48/10(4).
It is not thought that any of the above was implemented.

Helmingham Hall, Stowmarket
Client: Mr J. Tollemache J.P.
Dates: 1848.
Existing Reports: Recommendations and criticisms.
Source: Nesfield Archives.

Orwell Park, Nacton, near Ipswich
Client: Mr Tomlin.
Source: Nesfield Archives C.M.

Somerleyton Hall, Lowestoft
Client: Sir S. Morton Peto.
Dates: 1846 onwards.
Summary of Work: 'Large formal gardens to the east of the house incorporating a terrace which overlooked an elaborate *parterre* with box edgings round an infill of white stone chippings' Equitorial sundial the whole bound by green and gold Irish yews. Maze of yew hedges with a central pagoda.'
Existing Plans: Plan of ground work and *parterre* and plan for a Maze.
Source: Somerleyton Archives.
According to the Sale Particulars of 1861, the design for the *parterre* was based on an old church hinge.

Sproughton Manor, Ipswich
Clients: Lt. Col. and Mrs Henry Phillips
Source: Nesfield Archives. C.M.
The manor was designed by William Eden Nesfield.

Tattingstone Place, near Ipswich
Client: Mr J.S. Western.
Source: Nesfield Archives. C.M.

Woolverstone Hall, near Ipswich
Client: Mr W. Berners.
Dates: Late 1860s.
Summary of Work: large formal garden containing a *parterre.*
Source: Suffolk Record Office Ipswich (HE7 2855); *Gardeners Chronicle* 1867 pp. 156-158; *Journal of Horticulture Cottage Gardener* 1905 N.S. v. 50, pp. 557-558.
Arthur Markham Nesfield also worked here.

Surrey

Busbridge, Godalming
Client: Mr Ellis Gosling, M.P.
Source: Nesfield Archives C.M. together with an Abstract of Professional Accounts dated September 1859.

Denbies, near Dorking
Client: Mr T. Cubitt.
Source: Nesfield Archives C.M.
House Demolished.

Eastwick Park, Leatherhead
Client: Mr C. Barclay.
Dates: 1840s.
Existing Plans: Ground plan for a rosarium, December 1843.
Source: Nesfield Archives. C.M.

The Ellery, Caterham
Client: Mr T. Leonino.
Source: Nesfield Archives. C.M.

Goring Park
Client: David Lyon.
Existing Reports: Recommendations and criticisms.
Source: Nesfield Archives.

Hatchford Park, Weybridge
Client: Earl of Ellesmere.
Source: Nesfield Archives. C.M.

Marshall Vale, Godalming
Client: Mr T. Fisher.
Source: Nesfield Archives. C.M.

Milton Heath, Dorking
Client: Mr A. Powell.
Source: Nesfield Archives C.M. Arthur Markham Nesfield married the daughter of the house.

Norbury Park, Leatherhead
Client: Mr T. Grissell.
Source: Nesfield Archives C.M.

Oatlands Lodge, Shepperton
Client: Mr William Drake.
Source: Nesfield Archives C.M.

Park Hatch, Godalming
Client: Mr Joseph Godman.
Source: Nesfield Archives C.M.

Peper Harow, House near Godalming
Client: 5th Viscount Midleton.
Existing Reports: Recommendations and criticisms.
Source: Nesfield Archives C.M.

Grove House, Roehampton
Client: Stephen Lyne-Stephens.
Source: Nesfield Archives C.M.

Rokefield House
Dates: 1869.
Existing Plans: Plans for details of general arrangements November 1869.
Source: Nesfield Archives C.M.
Arthur Markham Nesfield also worked here.

Royal Botanic Gardens Richmond, Kew
Client: Lord Lincoln.
Dates: 1844 onwards.
Summary of Work: 'Designed parterres and gravelled walks and formalized the lake in the vicinity of the Palm House, the three vistas radiating from the Palm House and a fourth Cedar Vista which connects the Pagoda with the Sion end of the Sion Vista. The broad walk and avenue linking the main gate and an Arboretum.'
Existing Plans: Plan of proposed Arboretum and designs for the *parterres* to accompany the Palm House.
Existing Reports: Report for the formation of an Arboretum dated July 1845.
There is also in the Nesfield Archives a Watercolour by William Nesfield of the formalized lake in front of the Palm House.
Source: Nesfield Archives; Royal Botanic Gardens English Letters L-Z 585, 22: 129-140, 23: 517-518, 24: 432-433, 25: 378, 26: 403-407, 28: 126-128, 35: 338-339, 38: 429, 40: 165; Public Record Office, Kew Work 32/114 x 4, 32/115 x 4.

Ruxley, near Maidenhead
Client: Mr William Beckford.
Source: Nesfield Archives. C.M.

Shalford, Guildford
Mr Henry Edward Austin.
Existing Reports: Report on injury to be sustained by introduction of Guildford Extension Railway and recommendations and criticisms.
Nesfield Archives. C.M.

Sompting Abbotts, near Sompting, West Sussex
Client: Captain Crofts.
Source: Nesfield Archives. C.M.

Sussex

Arundel Castle, Arundel, West Sussex
Client: 13th Duke of Norfolk.
Existing Plans: Plan for parkland, re-designing grounds, new kitchen garden, layout of elaborate formal *parterre* in north bailey.
Existing Reports: Recommendations and criticisms dated September 1850.
Source: Nesfield Archives.

Ashdown Park, near East Grinstead
Client: Earl of Craven.
Existing Plans: Design for *parterre.*
Source: Nesfield Archives.

Coghurst Hall, Hastings, East Sussex
Client: Musgrave Brisco, M.P.
Existing Reports: Report on proposed railway effects and summary of work together with recommendations and criticisms.
Source: Nesfield Archives. C.M.

Crowhurst Park, near Battle, East Sussex
Client: Thomas Papillion.
Source: Nesfield Archives. C.M.

Goring Park, West Sussex
Client: Mr David Lyon.
Existing Reports: Report on parkland and recommendations and criticisms.
Source: Nesfield Archives.

Paxhill Park, West Sussex
Client: P.N. Laurie.
Source: Nesfield Archives. C.M.

Worth Park, West Sussex
Client: J. M. Montefiore.
Source: Nesfield Archives C.M.

Warwickshire

Barford House, Barford Hill
Client: Miss Louisa Ann Ryland.
Source: Nesfield Archives C.M.
Arthur Markham Nesfield also worked here.

Berkswell Hall, Coventry
Client Mr T. Walker.
Dates: After 1861
Source: Nesfield Archives. C.M.

Claverdon Leys, Warwick
Client: Mr Darwin Galton.
Source: Nesfield Archives. C.M.

Hampton Manor, Hampton-in-Arden
Client: Rt Hon. Frederick Peel.
Source: Nesfield Archives. C.M. Arthur Markham Nesfield engaged on landscape design work at Hampton between 1867-1870. William Eden Nesfield carried out extensive work on the estate in the mid 1860s.

Merevale Hall, Atherstone
Client: Sir William Dugdale.
Dates: 1842.
Existing Plans: Plan of *parterres* and terraces together with a plan of 1842 for Merevale Parsonage.
Existing Reports: Recommendations and criticisms.
Source: Nesfield Archives.

Offchurch Bury, Offchurch
Client: Lord Guernsey.
Existing Reports: Recommendations and criticisms.
Source: Nesfield Archives.

Stoneleigh Abbey, Kenilworth
Clients: Lord and Lady Leigh.
Dates: 1852.
Summary of Work: Large formal garden which included an equatorial sundial
Source: Nesfield Archives C.M. together with a drawing by William Nesfield for a Grille.

Studley Castle Studley
Client: Sir F. Holyoake-Goodricke.
Source: Nesfield Archives C.M.

Welcombe Hall, near Stratford-Upon-Avon
Client: Mark Phillips.
Summary of Work: Terraced formal gardens to the rear of the house.
Source: Nesfield Archives C.M.
Arthur Markham Nesfield also worked here.

Westmorland

Dalton Hall, Kirkby Lonsdale
Client: Mr E.G. Hornby, M.P. for Preston.
Source: Nesfield Archives C.M.
House Demolished

Wiltshire

Amesbury Abbey, Amesbury
Client: Sir E. Antrobus.
Source: Nesfield Archives C.M.

Bowood, near Calne
Client: 3rd Baron Lansdowne.
Dates: 1849.
Existing Plans: Plan for the lower terrace.
Existing Reports: Report on the poor appearance and location of the house together with recommendations.
Source: Nesfield Archives. C.M.
William Nesfield was asked to submit a plan for the lower terrace but declined as he was too busy on his Buckingham Palace designs.

Fonthill Abbey, Fonthill Bishop
Client: Marquess of Westminster.
Source: Nesfield Archives. C.M.
House demolished 1955.

Northlands, near Salisbury
Client: Mr J.R. Wigram.
Source: Nesfield Archives C.M.

Worcestershire

Hadzor, near Droitwich
Client: Mr J. Howard Dalton.
Source: Nesfield Archives C.M.

Witley Court, Great Witley
Client: Lord Ward (later 1st Earl Dudley).
Dates: 1860s.
Summary of Work: Large formal gardens.
Source: Nesfield Archives elevation and section of shell tazza to be added to pedestal of central figures on east fountain; Motto for use on the fountain 'Hear with favour O Neptune him who prays to thee, Ovid'; Pedestal on which stands figure of Hercules; Sketch of Pavilion by Daukes; drawing of grounds; Perseus and Andromeda central group.

Yorkshire

Aske Hall, near Richmond
Client: Lord Zetland.
Existing Plans: Survey of Landscape previous to cutting.
Source: Nesfield Archives. C.M.

Birdsall House, near Wharram le Street
Client: 8th Baron Middleton.
Existing Reports: Report on parklands and improvements to house and recommendations and criticisms.
Source: Nesfield Archives. C.M.

Bishopthorpe Palace, Skipton
Client: Thomas Musgrave, Archbishop of York, 1847-1860
Existing Plans: Plan of *parterres*.
Existing Reports: Report regarding the parkland and recommendations and criticisms.
Source: Nesfield Archives.

Broughton Hall, Skipton
Client: Sir Charles Tempest.
Dates: 1855 onwards.
Summary of Work: Formal gardens around the house on steeply sloping ground and with very limited space available. This estate is another example, together with Alton Towers in Staffordshire, where William Nesfield designed a garden which was completely at variance with how *parterres-de-broderie* should be displayed. He told his client that: 'you have certainly given me the most difficult job I have experienced but I am one of those who cannot endure to be beaten, hence my endeavours shall be untiring.' (Letter from William Nesfield to Sir Charles Tempest 12 January 1855: Broughton Hall Archives). His solution was to design a small *parterre*, with support walls and steps. He also provided a basin with shells and dolphins and reshaped the curving shrubs above the high ground. To the east he designed a *parterre* on the steep slope, into which he introduced a scroll and feather design within two lines of box on coloured gravels, with yellow spar round the outside and crushed tile and spar in red, white and blue to fill the interstices of the box. On the north east corner he placed a gazebo whilst above, on the high ground, where space was at a premium, he introduced statues of a Piping Shepherd and Shepherdess, Haymakers and three figures known as Faith, Hope and Charity. From the gazebo a path led along a woodland walk to Broughton Brook where he placed a shepherd boy with a dog.
Source: Nesfield Archives and Broughton Hall Archives.

Burton Field, Stamford Bridge
Client: Mr Charles Darley.
Source: Nesfield Archives C.M.
Charles Darley married Marianne Nesfield, step-sister to William Nesfield.

Castle Howard, near York
Client: 7th Earl of Carlisle.
Dates: 1849-64.
Summary of Work: Embroidered *parterres*, Atlas and Prince of Wales fountains. Alterations to north and south lakes. Development of south waterways, cascade, basin and waterfall, planting of lime avenue, Plan of Boar on pedestal, gilded dial, Castle Howard from mausoleum, watercolour September 1862 to commemorate the visit of Queen Victoria.
Source: Nesfield Archives where there a number of watercolours relating to the garden, Royal Library, Windsor Castle, Berkshire 229/88 where there is a watercolour by William Nesfield dated September 1862 commemorating Queen Victoria's visit. County Record Office York, Castle Howard Archives.

Grimston Park, Grimston
Clients: John Hobart Caradoc, 2nd Baron Howden.
Dates: 1840s.
Summary of Work: Laid out formal gardens and an avenue of marble statuary of 12 Caesars upon full pedestals leading to a temple where there was a bust of Napoleon. Also a garden with a *parterre* on each side of a walk 120 metres long and an informal garden planted with conifers and ground cover.
Existing Plans: Ground plan of rosarium &c January 1843.
Existing Reports: Report stating reasons for determining that a statue of a boar should occupy the centre of the *parterre* bastion.
Source: Nesfield Archives.

Harewood House, near Leeds
Client: Lord Harewood.
Dates: 1843.
Existing Plans: Plan for a *parterre* 1843.
Source: Nesfield Archives.

Helbeck Hall, Warsop
Existing Reports: Three recommended sites for the positioning of a mansion.
Source: Nesfield Archives.

Kirklees Park, near Huddersfield
Client: Sir George Armytage.
Existing Reports: Report on proposed viaduct's affects on park from the Huddersfield and Manchester Railway and recommendations and criticisms.
Source: Nesfield Archives.

Methley Hall, West Riding
Client: 3rd Earl of Mexborough.
Dates: Late 1830s.
Summary of Work: Not known, but this was extensive according to William Nesfield's remarks about the importance of this commission.
Existing Plans: Plan and *parterres* for Methley Rectory.
Source: Nesfield Archives.
Between 1830 and 1836 Anthony Salvin carried out alterations and additions to Methley Hall.

Nawton Grange, Nawton
Client: C. Dunscombe.
Source: Nesfield Archives. C.M.

Oulton Park, near Leeds
Client: John Blayds (changed his name back to John Calverley in 1852).
Dates: 1851-52.
Source: Leeds District Archives who hold drawings, Farrar 161-163.

Stanmore, Richmond
Client: Duke of Northumberland.
Source: Nesfield Archives where there is a 'Before and After' watercolour of the church.

Pepper House, near Newby
Client: Lord Annesley.
Source: Nesfield Archives. C.M.
Arthur Markham Nesfield also worked here.

Sessay, Easingwold
Client: Viscount Downe.
Source: Nesfield Archives. C.M.

Scutterskele [sic]
Client: Lord Falkland
Source: Nesfield Archives. C.M.

Swillington Hall, near Leeds
Client: Sir John H. Lowther.
Dates: 1857.

Existing Plans: Drawing for a vase and a plan of proposed treatment of dressed ground in connection with the house and alteration of approaches.
Source: Nesfield Archives.

Upleatham Hall, Upleatham, Cleveland
Client: Lord Zetland.
Source: Nesfield Archives. C.M.

Wiganthorpe, near Terrington
Client: W. Garforth.
Source: Nesfield Archives. C.M
House demolished.

Wykeham Abbey, Wykeham
Client: Lord Downe.
Source: Nesfield Archives. C.M.

Miscellaneous

Rudding Park
Existing Plans: Plan of ground work preparatory to the formation of terraces and *parterres*.
Source: Nesfield Archives.

Upton
Source: Nesfield Archives, where there is a plan for *parterres*.

List of William Eden Nesfield's Commissions

Editor's Note

William Eden's commissions are arranged by decade, as he worked for many clients over a period of years. His clients also requested his services in more than one part of the country.

1850s

Assize Court, Manchester
Working with Richard Norman Shaw: unexecuted plan.
Source: Andrew Saint, *Richard Norman Shaw*, Yale University Press, 1983.

Belvoir Castle, Leicestershire
Working for the 7th Duke of Rutland: Grantham Lodge.
Source: Royal Institute of British Architects: holds preliminary study and designs for Lodge.

Clumber, Nottinghamshire
Working for the Duke of Newcastle: boat house, pavilion, terrace and seats.
Source: Royal Institute of British Architects *

Crewe Hall Estate, Cheshire
Working for Lord Crewe: commemorative tomb in St Bertoline's Church, Barthomley for 3rd Baron Crewe.
Source: Journal of the Royal Institute of British Architects.

Keele Hall, Staffordshire
Working for Ralph Sneyd: while in Anthony Salvin's office he assisted the Clerk of Works during the re-building of the manor house.
Source: Jill Allibone, *Anthony Salvin – Gothic Revival Architect,* The Lutterworth Press, 1987.

Kirtlington Park, Oxfordshire
Working for Sir John Dashwood: two Gothic-style lodge houses.
Source: Royal Institute of British Architects. *

New Lodge, Windsor
Working for Mdm Van de Weyer: summer house, lodge and laundry.
Source: Royal Institute of British Architects. *

West Derby village, Liverpool
Working for William Molyneux, 4th Earl of Sefton: cottages.

West Derby village, Liverpool
Working for J. Pemberton Heywood: Gothic Cross.
Source: Journal of the Royal Institute of British Architects. *

Woolverstone Hall, Suffolk
Working for John Berners: Holbrook Lodge.
Source: Journal of the Royal Institute of British Architects.

1860s

Bradfield Hall, Bradfield Combust, near Bury St Edmunds, Suffolk
Working for Arthur J. Young: new house and entrance lodge, flint faced.
Source: Suffolk County Record Office, Bury St Edmunds: Bradfield Hall exteriors K 717/1, HD 526/18/6-7.
Royal Institute of British Architects *

Callore, Mor
Working for John Malcolm: sundial, pavement, flower basin.
Source: Royal Institute of British Architects. *

Coombe Abbey, Warwickshire
Working for 2nd Baron Craven, major re-build of the Abbey and farm buildings.
Source: Victoria & Albert Museum (Prints Room): DD 11 D 1381-1400.
Royal Institute of British Architects: Design for arches, connected with additions and alterations; elevations and details.*
Architectural Review, 1897-2.
Country Life, December 11 1909.
A History of Coombe Abbey, Robin Moore, 1983, Bodleian Library, Oxford.

Crewe Hall estate, Crewe, Cheshire
Working for Lord Crewe: estate cottages.

Old Hall, Sandbach, Cheshire
Working for Lord Crewe: new inn sign.
Source: Royal Institute of British Architects: design for new inn sign 1863; cottages and farmhouse in Weston Village, 1864-65; Detached cottage in Weston Village, ground plan, chamber plan, diagram of roof, front, back and side elevation, two sections and elevation of framing of gable over living room/window. *
County Record Office, Chester: MSS DCR/ 15/2.
Architectural Review, 1897-2.
Country Life, 20 March, 1902.

Croxteth Hall, Liverpool
Working for 4th Earl of Sefton: laundry and dairy.
Watercolour plans were also submitted for the remodelling of the interior of the Hall and for adding a new wing dated October 1863 – not executed.
Source: Royal Institute of British Architects. *

Great Budworth, Cheshire
Working for Rowland Egerton-Warburton of Arley Hall: small cottage on south side of High Street on corner of Mount Pleasant, brick half-timbered, originally with pargetting, 1862.
Source: Arley Hall Archives.

Hampton-in-Arden Estate
Working for Rt Hon. Frederick Peel: Manor house restoration, octagonal Gothic style clock tower, lodge house and cottages in the village with brick and ornamental plasterwork, tile hanging, heavily modelled chimneys.

SS Mary & Bartholomew Parish Church, Hampton-in-Arden, Warwickshire
Restoration work.

23 Chesham Place, London
Alterations.
Sources: Institute of British Architects: revised design for proposed new clock tower, 1869. *
County Record Office, Warwick
Plan for additions and alterations and photography of interior and exterior with figures of SS Mary & Bartholomew Church in the Parish of Hampton-in-Arden, Warwickshire, Signed W. Eden Nesfield Architect, 30 Argyll Street, Regent Street W. May 16 1869.
Architectural Review, (clock tower) 1897-2.

Kinmel Park, North Wales
Working for H.R. Hughes.
Sources: Royal Institute of British Architects: survey drawing; sketch plan of Kinmel Village; preliminary design for rebuilding Kinmel Hall; elevation; design for a table; sketch plan and elevation.
Architectural Review, 1897-1 and (Gate lodge) 1897-2.
Royal Institute of British Architects. *

King's Walden, Hertfordshire
(St Mary's Church) for S.L.C. Cholmeley, Hale: contemporary of William Eden Nesfield's at Eton: outer walls refaced, chancel and aisles partly rebuilt and porch added.
Sources: Royal Institute of British Architects: design for restoration for C. Cholmeley Hales, 1867.
Victoria & Albert Museum (Prints Room): DD 11 D 1349-54, 1867/1868.
Architectural Review: 2 June 1897.

Kiplin Hall, near Northallerton, Yorkshire
Working for Captain (later Admiral) Walter Carpenter. The ancestral seat of the Barons Baltimore, one of whom George Calvert,

1st Baron Baltimore founded Maryland in the United States of America. Fifty letters exist from between Eden Nesfield and Capt. Carpenter and the agent John Topham. The captain's daughter Sarah married Christopher Turnor of Stoke Rochford Hall, Lancashire, where Nesfield's Snear had a commission: entrance gates, home farm, coachman's house, redesigned the drawing room in the Hall, built a library and left behind a drawing of his dog, 'Poor Bumble', dated 1873.
Sources: *Country Life*, Richard Haslem, 28 July and 4 August 1983.
North Yorkshire County Council hold the letters between William Eden Nesfield and John Topham and Captain Carpenter.
Royal Institute of British Architects. *

Linton Park, Kent
Working for Viscountess Holmesdale: conservatory and ferneries.
Source: Royal Institute of British Architects. *

Loughton Hall, Loughton, Essex
Working for the Revd R. J. Whittaker Maitland, brother-in-law to Anthony Salvin's son Osbert: manor house similar to Plas Dinas, but Queen Anne Revival. Entrance off centre, high chimneys and canopied bell tower.
St Mary's Parish Church, Loughton, Essex: restoration and memorial chapel.
Sources: Royal Institute of British Architects. *
Victoria & Albert Museum (Prints Room): plans dated 1871-1878.

Palace at Potsdam
Working for the Crown Princess of Prussia (later Empress Frederick), dairy.
Source: Royal Institute of British Architects. *

Regent's Park, London
Lodge House.
Sources: Victoria & Albert Museum (Prints Room): DD 11 D 1316-1318.
The Magazine of Art, 22, 1898 by R.P. Spiers.
Architectural Review: 1897-1.
Royal Institute of British Architects. *

Royal Botanic Gardens, Kew, Richmond, Surrey
Entrance Lodge.
Sources: Victoria & Albert Museum (Prints Room): Entrance Lodge DD 11 D 1330-1332.
Journal of the Kew Guild: 1964 p. 452.
Country Life: 23 March 1978 pp. 766-768.
Victoria & Albert Museum: Marble Halls: Drawings and Models from Victorian Secular Buildings, Exhibition August-October 1973.
Architectural Review: (lodge) 1897-1.
Royal Institute of British Architects. *

Royal Horticultural Society Gardens, South Kensington
Working for the Committee: Terrace walls, steps and fountain basins.
Source: Royal Institute of British Architects. *

Shipley Estate, Derbyshire
Working for A.M. Mundy: farm house, lodge, cottages, new porch to hall and octagonal dairy.
Source: Royal Institute of British Architects. *

Sproughton Manor, Suffolk
Working for Lt Col. and Mrs Phillips: new manor house.
Source: Royal Society of British Architects. *

Swillington Hall, Leeds
Working for Sir John Lowther: pavilion and iron gates.
Source: Royal Institute of British Architects. *

Tregothnan, Cornwall
Working for 6th Viscount Falmouth: Drawing for proposed Decorative heating grilles sent from 15 Bedford Row, London and Wrought Iron Gate.
Source: Victoria & Albert Museum for wrought iron gate M 24 D 1576-1580.

1870s

5 Aubrey Road, Notting Hill, London
Working for Dr Whistler: alterations and additions.
Source: Royal Institute of British Architects.

Bank Hall, Chapel-en-le-Frith, Derbyshire
Working for Henry Renshaw: oak sideboard, lodge house and single room in house.
Sources: Royal Institute of British Architects: design for chimney-piece, incorporating a bracket supporting a Japanese vase, 1871. *
Architectural Review 1897-2 p. 32.

Bettws Church, Newtown, Powys, North Wales
New aisle, vestry and organ.
Source: Royal Institute of British Architects. *

Bodrhyddan, North Wales
Working for Captain Conwy Grenville Hercules Rowley-Conwy: Queen Anne additions and alterations.
Source: Victoria & Albert Museum Prints Room: DD 11 D 1564-1573.
Royal Institute of British Architects. *

Broadlands, Romsey, Hampshire
Working for Lord and Lady Mount Temple: waterworks, fountain, orangery, library, estate cottages and lodge houses.
Marine Villa, Babbacombe, Devon
Working for Lady Mount Temple.
Grammar School, Station Road, Romsey, Hampshire.
Now a public library with a blue plaque to commemorate its history and the architect.
Sources: Royal Institute of British Architects: Four contract drawings for additions and alterations for Babbacombe Marina Villa, 1874, Elevation in Courtyard, Elevation facing Approach, End Elevation and Elevation at X, half-elevation and sections of Gable, detail of Balcony including plan, side elevation, elevation facing road, section of floor. Design for Grammar School, Romsey 1870-72.*
Devon Record Office: Babbacombe Marine Villa SX 9265 7/31, 5183.
Victoria & Albert Museum (Prints Room): Entrance Lodge and Cottages at Broadlands DD 11 D 1340-41, March 1869.

Boys' Grammar School, Newport, Essex
Working for the Governors: Plan consisted of a cloister on the south flanked by the Headmaster's house, dormitories, dining room and schoolroom with a projection to the west of the outhouses. Tall chimneys, varying rooflines and hipped dormer windows of red brick, (first plan dated 26 May 1875). Final plan and specifications approved 19 October 1875.
Sources: Essex Record Office, Ipswich: Specification and Plans regarding a new school 25/75 Acc 3904.
Royal Institute of British Architects. *

Cloverley Hall, Calverhall, Shropshire
Working for A. Pemberton Heywood-Lonsdale: Manor House, Old English with French flavour 1864-5, but these omissions also spanned the 1870s.
Cora Church, Calverhall, Shropshire for A. Pemberton Heywood-Lonsdale: alabaster reredos, new nave, two aisles and tower. Nave had roof pie discs used on the internal window facings and on the semi-circular lectern. South window in the chancel Morris & Co. Externally by main door inscribed panel commemorating the building work. Church furniture.

23 Grosvenor Square, London
Alterations and additions.
Sources: Lichfield Joint Record Office and Public Library: Cora Church, B/C/12 Calverhall, 27 May 1871 for Permission to enlarge north transept and chancel and remove gallery approved 12 June 1871.
Shropshire County Council, Shrewsbury
Vestry Minute Book (2477/2/9).
Architectural Review: (26 Grosvenor Square).
Royal Institute of British Architects.*

Gibson's Bank, Saffron Walden, Essex
Working for the Gibson Family: new Bank building on the Market Square.
Sources: Royal Institute of British Architects.
Victoria & Albert Museum (Prints Room): DD 11 D 1342-44.

Gloddaeth Hall, Gloddaeth, near Llandudno, North Wales
Working for Lady Augusta Mostyn: alterations and additions to 16th manor house.
Plas Uchaf Farm, Mostyn Estate for Lady Augusta Mostyn.
Sources: Royal Institute of British Architects. *
Victoria & Albert Museum (Prints Room): DD 11 D1355-56 June 1875.
Architectural Review: 1897-2 p. 32.
Country Life: Gloddaeth, Gwynedd, Richard Haslem, 7 December 1978.

Greenock, Scotland
Greenock for John Stewart: new house.
Source: Royal Institute of British Architects. *

Gregynog Hall, Montgomeryshire
Greenock for Charles Douglas Richard Hanbury-Tracy, 4th Baron Sudeley.

7 Buckingham Palace Gate
Working for Lord Sudeley: alterations and additions.

Ray Meadow Farm, Toddington, Evesham, Gloucestershire
Working for Lord Sudeley.
Toddington Estate, Evesham for Lord Sudeley: estate cottages, sculpture.
Sources: *Architectural Review* (7 Buckingham Palace Gate) 1897-2.
The Building News, 22 December, 1882. Reproduction of architectural drawing entitled: 'A Prospect of Gregynog Hall, Montgomeryshire' executed by William Eden Nesfield, copy of the drawing from Mary Oldham, Librarian, University of Wales.
Royal Institute of British Architects.*

Holy Trinity Church, Paddington, London
New organ chamber and alterations to vestry.
Sources: Architectural Review 1897-1 p. 283.
Source: Royal Institute of British Architects. *

Hutton Bonville Hall, Northallerton, Yorkshire
Working for T.R.W. Hilyard
Source: Royal Institute of British Architects.

Lea Wood, near Dethick, Derbyshire
Working for William Walker: Old English style manor house, external stonework, half-timbering, moulded pargetting, hipped roof, half timbered, full height bays, WW, heraldic devices, rose in vase and pies on front elevation and internally the mullioned windows on the stair had stained glass (reminiscent of Bodrhyddan Hall).
Sources: Royal Institute of British Architects. *
Victoria & Albert Museum (Prints Room): DD 11 D1319-1329, 1854.
Architectural Review 1897-1.

Llandyrnog Church, Denbighshire
Working for Captain Mesham at the request of the Rector and Committee: restoration work and font.
Sources: Royal Institute of British Architects.
Victoria & Albert Museum (Prints Room): DD 11 D 1345, May 1871.
Architectural Review, 1897-2.

Maesmawr Hall Farmhouse, Powys, North Wales
Working for John Pryce Davies.
Architectural Review, 1897-2.
Sources: Royal Institute of British Architects. *

Melchet Court, near Sherfield English, Hampshire
Working for Louisa Caroline, Lady Ashburton.
Source: Royal Institute of British Architects. *

Loch Lincart Lodge
Working for Lord and Lady Ashburton: double cottages.
Source: Royal Institute of British Architects. *

Newbattle Abbey, Midlothian
Working for the Marquess and Marchioness of Lothian: turnpike, double cottages on estate and new public library and reading room in village.
Source: Royal Institute of British Architects: plan for proposed Reading Room and Library, 1872.
Source: Royal Institute of British Architects.*

Plas Dinam, Llandinam, Powys, North Wales
Working for Captain Crewe-Read: Old English style manor house, lower storey stone, pointed arch entrance below double jettied half-timbered two storey bay, terminating in a gable. Tall ribbed brick chimneys, pargetting, vertical tile-hanging and heavily mullioned windows. Internally, Great Hall.
Source: Royal Institute of British Architects: mostly working drawings for a house for Capt. Crewe-Read, 1872-73; Plan of stable yard. *

Poltalloch, Scotland
Plan for a Gardener's Cottage dated 20 February 1862.
Source: Nesfield Archives.

Portland Place, London
Valued for mortgage (January 10 1870).
Source: *A Deuce of an Uproar.*

Radwinter Parish Church, Essex
Working for the Revd Frederick Bullock: additions and alterations.
Radwinter Village, Essex: almshouses, shops and cottages.
Sources: Victoria & Albert Museum (Prints Room): shops and cottages DD 11 D1339-1907, 1868-1869; Church Radwinter DD 11 D1333-1338, February 1871.
Architectural Review: 1897-2.
Royal Society of British Architects.*

Rose and Crown Hotel, Market Square, Saffron Walden, Essex
Front refaced in plaster with a pargetted decoration of Roses and Crowns and new stabling.
Sources: Victoria & Albert Museum (Prints Room): DD 11 D 1576-1580, July 1874.
Royal Institute of British Architects: Elevations and detail showing section of cornice; design for alteration to front in Queen Anne style. Elevations and detail of stamped plaster between windows, 1874.
Architectural Review: 1897-2.
Royal Institute of British Architects.*

Scorton Schools, Catterick-on-Swale, Yorkshire
Working for Christopher Craddock.
Source: Royal Institute of British Architects.*

St Mary's Church, Bolton-on-Swale, Yorkshire
Working for Charles Craddock: chancel with Spanish style Minton Majolica tiles tiled floor and dado with wood carvings and wall paintings on each side of the east window with angels – reminiscent of the drawings produced by Eden Nesfield during his Italian journeys. In the Carpenter Chapel, which was built by the Carpenter family from nearby Kiplin Hall to commemorate their family, the tiling motif is repeated, together with stained glass and plaster reliefs depicting workers in the fields. There is a richly decorated altar-piece with texts and paintings in the Pre-Raphaelite manner by Albert Moore. The Arts and Crafts influence was instigated by Captain Walter Carpenter's second wife Beatrice de Grey.
Source: Royal Institute of British Architects.*

St Mary and All the Saints Church, Walsingham, Norfolk
Reredos.
Source: Royal Institute of British Architects.*

Westcombe Park, Greenwich
Working for F. Gerrard: manor house.
Sources: Royal Institute of British Architects.
Victoria & Albert Museum (Prints Room): DD 13 D1357-60.
Architectural Review: 1897-2.

Welcombe Hall, Stratford-upon-Avon, Warwickshire
Working for Mark Phillips.
Sources: Architectural Review: 1897-2.
Royal Institute of British Architects.*

Wigfair Hall, Denbighshire
Working for the Revd R. H. Howard.
Source: Royal Institute of British Architects.*

1880s

Crichel House, Dorset
Gate house.
Source: Royal Institute of British Architects: Lodge – ground plan, chamber plan, back elevation and 2 side elevations, 1871.

Eton College Chapel, Durnford
Memorial brass.
Source: Royal Institute of British Architects.

Farnham Park, Farnham Royal, Buckinghamshire
Working for Henry Vallance: improvements and additions to manor house including pyramid roofed tower, shallow relief carving by the clock showing the sunflower motif of the Aesthetic Movement, an inglenook reminiscent of Bodrhyddan Hall stained glass by Morris & Company.
St Mary's Church, Farnham Royal Church, for Henry Vallance: rebuilt chancel, nave and aisles.
Sources: Royal Institute of British Architects.*
Architectural Review, 2 June 1897.
Victoria & Albert Museum (Prints Room): DD 11 D 1368-69.

Faulkbourne Hall, Bishops Stortford, Essex
Working for Matilda Holland, wife of the Revd William Holland and sister of the Revd Frederick Bullock of Radwinter: alterations and additions.

St Margaret's Parish Church
New aisle, vestry and organ.
Source: Royal Institute of British Architects.*

Gwernyfed Park, Llandinam, Brecon
Working for Colonel Thomas Wood: estate cottages, gas works, iron gates, Powis lodge and manor house with an Elizabethan style front, stone built with three gables.
Source: Royal Institute of British Architects.*

Holbrook House, Wincanton, Somerset
Lodge house.
Source: Royal Institute of British Architects.*

Houghton Hall, Norfolk
Working for Henry Lee Warner.

Houghton Church, Norfolk
Working for Henry Lea Warner: restoration.
Source: Royal Institute of British Architects.*

Memorials

Lady Peel
Monument.
Source: *Journal of the Royal Institute of British Architects.*

Lady Geary
Monument.
Source: Royal Institute of British Architects.

Earl of Craven's son
Monument.
Source: *Journal of the Royal Institute of British Architects.*

Lady Cowper Temple
Memorial.
Source: *Journal of the Royal Society of British Architects.*

Willesden Church, North West London
Tomb.
Working for Mrs H. Vallance.
Source: Royal Institute of British Architects.*

St Mary the Virgin, Ingestre Church, Staffordshire
Monument.
Working for the 18th Earl of Shrewsbury.
Source: Royal Institute of British Architects.*

Manchester
Memorial Cross for T. Armstrong.
Source: Royal Institute of British Architects.

Avington, Berkshire
Monument to Sir John Shelley.
Source: Royal Institute of British Architects.*

West Auchmade House, Greenock
Working for T.R. Lamont.
Source: Royal Institute of British Architects.

Further Sources

1. *Canterbury School of Architecture Review*, 1990: William Eden Nesfield (1835-1888), *Some Houses* by Roger Turner, pp. 16-26.
2. *Architectural Review*: An Impression of William Eden Nesfield by Bulkeley Cresswel, 1 1897, pp. 23-32.
3. *Architectural Review*: J.M. Brydon 1 and 2 May (1897) pp. 235-247. An assessment of William Eden Nesfield's commissions.
(John McKean Brydon was chief assistant to William Eden Nesfield and Richard Norman Shaw between 1867-71).
4. *Country Life*: The Country Houses of William Eden Nesfield by Clive Aslet, Parts 1 and 2, 16 and 23 March 1978.
5. *Royal Institute of British Architects Journal*: John Hebb, 23 May (1903), pp. 396-400. Includes a list of William Eden Nesfield's main works.
6. Royal Institute of British Architects hold Sketchbook 1 – volume containing 167 pages of topographical views of buildings, a few plans and architectural details and sketches of furniture executed in 1859 in Normandy and other parts of northern France.
Sketchbook 11 – volume containing 180 pages of topographical views of buildings and occasional plans, architectural details and sketches of furniture, a few sketches of museum exhibits from books and MSS. Sketch by Albert Moore of the glazing bars of a cottage window and page from medieval Book of Hours. Design for a Gothic bier for a parrot 1863. Design for the restoration of Kings Walden Church, Hertfordshire 1868.
Sketchbook 111 containing 180 pages.
Design for capital S for title page of *Specimens of Medieval Architecture*.
Restored plans of Jervaulx and Easby Abbeys, Yorkshire and sketches of architectural details and furniture, some to scale and some not to scale, but with dimensions given.
Ten loose sheets of topographical sketches, probably perspective views of buildings and architectural details.

Volume of 55 leaves, topographical views of buildings, details of architecture, furniture and *objets d'art*, many drawn to scale, sketches of scenery, copies from paintings and books and illustrations cut from books. Executed between 1853 and 1880 in England and Wales 1853-54 and 1879-80, France 1854, 1857 and 1859 and Italy, Greece and Turkey 1858.
Volume of 60 leaves, topographical views of buildings and details of old and contemporary architecture and furniture, many drawn to scale, some copied from books and museum exhibits, also miscellaneous sketches of scenery, people, animals, etc.
Volume of 82 leaves, topographical views of buildings, architectural details and sketches of furniture.
Volume of 105 leaves – design for the frontispiece of *Specimens of Medieval Architecture*; also topographical views of buildings, architectural details and sketches of furniture.
7. Architectural Association Notes: An article by R. Phené Spiers on the drawings of William Eden Nesfield vol. 11, 3rd Series 1895 pp. 47-49.
8. Architectural Association Notes: Appreciation by James Forsyth, vol. 16, August 1901, pp. 109-111.
9. Victoria & Albert Museum (Prints Room): A colour wheel as a palette PD; Study of Trees, Ash entwined, Thick copse dated 5 September 1870. MD 183-1874.

* Some of the material held by the Royal Institute of British Architects is taken from a list compiled by Mrs Annetta Nesfield from account books after the death of her husband.

Watercolours Exhibited by William Andrews Nesfield at The Old Watercolour Society 1823-1852

The following items are spelled as in the List of the Watercolour Society's Victorian Archives.

19th Exhibition 1823

1. Chateau di Jaro, near Aosta, Piedmont.
2. New Bridge, Canton of Ticino, near Dazio Grande, Switzerland.
3. Study near Witton-le-Wear, Durham (sold to Col. Grenville 5 gns).
4. Chateau de Dussel near Chatillon, Val d'Aosta, Piedmont.
5. Bridge over the Reichenbach, Canton of Berne, Switzerland.
6. Falls of Teufels Bruke, Canton of Uri, Switzerland.
7. Study from Nature (sold to B. Windus, Esq. for 5 gns).
8. Study from Nature.

20th Exhibition 1824

1. Study near Burn Hall, Durham.
2. A Brook Scene:

   But should you lure from his dark haunt,
   beneath the tangled roots of pendant trees,
   the monarch of the brook Behoves you then
   to ply your finest . . . [unattributed].
3. Birch Trees from Nature.
4. A Brood Mare and Foal, Study from Nature.
5. Scene from Breadalbane:

   Around th' adjoining brook, that purls along
   The vocal grove, now fretting o'er a rock
   Now scarcely moving from a reedy pool
   A various group of herds and flocks compose
   Rural confusion [unattributed].
6. Gordale Scar, near Malham, Yorkshire.
7. Study above the High Force of the Tees, Yorkshire.
8. Scene in Brancepeth Park, Durham,
9. Falls of Niagara, from a sketch taken on the spot in 1814.

   Down the steep it thundering shoots,
   and shakes the country round
   And from the loud resounding rocks below
   Dash'd in a cloud of foam, it sends aloft
   A hoary mist, and forms a ceaseless show
   (unattributed).
10. North-west view of Brancepeth Castle, to be engraved for Surtees' *History and Antiquities of Durham*. (Unfortunately Surtees died before the section on Brancepeth could be completed).

21st Exhibition 1825

1. Red-legged Partridge (sold £12).

22nd Exhibition 1826

1. West Point of Staffa, called the Stirk Hill (sold).
2. Treshnish Isles, Coll and Rum in the Distance.
3. Clam Shell Cave, Staffa, Coast of Mull in the Distance (sold).

23rd Exhibition 1827

1. Fingal's Cave, Staffa (sold).
2. View from the Summit of Goat Fell, Arran (sold).
3. Periwinkle Bay, Staffa (sold).
4. Falls of Fyers (sold).
5. Kirch-na-heen, at the head of Glen Sannox, Arran (sold 20 gns).

24th Exhibition 1828
1. Framwellgate Bridge, Durham (sold £20).
2. Glacier of Brenta in the distance Mont Blanc (sold £45).
Round whose stern cerulean brows
White winged snow, and cloud and pearly rain
Frequent attend, with solemn majesty (unattributed).
3. Druidical Temple of Tormore, Arran (sold to Earl Brownlow £20).
4. Falls of the Tummel, near Blair Atholl (sold £40).
5. Deer in Brancepeth Park (sold to T. Griffiths, Esq. £50).
(Appeared in the Sale Rooms in 1875 and 1974 (sold 1984).
6. Force of the Tees, Durham (sold).

25th Exhibition 1829
1. Near Ffestiniog, North Wales (sold 5 gns).

26th Exhibition 1830
1. Mill at Inveraray (sold 6 gns).

27th Exhibition 1831
1. The Laird at the Dinner Spring. Loch Etive, Argyllshire.
2. Dressing a Fly at Stonebyers Falls, on the Clyde (sold 25 gns).

28th Exhibition 1832
1. Hartlepool, Near Durham (sold to Mrs. Griffiths of Norwood 6 gns).
2. Milking (sold 5 gns).
3. Brancepeth Park, Durham (sold 8 gns).
4. Bamborough Castle (sold to Mrs Olive of 4 York Terrace, Regent's Park 15 gns).
(Now in the Victoria & Albert Museum).

29th Exhibition 1833
1. Glen Coe (sold 10 gns).

30th Exhibition 1834
1. Eagles of the Hebrides (sold 25 gns).
2. Castle Howard Park (sold 25 gns).
3. Fingal's Cave, Staffa (sold).

3lst Exhibition 1835
1. Kilchurn Castle, Loch Awe, Strathclyde (sold to J. Ryman, Esq. of Oxford 8 gns).
There is a watercolour of Kilchurn Castle in the Wallace Collection where it is catalogued as being 26'5 x 36'8 and purchased by the 4th Marquess of Hertford, 1863. Wrongly attributed to W.A. Naysmth but corrected in the 2nd Edition of their Catalogue in 1902.

32nd Exhibition 1836
1. Scene near Rothsay, Isle of Bute (sold 8 gns).
2. Loch Fad, Isle of Bute and the House of the late Edmund Keen, Esq. Mountains of Arran in the distance (sold to William Hobson, Jnr. Esq. of 43 Hailey Street 15 gns).
(Sold in the Sale Room 1994).
3. Head of Glen Sannox, Isle of Arran (sold for 20 gns).
4. Kidwelly Castle, South Wales (sold for 10 gns).
(Sold in the Sale Room 1994).
5. Interior of Fingal's Cave, Staffa, Isle of Iona in the distance.
6. Farmyard, Near Durham (sold for 8 gns).

33rd Exhibition 1837
1. Highlanders, at Loch Leven, near Ballahulish (sold to the Marquess of Abercorn 1 Carlton House Terrace.
2. Dovedale, Derbyshire (sold to H. Ashton, Esq. 22 Edward Street, Hampstead Road).
3. Isolated Rock on the Tummel, near Mount Alexander, Blair Athol (sold for 25 gns).
4. Chatsworth Park (sold for 25 gns).

34th Exhibition 1838
1. Cora Castle on the Clyde.
2. Bamborough Castle (re-sold in 1980).
3. Fall, near Dalmally, Argyllshire.
4. Holy Island, Lamlash Bay, Arran.

35th Exhibition 1839
1. Gordale Scar, Yorkshire (sold).
2. Red Deer.
(Attributed to W. Nesfield and R. Hills, sold in 1977).
3. Near the Village of St Remi, Val d'Aosta – Glacier of Brenva and Mont Blanc in the distance (sold 50 gns).
(Re-sold in 1977).
4. In Windsor Park (sold).
5. Peat Bog, near Harlech Castle, North Wales (sold).

6. Kilchurn Castle, Loch Awe (sold 30 gns. To Franz Baron v Kreusser, 141 Regent Street.
A smaller picture under this title was shown in 1835. There is a picture under the same title in the Wallace Collection.
7. Hartlepool Rock (sold 30 gns. to W. Strachan, Esq., Hill Street).

36th Exhibition 1840
1. Rhaiadyr y Mawdach, North Wales.
2. Stack Rocks, Pembrokeshire.
3. Near Loch Rannoch, Shihallion in the distance.
4. Eton College.
5. Flint Castle.

37th Exhibition 1841
1. Gougan Barra, near Bantry (animals by R. Hills) (sold for 50 gns).
2. Falls of the Tunel (sold)
Appeared in the Sale Rooms in 1891 and 1981.
3. A Day in the Highlands (sold for 80 gns to Charles Burrow, 12 The Grove Terrace, Kentish Town).

38th Exhibition 1842
1. Torc Fall, Killarney – from a sketch made during the clearing, under the superintendence of the artist in September 1841.
2. A Day on the Upper Lake, Killarney.

39th Exhibition 1843
1. Entrance to the Gap at Dunloe (sold for 60 gns).

40th Exhibition 1844
1. On the Wharfe, Bolton, Yorkshire (sold)
In the Laing Gallery.
2. In the Vale of Neath (sold for 50 gns).

4lst Exhibition 1845
1. Eagle's Nest, Glengariff, County of Kerry (sold for 50 gns to James Coles, Esq. of Old Park, Clapham).

42nd Exhibition 1846
1. Ross Castle, Killarney (sold for 50 gns. To Hobson Esq).
2. Inverannon, Glen Falloch (sold for 45 gns. To Revd E. Coleridge of Eton).

43rd Exhibition 1847
1. Drumadoun (sold for 60 gns, to Moon, Durham).
2. Ben Noosh, Arran (sold for 60 gns. Frame and glass £9 10).

44th Exhibition 1848
1. Aurora Borealis, Western Isles (sold for 80 gns).
2. Glen Rossie, Arran (sold for 80 gns).

45th Exhibition 1849
1. Buchal Etive, Argyllshire.
2. The Giant's Amphitheatre, near the Causeway (sold for 65 gns).

46th Exhibition 1850
1. The Swan's Nest (sold for 35 gns), frame and glass £5 8s, to Revd John Middleton, King's College, Cambridge (Revd S. Marshall, Eton College).

47th Exhibition 1851
1. Ben Noosh, Arran.

Examples of William Andrews Nesfield's Paintings can be seen in:
1. The Nesfield Archives
2. Other Private Collections
3. The Royal Collection
4. The British Museum
5. The Victoria & Albert Museum
6. The Wallace Collection
7. Eton College
8. The Birmingham Museum & Art Gallery
9. The Laing Gallery, Newcastle-on-Tyne
10. Leeds City Art Gallery
11. The National Gallery of Ireland

Glossary

Some words and terms used in this book

Arboretum: A collection of specimen trees grouped together to demonstrate the diversity of a variety of forms and species. One of the most important collections in Britain is at Westonbirt in Gloucestershire.

Arts and Crafts Movement: This movement came to the fore in the late nineteenth century. It developed as a reaction against mass-production and a desire on the part of a number of artists and craftspeople, to work with their hands, and with local materials. One of its most important proponents was the designer, poet and calligrapher William Morris (1834-1896).

Brick-angle corbels: Ornamental brackets that jut out from a wall.

Camera lucida: Optical instrument used in drawing and painting which, with the aid of mirrors, enables the artist to reproduce his work directly onto to the paper from the object in front of him.

Carpet bedding: Dense formal bedding, replaced seasonally, and usually made up of hardy annuals and Spring bulbs. It is sometimes laid out to represent the pattern on Oriental carpets and was a device that was very popular in municipal parks in the nineteenth early twentieth century.

Clerestory: High window situated above eye level.

Corbeilles: When used in a garden, corbeilles are baskets, round or oval in shape, sometimes made of wickerwork. Raised up in a lawn they were intended for the display of flowers. For example the baskets used by Humphry Repton in the nineteenth century in the gardens at the Royal Pavilion, Brighton.

Diligence: Public, horse-drawn stage coach.

Encaustic tiles: Inlaid ceramic tiles in which the pattern is not a product of the glaze.

Fabrique: An ornamental construction erected in a garden, to enhance the fashion prevalent at the time. For example the Pagoda erected in the Royal Botanic Garden, Kew in the eighteenth century by Sir William Chambers when Chinese art, known as Chinoiserie, was the fashion.

Façade: The exterior front of a building.

Gazebo: Literally to mean 'gaze out'. A small, pavilion-type building.

Gothic: A style of architecture derived from the European architecture of the twelfth to sixteenth centuries. Its main features were ribbed vaults, pointed arches, flying buttresses and tracery. It also featured large windows, ornate facades, towers and pinnacles. It was used in the cathedrals, abbeys and churches of the day.

Gothick: A confectionary use of true Gothic, this style was a pick-and-mix attempt at achieving authenticity. The eighteenth-century house, Strawberry Hill at Twickenham, London, the home of Horace Walpole, is a good example of Gothick architecture.

Guilloche: Oblong, formal beds, usually bordered with clipped evergreens such as box and filled with brightly-coloured, low-growing flowers and bulbs. Often used to divide one area of the garden from another.

Ha-ha: A hidden, sunken ditch designed to give the impression of uninterrupted terrain, intended to exclude livestock from the environs of a property. Reputedly the term Ha-ha is derived from the exclamation of surprise when the viewer came across it in the landscape. Possibly developed from a military defensive ditch.

Half-hipped: A roof with sloping ends as well as sides.

Heraldic devices: Aristocratic, family devices used on seals, banners, badges and coats-of-arms, originally by knights in battle to distinguish adversaries, one from another. In Tudor times they were used on ornamental wooden, brightly coloured poles to denote the power and status of their owners.

Knot gardens: Formal, geometrical gardens, popular in the Tudor period, they used low hedges within the design interwoven into patterns to resemble knots, as a symbol of infinity. Often infilled with herbs.

Liber studiorum: Series of landscapes and seascapes drawn by the landscape painter Joseph Mallord William Turner into a small volume as an *aide memoire.*

Linenfold panels: Relief carving imitating folds in linen used to decorate wooden panels in a house, a feature in the fourteenth to sixteenth centuries.

Mazes: From the word 'amazed', they were puzzle devices made from living, high hedges.

They were devised to ensure that the participant was required to follow a path with no entry areas that would eventually lead him to the centre of the maze.

Mullion: The upright portion, in wood or stone, subdividing a window opening.

Parterre: A garden device that originated in Italy where the arid conditions often meant that flower gardening was difficult. They are strictly symmetrical designs laid out on oblongs or squares and enclosed by clipped evergreens, often of box. Clipped evergreens were also used to form the outlines of thc geometrical shapes which were infilled with coloured gravels.

Parterre-de-broderie: Derived from the Italian model but used in France in the seventeenth century, they featured flowing, plant-like shapes of volutes and scrolls instead of the geometrically-conceived designs found in Italy.

Picturesque: The word picturesque is one that has been used in a variety of ways by artists, poets and writers to describe a landscape. Words such as beautiful, to denote a calm and serene view, and sublime, evoking raging seas, gloomy chasms and mountains, have also been used in connection with it. However, no matter how the word was defined, it conjured up for the artist the notion of the perfect picture. It was first used by the Revd William Gilpin in his *Observations on the River Wye.*

Pies: An ancient device that can be seen in the Cosmati Pavement in Westminster Abbey. Originally probably used to denote infinity. They became popular in the 1850s when the painter Dante Gabriel Rossetti used them to decorate his picture-frames. They were adapted as ornamental, formalized roundels, using a variety of patterns incised into buildings by Eden Nesfield.

Quincunx: In a garden it was an arrangement of five, usually trees, one in each corner of a piece of ground and one in the middle.

Rosarium: A garden intended for the display of roses

Tazza: A large urn or vase, usually part of a formal garden design.

Treillage: A support for climbing plants, usually made of wood or iron.

Bibliography

Books

Abrams, M.H. *The Mirror and the Lamp: Romantic Theory and the Critical Tradition*, Oxford University Press, Oxford (1953).

Ackerman, J.S. *The Villa: Form and Ideology of Country Houses*, Thames & Hudson, London (1990).

Ackroyd, Peter. *Dickens*, Sinclair Stevenson, London (1990).

Agnelli, Mariella. *Gardens of the Italian Villas*, Weidenfeld & Nicolson, London (1987).

Anderson, Perry. *English Questions*, Verso, London and New York (1992).

Allibone, Jill. *Anthony Salvin: A Pioneer of Gothic Revival Architecture*, Lutterworth Press, Cambridge (1988).

Andrews, A. *The Search for the Picturesque Landscape: Aesthetics and Tourism in Britain 1760-1800,* Scolar Press, Aldershot (1989).

Anon., T.S. 'William Andrews Nesfield (1794-1881)' in Stephen, L. and Lee, S. (eds) *The Dictionary of National Biography From the earliest times to 1900* (1894-1895) vol. XV, pp. 226-227, Oxford University Press, Oxford.

Anstruther, Ian. *The Knight and the Umbrella: An Account of the Eglinton Tournament 1839*, Geoffrey Bles, London (1963).

Aslet, Clive. Gray, Victor W. Rowell, Geoffrey. Saint, Andrew. *A Deuce of an Uproar: William Eden Nesfield's Letters to The Rector of Radwinter in Essex*, Friends of Radwinter Church, Radwinter, Saffron Walden, Essex

Attlee, Helena. *Italian Gardens: A Cultural History*, Frances Lincoln Limited, London (2006).

Auger, Suzy (ed.). *Knowing the Past: Victorian Literature and Culture*, Cornell University Press, Ithaca and London (2001).

Bailey, Anthony. *Standing in the Sun: A Life of J.M.W. Turner*, Sinclair Stevenson, London (1997).

Banham, J. and Harris, J. (eds.) *William Morris and the Middle Ages*, Manchester University Press, Manchester (1984).

Barbier, C.F. *William Gilpin: His Drawings, Teaching and Theory of the Picturesque*, Clarendon Press, Oxford (1963).

Barrell, John. *The Idea of Landscape and the Sense of Place 1730-1840*, Cambridge University Press, Cambridge (1972).

Batey, Mavis. Alexander Pope: *The Poet and the Landscape*, Barn Elms (1999).

Bean, W.J. *Botanic Gardens, Kew: Historical and Descriptive*, Cassell & Company Limited, London (1908).

Benson, E.F. *As We Were: A Victorian Peep Show*, The Hogarth Press, London (1985).
Berger, R.W. *Antoine Le Pautre: A French Architect of the Era of Louis X1V*, New York University Press for the College Art Association of America (1969).
Bermingham, A. *Landscape and Ideology: The English Rustic Tradition 1740-1860,* Thames & Hudson, London (1987).
Binney, M. and Hill, A. *Elysian Gardens: Save Britain's Heritage* (May 1979).
Bisgrove, Richard. *William Robinson: The Wild Garden*, Frances Lincoln Limited (2008).
Blanning, T.C.W. *Short Oxford History of Europe: the Nineteenth Century*, Oxford University Press, Oxford (2000).
Blomfield, R. and Thomas, F.I. *The Formal Gardens of England*, Waterstone, London (1892).
Blunt, Wilfred. *In For a Penny: a Prospect of Kew Gardens*, Hamish Hamilton, London (1978).
Boniface, Priscilla (ed.). *In Search of English Gardens: The Travels of John Claudius Loudon and his Wife Jane*, Guild Publishing, London (1987).
Boxhall, Elaine. *The Seven Lives of Kinmel Hall* (1984).
Boydell, J. *History of the River Thames* W. Bulmer & Co., London (1794).
Briggs, Asa. *A Social History of England*, Weidenfeld & Nicolson, London (1983).
Bright, H.A. *The English Flower Garden*, Macmillan & Company, London (1881).
Brooke, E. Aveno. *The Gardens of England*, T. McLean, London (1857).
Brookes, J.A. *A Place in the Country*, Thames & Hudson, London (1984).
Brooks, Christopher. *The Gothic Revival*, Phaidon, London (2001).
Brooks, Christopher. *Signs of the Times*, George Allen & Unwin, London (1985).
Brown, Jane. *Eminent Gardeners 1880-1980,* Viking, London (1990).
Brown, Jane. *The Art and Architecture of Gardens,* Weidenfeld & Nicolson, London (1989).
Brown, Jane. *The Omnipotent Magician: Lancelot 'Capability' Brown 1716-1783*, Chatto & Windus, London (2011).
Brown, G.N. *This Old House: A Domestic Biography*, Betley Court Gallery, Betley, Staffordshire (1987).
Brewer, John. *The Pleasure of the Imagination: English Culture in the Eighteenth Century*, Harper Collins, London (1979).
Buchan, Ursula and Lawson, Andrew. *The Gardens of English Heritage*, Frances
Lincoln Limited, London (2006).
Bury, Adrian (ed.) *The Old Watercolour Club*, 27th Annual volume, London (1949).
Cannadine, David. *The Pleasures of the Past*, William Collins Sons & Company Press (1989).
Cannadine, David. *The Decline and Fall of the British Aristocracy*, Yale University Press (1990).
Carter, T. *The Victorian Garden, Bell & Hyman*, London (1984).
Chadwick, G.F. *The Park and the Town*, The Architectural Press, London (1966).
Chadwick, G.F. *The Works of Sir Joseph Paxton*, The Architectural Press, London (1961).
Chaloner, W.H. *Social and Economic Development of Crewe 1780-1923*, Manchester University Press, Manchester (1950).
Chandler, Alice. *A Dream of Order, Routledge & Kegan Paul*, London (1971).
Clark, Kenneth. *The Gothic Revival: An Essay on the History of Taste*, John Murray, London (1962).
Clemenson, Heather A. *English Country Houses and Landed Estates*, Croom Helm, Beckenham, Kent (1982).
Clifford, Derek. *History of Garden Design*, Faber & Faber, London (1966).
Clifton Taylor Alex. *Another Six English Towns*, British Broadcasting Corporation, London (1984).
Cole, M. *The Tempting Prospect: A Social History of English Watercolours*, British Museum, London (1981).
Colquhoun, Kate. *A Thing in Disguise: the Visionary Life of Joseph Paxton*, Harper Perennial (2003).
Conway, Hazel. *People's Parks: The Design and Development of Victorian Parks in Britain*, Cambridge University Press, Cambridge (1991).

Cousin, Victor. *The Philosophy of the Beautiful*, translated with notes and an introduction by Jesse Cato Daniel, William Pickering, London (1848).

Crossley, Ceri and Small, Ian. *The French Revolution and British Culture*, Oxford University Press, Oxford (1989).

Daniels, Stephen and Watkins, Charles (eds.) *The French Revolution and British Culture*, Oxford University Press, Oxford (1989).

Davis, John P.S. *Antique Garden Ornament 300 Years of Creativity: Artists, Manufacturers and Materials*, Antique Collectors Club, Woodbridge, Suffolk (1991).

Deane, P. and Cole, W.A. *British Economic Growth 1688-1959*, Cambridge University Press, Cambridge (1962).

Desmond, Ray. *Kew: The History of the Royal Botanic Gardens*, The Harvill Press and the Royal Botanic Gardens, London (1995).

Desmond, Ray. *Bibliography of British Gardens*, St Paul's Biographies, Winchester, Hampshire (1988).

De Figeirdeo, Paul and Treuherz, Julian, *Cheshire Country Houses*, Phillimore, Chichester, West Sussex (1988).

Dickens, A.G. and Gash, N. (eds.) *Aristocracy & People: Britain 1815-1865*, Edward Arnold, London (1979).

Digby, George Wingfield. *Elizabethan Embroidery*, Faber & Faber, London (1963).

Dixon Hunt, John and Conan, Michael (eds.). *Tradition and Innovation in French Garden Art: Chapters of a New History*, University of Pennsylvania Press (2002).

Dixon Hunt, John. *A World of Gardens*, Reaktion Books Limited, London (2012).

Dixon Hunt, John. Greater *Perfections: The Practice of Garden Theory*, Thames & Hudson, London (2000).

Dixon Hunt, John. *Gardens and the Picturesque: Studies in the History of Landscape Architecture*, The MIT Press, Cambridge, Massachesetts, U.S.A. (1994).

Dixon Hunt, John. *Garden and Grove: The Italian Renaissance Garden in the English Imagination 1600-1750*, J.M. Dent & Sons Limited, London (1986).

Dixon Hunt, John. *The Wider Sea: A Life of John Ruskin*: J.M. Dent & Sons Limited, London (1982)

Dixon Hunt, John. *The Figure in the Landscape*, John Hopkins University Press, Baltimore, U.S.A. (1976).

Dixon Hunt, John and Willis, Peter (eds.) *The Genius of the Place*, Paul Elek, London and New Hampshire, U.S.A. (1975).

Eastage, C.L. *The Gothic Revival*, Loughborough University Press, Loughborough (1972).

Eliot, Simon and Stern, Beverley. *The Age of Enlightenment: An Anthology of Eighteenth-Century Texts*, Oxford University Press, Oxford (1981).

Elliott, Brent. *Victorian Gardens*, B.T. Batsford Limited, London (1986).

Engell James, *The Creative Imagination*, Harvard University Press, Cambridge, Massachusetts (1981).

Evans, E.J. *The Forging of the Modern State: Early Industrial Britain* 1783-1870, Longmans, London (1983).

Evans, Shirley. *Nesfield's Monster Work: The Gardens of Witley Court*, A Peter Huxtable Designs Publication, Worcestershire (1994).

Evans, Leslie. *Crewe Hall Estate Lands: Past and Present*, unpublished B.A. Hons. Thesis, Manchester Metropolitan University, Manchester (1986).

Everett, Nigel. *The Tory View of Landscape*, The Paul Mellon Centre for Studies in British Art, Yale University Press, London and New York (1994).

Ferris, F. *The Parterre or Whole Art of Forming Flower Gardens*, Bull, Holles, London (1837).

Finsberg, A.J. *The Life of J.M.W. Turner R.A.*, Oxford Univesity Press, Oxford (1967).

Fleming, Laurence and Gore, Alan. *The English Garden*, Michael Joseph, London (1979).

Fletcher, H.R. *The Story of the Royal Horticultural Society 18904-1968*, Oxford University Press, Oxford (1969).

Flint, Kate. *The Victorians and the Visual Imagination,* Cambridge University Press, Cambridge (2006).
Focilon, H. *The Art of the West: II Gothic Landmarks in Art History*, Phaidon, London (1980).
Forsyth, A. Yesterday's Gardens, The Royal Commission for Historical Monuments, London (1980).
Foster, R. *Patterns of Thought*, Jonathan Cape, London (1991).
Fox, H.M. *André Le Nôtre: Garden Architect to Kings*, B.T. Batsford Limited, London (1962).
Gage, J. *Colour & Culture Practice and Meaning from Antiquity to Abstraction*, Thames & Hudson, London (1995).
Galinou, M. (ed.) *The Glorious History of London's Parks and Gardens*, Anaya Publishers Limited, London (1990).
Gambier-Parry. *Annals of an Eton House*, John Murray, London (1907).
Garner-Wilkinson, J. *On Colour and on the Necessity for A General Diffusion of Taste Among All Classes,* John Murray, London (1958).
Gash, Norman (ed.) *The Age of Peel*, Edward Arnold, London (1969).
Gilpin, William Sawrey. *Practical Hints upon Landscape Gardening with some remarks on Domestic Architecture as connected with scenery*, T. Cadell, Strand, London (1835).
Golby, J.M. (ed.) *Culture and Society in Britain 1850-1890: A Source Book of Contemporary Writings*, Oxford University Press, Oxford (1990).
Girard, Jacques. *Versailles Gardens: Sculpture and Mythology*, Sotheby's Publications, London (1985).
Girouard, Mark. *Return to Camelot: Chivalry and the English Gentleman*, Yale University Press, London and New Haven (1981).
Girouard, Mark. *The Victorian Country House,* Clarendon Press, Oxford (1971).
Girouard, Mark. *Life in the English Country House*, Book Club Associates in arrangement with Yale University Press, London and New Haven (1971).
Girouard, Mark. *The English Town*, Yale University Press, London and New Haven (1990).
Graham, G.S. *A Concise History of Canada,* Thames & Hudson, London (1968).
Gratton, A. *Alberti: Master Builder of the Italian Renaissance*, Allan Lane the Penguin Press, Middlesex, England (2000).
Green, Nicholas. *The Spectacle of Nature: Landscape and Bourgeois culture in nineteenth-century France*, Manchester University Press, Manchester (1990).
Griswold, Mae and Weller, Eleanor. *The Golden Age of American Gardens: Proud Owners and Private Estates 1890-1940*, Harry N. Abrahams Inc., New York (1991).
Hadfield, M.A. *A History of British Gardens*, The Hamlyn Publishing Group Limited, London (1969).
Hamilton Finlay, Ian. *Nature Over Again After Poussin*, Collins, Exhibition Hall University of Strathclyde, Glasgow (1980).
Hamilton Hazelhurst, Franklin. *Gardens of Illusion*, Vanderbilt University Press, Nashville, Tennessee, U.S.A. (1980).
Hamilton Hazelhurst, Franklin. *Jacques Boyceau and The French Formal Garden*, University of Georgia Press, Athens, Georgia, U.S.A. (1966).
Harris, J. *The Artist and the Country House*, Sotheby's Publications, London (1979).
Harrison, C. (ed.) *A History of Keele*, University of Keele, Keele (1989).
Haskell, Francis and Penny. *Taste and the Antique: The Love of Classical Sculpture 1500-1900:* Yale University Press, London and New Haven (1982).
Herrmann, Frank. *The English Collectors: A Documentary Source Book*, John Murray, London (1999).
Herrmann, Luke. *British Landscape Paintings of the Eighteenth Century*, Faber & Faber, London (1973).
Herrmann, Luke. *Ruskin and Turner*, Faber & Faber, London (1968).
Hibberd, Shirley. *Rustic Adornments for Homes of Taste*, (3rd ed.) Groombridge & Sons Limited, London (1870).
Highstone, J. *Victorian Gardens*, Harper & Row, London (1982).

Hill, C. *British Economic and Social History 1700-1975*, Edward Arnold, London (1977).
Hill, C. *Reformation to Industrial Revolution 1530-1780*, The Pelican Economic History of Britain, Penguin Books, Middlesex, England (1969).
Hinchliffe, Edward. *Barthomley*, Longman, Brown, Green 7 Longmans, London (1856).
Hitchcock, Henry Russell. *Early Victorian Architecture*, vol. 1, Penguin Books, Middlesex, England (1954).
Hobhouse, Hermoine. *Prince Albert His Life and Work*, Hamish Hamilton Limited in conjunction with the Observer, Midland Bank Group and The Royal College of Art (1983).
Hobhouse, Penelope and Wood, Michael. *Painted Gardens, English Watercolours 1850-1914*, Pavilion Michael Joseph, London (1988).
Hobsbawm, E.J. *The Age of Capital 1848-1875*, Abacus, London (1980).
Hobsbawm, E.J. *The Age of Revolution 1789-1848*, Cardinal Publishing Group, Indianapolis, U.S.A. (1962).
Honour, Hugh. *Neo-Classicism*, Penguin Books, Middlesex, England (1980).
Hope Nicolson, Marjorie. *Mountain Gloom Mountain Glory: Development of the Aesthetics of the Infinite*, Cornell University Press, New York (1959).
Horfe, S. *John Leech and the Victorian Scene*, Antique Collectors Club, Woodbridge, Suffolk (1984).
Horn, Pamela. *The Changing Countryside in Victorian and Edwardian England and Wales*, The Athlone Press, London (1984).
Horn, Pamela. *The Rural World: Social Change in the English Countryside 1780-1850,* Hutchinson, London (1980).
Houghton, Walter E. *The Victorian Frame of Mind 1830-1870*, Published for Wellesley College by Yale University Press, London and New Haven (1985).
Hussey, Christopher. *The Picturesque: Studies in a point of view*, Frank Cass & Company Limited, London (1983).
Hussey, Christopher. *English Country Houses: Late Georgian 1800-1840*, Antique Collectors Club, Woodbridge, Suffolk (1985).
Huxley, Anthony. *An Illustrated History of Gardening*, published in association with the Royal Horticultural Society, London (1983).
Huxley, Anthony. *The Painted Garden: Through the Artist's Eye*, London (1988).
Hyams, Edward. *The English Garden*, Thames & Hudson, London (1964).
Hyams, Edward. *Capability Brown & Humphry Repton*, Charles Scribner & Sons, London (1971).
Inglis-Jones, Elizabeth. *Peacocks in Paradise*, Gormer Press, Llandysul, Dyfed (1990).
Jackson-Stops, Gervase. *An English Arcadia 1600-1990, The* National Trust (1991).
Jackson, W.T. *The Development of Transportation in Modern England,* Frank Cass & Company Limited, London (1966).
Jacques, David. *Georgian Gardens: The Reign of Nature,* Butler & Turner Limited, London (1983).
James, J. *The Theory and Practice of Gardening*, printed by George Jones and told by Maurice Atlas at the Golden Bell in St Paul's Churchyard, London (1712).
Jekyll, G. *Garden Ornament*, published originally in *Country Life*, George Newnes Limited, London (1918) Antique Collectors Club (1982).
Jekyll, G. and Elgood, G.S. *Some English Gardens*, Longmans, London (1904).
Jellicoe, Goode and Lancaster (eds.) *The Oxford Companion to Gardens*, Oxford University Press, Oxford (1986).
Johnson, George William. *A History of English Gardening*, Baldwin & Cradock and Longman & Company, London (1829).
Kemp, F. *How to Lay out a Garden*, Bradbury & Evans, London (1864).
Laird, Mark. *The Flowering of the Landscape Garden: English Pleasure Gardens 1720-1800,* University of Pennsylvania Press, Philadelphia, U.S.A. (1999).

Laslett, P. *The World We Have Lost*, Methuen & Company, London (1965).
Lazzard, C. *The Italian Renaissance Garden*, Yale University Press, London and New Haven (1990).
Le Dantec, Denise and Jean-Pierre, *Reading the French Garden: Story and History*, Le Roman des Jardins de France, Libraire Plon, Paris (1987) Massachusetts Institute of Technology, Massachusetts, New England, U.S.A. (1990).
Lees-Milne, James. *People and Places*, John Murray, London (2001).
Levin, H. *The Myth of the Golden Age in the Renaissance,* Faber & Faber, London (1970).
Lindsay, J.G. and Cash, M. *Inveraray and the Dukes of Argyll*, Edinburgh University Press, Edinburgh (1973).
Lorenz, Eitner. *Neo-Classicism and Romanticism 1750-1850*, Prentice-Hall International Press, London (1971).
Loudon, John Claudius. *The Suburban Gardens and Villa Companion,* London (1838).
Loudon, John Claudius. *The Landscape Gardens and Landscape Architecture of the late Humphry Repton being his Entire Works on the Subjects.* New edition, Longman & Company, London and A. & C. Black, Edinburgh (1840).
MacCloud, Dianne Sachko. *Art and the Victorian Middle Class: Money and the Making of Cultural Identity,* Cambridge University Press, Cambridge (1998).
Mackay Hitsman, J. *The Incredible War of 1812: A Military History*, University of Toronto Press, Canada (1965).
Mallalieu, H.C. *William Andrews Nesfield*, New Dictionary of National Biography, Oxford (2004).
Masson, Georgina. *Italian Gardens*, Thames & Hudson, London (1996).
Matson, John. *Dear Osborne*, Hamish Hamilton, London (2000).
McCarthy, Michael. *The Origins of the Gothic Revival,* The Paul Mellon Centre for Studies in British Art, Yale University Press, London and New Haven (1987).
McLean, Teresa. *Medieval English Gardens*, William Collins Sons & Co. Ltd., London (1981).
McIntosh, Charles. *The Flower Garden*, William S. Orr & Company Limited, London (1838).
McIntosh, Charles, *The Book of the Garden*, vol. 3, William Blackwood and Sons, Edinburgh and London (1853).
Mingay (ed.) *History of Coombe Abbey*, Jones-Sands Publishing, Wirral, Merseyside (1981).
Moffett, Marian and Fazio Michael. *A World History of Architecture*, Laurence King Publishing London (2003).
Mordaunt Crook, J. *The Rise of the Nouveaux Riches: Style and Status in Victorian and Edwardian Architecture,* John Murray, London (1999).
Mordaunt Crook, J. *William Burges and the High Victorian Dream*, John Murray, London (1981) Revised Frances Lincoln (2013).
Mosser, Monique and Teysott, Georges (eds.) *Garden Design: The Western Tradition from Renaissance to the Present Day,* Thames & Hudson, London (1991).
Mowl, Timothy. *Historic Gardens of Cornwall,* Tempus, Stroud, Gloucestershire (2005).
Mowl, Timothy. *Historic Gardens of Gloucestershire*, Tempus, Stroud, Gloucestershire (2002).
Mowl, Timothy. *Gentlemen and Players: Gardens of the British Landscape*, Sutton Publishing Limited, Stroud, Gloucestershire (2000).
Munro, Jane. *British Landscape Watercolours 1750-1850,* The Herbert Press in Association with the Fitzwilliam Museum, Cambridge (1994).
Nagler, A.M. *Theatre Festivals of the Medici 1539-1637*, Yale University Press, London and New Haven (1964).
Nesfield, William Eden, *Specimens of Medieval Architecture of the Twelfth and Thirteenth Centuries in France and Italy,* London (1862)
Nesfield, Henry William. *A Chequered Career: 15 Years in New Zealand & Australia,* London (1881).
Nevison, J.L. *The Embroidery Patterns of Thomas Trevelyon*, University Press, Glasgow (1968).

Newsome, David. *Perspection & Introspection in an Age of Change*, John Murray, London (1997).

Orbach, J. *Victorian Architecture in Britain*, Blue Guide A. 7 C. Black, London (1987).

Orgel, Stephen (ed.) *The Renaissance Imagination*, University of California Press, California, U.S.A. (1975).

Ottewill, David. *The Edwardian Garden*, Yale University Press, London and New Haven (1989).

Paulson, Ronald, *Literary Landscapes: Turner and Constable*, Yale University Press, London and New Haven (1982).

Patterson, Allen. *The Gardens at Kew*, Frances Lincoln, London (2008).

Peckman, Morse. *Beyond the Tragic Vision: The Georgian Quest for Identity in the 19th Century*, George Braziller, New York (1962).

Pevsner, N. and Hubbard, F. *The Buildings of England: Cheshire*, Penguin, Middlesex, England (1971).

Perkin, Harold. *Origins of Modern English Society*, Routledge & Kegan Paul, London (1969).

Pizzoni, F. *The Garden: A History in Landscape and Art*, Aurum Press, London (1999).

Plumpton, George. *The Garden Makers: The Great Tradition of Garden Design from 1600 to the Present Day*, Pavilion, London (1993).

Price, Uvedale. *On the Picturesque 1796*, Reprint Woodstock Books and 2000 Books International.

Price, Uvedale, *Essays on the Picturesque*, Reprint Farnborough, vol. 1 (1971).

Price, Uvedale, *Essays on the Picturesque*, London (1842).

Quest-Ritson, Charles. *The English Garden: A Social History*, Viking, London (2003).

Rackman, Oliver. *The History of the Countryside*, J.M. Dent & Sons Limited, London and Melbourne (1986).

Repton, Humphry. *Fragments on the Theory and Practice of Landscape Gardening*, London (1816).

Ridgway, Christopher (ed.) 1996a *William Andrews Nesfield*: Victorian Landscape Architect, Papers from the Bicentenary Conference, The Kings Manor, York, 1994, York Institute of Advanced Architectural Studies, The University of York.

Richardson, Tim. *The Arcadian Friends: Inventing the English Landscape Garden*, Bantam Prress (2007).

Roberts, D. *Paternalism in Early Victorian England*, Croom Helm, London and Rutgers University Press, New Brunswick, New Jersey, Aided by Research Committee of Dartmouth College (1979).

Robinson, William. *Garden Design and Architects Gardens*, John Murray, London (1892).

Roget, J. L. *History of the Old Water-Colour Society*, vols. 1-2 ,Longman, Green & Company (1892) reprinted Antique Collectors Club, Woodbridge, Suffolk (1972).

Rosen, Charles and Zovner, Henri. *Romanticism and Realism: The Methodology of 19th Century Art*, Faber & Faber, London (1984).

Royal Parks Survey, Directorate of Ancient Monuments and Historical Buildings, Department of the Environment, London (July 1981).

Ruskin, John. *Modern Painters*, vol. III, Smith, Elder & Company, London (1860).

Saint, Andrew. *Richard Norman Shaw*, Paul Mellon Studies in British Art, Yale University Press, London and New Haven (1976).

Saunders, A. *Regent's Park: A Study of the Development of the Area from 1096 to the Present Day*, David & Charles, Newton Abbot, Devon (1969).

Saward, J. *Magical Paths*, Mitchell Beazley and Imprint of Octopus Publishing Group Limited, London (2002).

Schultz, Max F. *Paradise Preserved: Recreations of Eden in Eighteenth and Nineteenth Century England*, Cambridge University Press, Cambridge (1985).

Schwitzer, Joan. *History and Association of Coleshill House*, Hornsey Historical Society, London.

Smith, C.H.J. *Parks and Pleasure Grounds*, Reece & Company, London (1952).

Smith, E.A. *Reform and Revolution: A Diary of Reform in England 1830-1832*, Alan Sutton Publishing, Stroud, Gloucestershire (1992).

Solkin, David H. *Painting for Money: the Visual Arts and the Public Sphere in Eighteenth-century England*, Yale University Press, London and New Haven (1993).

Soxby, J.J. *The Municipal Parks: Gardens and Open Spaces in London*, Elliot Stock, London (1898).
Steegman, John. *Victorian Taste: A Study of the Arts and Architecture*, Nelson's University Paperbacks, London (1970).
Strong, Roy. *Royal Gardens*, British Broadcasting Corporation, London (1992).
Strong, Roy. *The Renaissance Garden in England*, Thames & Hudson, London (1998).
Strong, Roy, *The Artist and the Garden*, The Paul Mellon Centre for Study in British Art by Yale University Press, New Haven and London (2000).
Stroud, Dorothy. *Capability Brown*, Faber & Faber, London (1957).
Summerson, J. *Royal Parks Survey*, Directorate of Ancient Monuments and Historic Buildings, Department of the Environment, London (1981).
Sweet, Rosemary. *Antiquaries: The Discovery of the Past in 18th Century Britain, Hambledon*, London and New York (2000).
Swindon, Nathaniel. *Beauties of Flora Display'd*, London (1778).
Tait, A.A. *The Landscape Garden in Scotland 1735-1835*, Edinburgh University Press, Edinburgh (1980).
Taylor, Geoffrey. *The Victorian Flower Garden*, Sheffington, London (1952).
Thomas, Graham Stuart. *Gardens of the National Trust*, Book Club Associates, London (1979).
Thompson, F.M. *The Rise of Respectable Society: A Society History of Victorian Britain 1830-1900*, Fontana Press, Harvard University Press, Cambridge, Massachusetts, U.S.A. (1988).
Thorn, M. *Tennyson*, Little, Brown & Company, London (1992).
Tooley, M.J. 1994a *William Andrews Nesfield* 1794-1881 Exhibition Guide (iv) + 25 pp. Michaelmas Books, Witton-le-Wear, Co. Durham.
Torelli, Giacomo and Bjurstrom, Per *Romantic Illusion: Baroque State Design*, Almquist & Wiksell, Stockholm (1961).
Tjaden, W.L. *The History of the Horticultural Club*, Oxford (1974).
Triggs, H.T. *Formal Gardens in England and Scotland*, B.T. Batsford Limited, London (1902).
Trollope, Anthony, *The Way We Live Now*, World's Classics, London (1875).
Walker, Robert O. Witley, *Worcestershire: A Record of a Parish*, Great Witley, Worcestershire (1985).
Walford, E (ed.) *County Familes of the United Kingdom*, Reprint Robert Hardwicke (1960).
Walpole Society, 41st Volume (1966-1968).
Waterhouse, Ellis. *Painting in Britain 1530-1720*, Pelican History of Art, Penguin Books (1953).
Watkin, David. *The English Vision: The Picturesque in Architecture, Landscape and Garden Design*, John Murray, London (1982).
Watkins, Charles and Cowell, Ben, *Uvedale Price (1747-1820): Decoding the Picturesque*, The Boydell Press (2012).
Who's Who in Architecture from 1400 to the Present Day, Weidenfeld & Nicolson, London (1977).
Whalley, Robin and Jennings, Anne. *Knot Gardens and Parterres*, Barn Elms, London (1998).
Wiebenson, Dora. *The Picturesque Garden in France*, Princetown University Prress, Princetown, New Jersey, U.S.A. (1978).
Williams, Iolo. *Early English Watercolours*, Kingsmead Reprints, Bath (1970).
Williams, Raymond. *The Country and the City*, Paladin, St Albans (1975).
Williamson, T. *Polite Landscapes: Gardens and Society in 18th century England*, Alan Sutton Publishing Limited, Stroud, Gloucestershire and John Hopkins University Press, Baltimore, Maryland, U.S.A. (1995).
Willis, Peter. *Charles Bridgeman and the English Landscape Garden*, Elysium Press Publishers, Macclesfield, Cheshire (2002).
Wilton, Andrew. *Turner in His Time*, Thames & Hudson, London (1987).

Wilton, Andrew. *Turner Abroad: France, Italy, Germany, Switzerland*, A Colonnade Book, British Museum Publications Limited, London (1982).
Woodbridge, Kenneth. *Princely Gardens: The Origins and Development of the French Formal Style*, Thames & Hudson, London (1986).
Woodbridge, Kenneth. *Landscape and Antiquity: Aspects of English Culture at Stourhead 1718-1836,* Clarendon Press, Oxford (1970).
Word and Image, January-June 1988, vols. 1 and 2.
Worsley, Giles. *England's Lost Houses* from the Archives of Country Life, Aurum Press, London (2002).
Yates, F.A. *Astraea: The Imperial Theme in the Sixteenth Century,* Routledge & Kegan Paul, London (1975).
Young, M. *Guide to the Botanic Gardens of Britain*, William Collins Sons and Company Limited, London (1987).

Articles

Acloque, Guy and Cornforth, John. 'The Eternal Gothic of Eaton: Eaton Hall, Cheshire I', *Country Life*, vol. cxlix 149 (11 February 1971) pp. 304-307.
Anon. 'Arley Hall, Cheshire', *Country Life,* vol. 16 (1904) pp. 942-950.
Anon. 'Barford Hill, Warwickshire: British Homes and Gardens', *The Garden,* 59 (1901) pp. 298-300.
Anon. 'Bayham Abbey, Kent: Bayham Abbey Gardens', *The Garden,* vol. 9 (1876) pp. 128-130.
Anon. 'Bayham Abbey, Kent', *Gardening World,* vol. 13 (1896) pp. 57-58.
Anon. 'Clumber, Nottinghamshire II', *Country Life,* vol. 24 (19 September 1908) pp. 384-389.
Anon. 'Crewe Hall, Cheshire: Garden Decoration', *The Gardeners Chronicle,* (7 February 1862) pp. 124.
Anon. 'Dogmersfield Park, Hampshire III', *Country Life Illustrated,* vol. 9 (27 April 1901) pp. 528-533.
Anon. 'Elizabethan Gardens', *Frazer's Magazine,* LXX (August 1864) pp. 179-191.
Anon. 'Garden Design: the Avenue Gardens in the Regent's Park', *The Garden* (21 June 1873) p. 474.
Anon. 'Hillingdon Court, Middlesex: Notes on Gardens', *Gardening World, i* (1884) p. 199.
Anon. 'Holkham Park: the Seat of the Earl of Leicester', *Gardeners Magazine,* vol. 16 (1840) pp. 666-667.
Anon. 'Holkham Hall, Norfolk', *Country Life,* vol. 2 (1897).
Anon. 'Linton Park, Kent', *Country Life Illustrated,* vol. 9 (1901) pp. 364-365.
Anon. 'Mentmore, Leighton Buzzard I', *Gardeners Chronicle* (1890) pp. 488-489.
Anon. 'Mentmore, Buckinghamshire: British Homes and Gardens', *The Garden,* vol. 62 (1902) pp. 305-306.
Anon. 'Newport Almeley', Hereford and Worcestershire Garden Trust (Summer 1998).
Anon. 'Preston Hall, Kent', *Gardeners Chronicle, ii* (1884) pp. 461-462.
Anon. 'Preston Hall, Kent', *Gardeners Chronicle, ii* (1893) pp. 236-238.
Anon. 'Regent's Park', *Gardeners Chronicle* (Saturday 26 April 1862) p. 379.
Anon. 'Royal Horticultural Society, Kensington', *Gardeners Chronicle* (Saturday 17 September 1864) pp. 889-890).
Anon. 'The New Garden of the Royal Horticultural Society', *Floral World and Garden Guide,* iv (1861) pp. 125-128.
Anon. 'Royal Horticultural Society, Kensington', *Gardeners Chronicle* (23 April 1854) pp. 391-392.
Anon. 'Somerleyton, Suffolk', *The Florist* (November 1857) pp. 327-329.
Anon. 'Stancliffe, Derbyshire', *Gardeners Chronicle* (1884) pp. 807-809.
Anon. 'Stancliffe, Derbyshire', *Gardeners Chronicle,* ii (1886) pp. 201-211.

Anon. 'Flower Gardening at Stoke Rochford, Lincolnshire', *Gardeners Chronicle* (1879) pp. 44-45.

Anon. 'Stoke Rochford, Lincolnshire', *Country Life Illustrated,* vol. 10 (1901) pp. 592-597.

Anon. 'Stoneleigh Abbey, Warwickshire', *Gardeners Chronicle,* (1890) p. 328.

Anon. 'Stoneleigh Abbey, Warwickshire', *Country Life Illustrated,* vol. 6 (1899) pp. 528-533.

Anon. 'Stoneleigh Abbey, Warwickshire', *Country Life Illustrated,* vol. 10 (1901) pp. 104-105.

Anon. 'Stoneleigh Abbey, Warwickshire', *Country Life,* vol. 160 pp. 1974-1975.

Anon. 'Tittenhurst, Sunninghill', *Gardeners Chronicle,* ii (1904) pp. 327-329.

Anon. 'The Gardens of Witley Court, Worcestershire', Gardeners Chronicle: (21 June 1873).

Antrobus, Florence C.M. 'Amesbury Abbey, Amesburym, Wilts.', *Country Life,* vol. xi, II, no. 269 (March 1902) pp. 272-279.

(Lady) Ashbrook. 'Arley Hall, Cheshire', *The Garden,* (1981) pp. 183-190.

Aslet, Clive. 'Bodrhyddan, Flintshire', *Country Life,* vol. 164 (1978) pp. 158-161, 226.

Beaton, D. 'Royal Horticultural Society', *Journal of Horticulture,* Cottage Gardener (13 August 1861) pp. 373-375.

Chambers, Douglas F. 'The Translation of Antiquiry: Virgil, Pliny the Landscape Garden', *University of Toronto Quarterly* (Spring 1991): vol 60 no 1 (1991) pp. 354-73.

(The) Conductor. 'Grenfell Pascoe Esq: Taplow House, Buckinghamshire', *Gardeners Magazine,* vol. 9 (1833) pp. 658-660.

Conway, Martin. 'Barham Court, Kent', *Country Life,* vol. 45 (1919) pp. 142-147.

Cornforth, John. 'Drayton House, Northamptonshire 11', *Country Life,* vol. cxxxvi 137 (20 May 1965) pp. 1216-1219.

Cornforth, John. 'Basildon House, Berkshire 1', *Country Life,* vol. 161 (1977) pp. 1158-1161.

Cornforth, John. 'Capesthorne Hall 1 Cheshire, Views of an Early Victorian House', *Country Life,* vol. clxii 162 (1 September 1977) pp. 535-538.

Cornforth, John. 'Capesthorne Hall 11 Cheshire Family Histories in Watercolour.' *Country Life* vol. clxii 162 (8 September 1977) pp. 607-610.

Crump, W.B. 'Methley Hall and its Builders', Thoresby Society Miscellany, vol. XXXII part IV (1942) pp. 313-348.

Curtis, Charles H. 'The Gardens of Tittenhurst, Berkshire', *Gardeners Magazine* (1906) pp. 253-257.

Diesdelkamp, Edward J. 'The Design and Building of the Palm House: Royal Botanic Gardens, Kew', Garden History, *Journal of the Garden History Society,* vol. 2, no 3 p. 23.

Dormant, Richard. 'David Cox: The Watercolour Weatherman.' *Daily Telegraph* (March 2000) p. 23.

Douglas, J. 'The Flower Garden and Pleasure Grounds: Worsley Hall, Lancashire.' *Journal of Horticulture,* Cottage Gardener vol. 31 (1876) pp. 237-239.

D.T.F. 'Lynford Hall, Norfolk', *Gardeners Chronicle* (Saturday 20 September 1884.

Dunkin, H. 'Barham Court, Kent', *Journal of Horticulture,* Cottage Gardener: NS vol. 33 (1896) pp. 223-224.

Durrant, Horatia. 'The Trials of a Landscape Gardener', *Cheshire Life* (February 1954) pp. 18-19.

Elliott, Brent. 'Victorian Garden Design' in Harris, John 'The Garden: A celebration of one thousand years of British gardening', Victoria & Albert Museum and New Perspectives Publishing Limited (1979).

Elliott, Brent. 'Master of the Geometric Art', *The Garden* 106 (1981) pp. 488-491.

ESS. 'Lynford Hall, Norfolk', *Country Life,* vol. 14 (1903) pp. 758-765.

Evans, Shirley. 'Master Designer', *The Antique Collector,* vol. 63 no 9 (October 1992) pp. 52-55.

Evans, Shirley. 'Talented Twice Over', *Country Life,* vol. xxxvii no. 14 (8 April 1993) pp. 64-66.

Evans, Shirley. 'Following in Turner's Footsteps', *Turner Society News,* no. 69 (August 1994) pp. 3-4.

Evans, Shirley. 'Life and Times of William Andrews Nesfield', in Tooley M.J. (ed.) (1994a) pp. 1-7.

Evans, Shirley, 'Arthur Markham Nesfield Remembered', *Garden History Society* news, 91, Spring 2013, pp. 14-19.

Evans, Shirley, 'Reflections on the connection between *Plein Aire* painting and its influence on the landscape designs of William Andrews Nesfield', *Garden History Society* news 92, Summer 2013, pp. 23-25.
Tooley, M.J. 'William Andrews Nesfield 1794-1881: soldier, painter, landscape gardener' in Batho, G.R. Durham Biographies, vol. 1, Durham, S. Durham County History Society.
Vagabond. 'Combermere Abbey, Cheshire', *Gardeners Chronicle,* ii (1892) pp. 363-364.
Visitor. 'Birdsall House, Yorkshire: The Seat of the Right Hon. Lord Middleton', *Journal of Horticulture,* Cottage Gardener (1879) vol. 61 pp. 326-328.
Warner, Tim. 'Line of Least Resistance', *Country Life* (4 April 1991) pp. 86-89.
Whitelaw, H.R. 'Bayham Abbey, Kent', *Gardeners Chronicle,* ii (1908) p. 170.
(A), Wiltshire Rector. 'A Day at Linton Park, Kent', *Journal of Horticulture,* Cottage Gardener: vol. 25 (1866) pp. 189-190.
W.I. 'Canford Manor, Dorset.' *Journal of Horticulture*, Cottage Gardener (1890) NS, vol. 21, pp. 182-183.
Wilkinson, Tom. and Targel, Anthea. 'Survey of Eighteenth Century Gardens', *Journal of Garden History,* (1991) vol. 11 nos. 1 and 2 pp. 5-16.
Woudstra, J. and Fieldhouse, Ken. 'The Regeneration of Public Parks', *Journal of the Garden History Society,* Landscape Design Trust and F. & F. N. Spon, London with support from English Heritage (2000).
Wright, J. 'Mentmore, Buckinghamshire', *Journal of Horticulture,* Cottage Gardener (1882) NS. vol. 5 pp. 478-481.
Wright, J. 'Stoneleigh Abbey', *Journal of Horticulture*, Cottage Gardener (1898) NS. vol 37 pp. 228-230.
W.S. 'Amesbury Abbey, Wiltshire', *Country Life,* ii, no. 269, pp. 272-279.
Zingari. 'Mentmore: The Seat of the Earl of Rosebery', *Journal of Horticulture,* Cottage Gardener (1900) NS. vol. 40 pp. 219-225.

Unpublished Works

I am grateful to the following individuals and organizations for permission to publish from their archives:

Arley Hall, Cheshire: The Trustees of Viscount Ashbrook.
Balcaskie, Fife, Scotland: Mr Toby Anstruther.
Bodleian Library, Oxford: University of Oxford.
British Architectural Library, Drawings and Archives Collections.
Broughton Hall, Skipton, Yorkshire: Mr Roger Tempest.
Holkham Hall, Norfolk: Viscount Coke and the Trustees of the Holkham Estate.
Royal Botanic Gardens, Richmond, Kew: The Board of Trustees.
Nesfield Archives: the Trustees of Mrs Sheila Nesfield.
Nottingham University, Manuscripts and Special Collections.
Oxon Hoath, Kent: Tindle Conferences and Education Limited.
Royal Watercolour Society, Blackfriars, London.
Stoke Edith, Herefordshire, Mr Rupert Foley.

Index